Cultural Reflection in Management

New Horizons in Management Sciences

Edited by Lukasz Sulkowski

Volume 11

PETER LANG

Łukasz Sułkowski

Cultural Reflection in Management

PETER LANG

Bibliographic Information published by the Deutsche Nationalbibliothek
The Deutsche Nationalbibliothek lists this publication in the Deutsche Nationalbibliografie; detailed bibliographic data is available online at http://dnb.d-nb.de.

Library of Congress Cataloging-in-Publication Data
A CIP catalog record for this book has been applied for at the Library of Congress.

"Publication is co-financed from grant of University of Social Sciences in Poland"

Printed by CPI books GmbH, Leck

ISSN 2194-153X
ISBN 978-3-631-64012-8 (Print)
E-ISBN 978-3-653-02218-6 (E-PDF)
E-ISBN 978-3-631-71188-0 (EPUB)
E-ISBN 978-3-631-71189-7 (MOBI)
DOI 10.3726/b16474

Peter Lang – Berlin · Bern · Bruxelles · New York · Oxford · Warszawa · Wien

This publication has been peer reviewed.

www.peterlang.com

Contents

Introduction

Culture in management is an important issue, and one that is still open, from both theoretical and practical points of view. Its essence lies in its significance to the functioning of an organisation as a whole. Culture is a universal medium, in which people act and organisations are submerged. It is a basis for all processes, such as communication, the exercise of power and valuation in the world of people and organisations. Culture, however, also remains an open and ambiguous phenomenon.

I began my research into cultural issues in management 20 years ago. Back then I assumed a functionalist approach, as I believed it to be the most mature stream of research, allowing for operationalisation of the notion of organisational culture. However, it turned out that an alternative approach to functionalism was developing more dynamically, and even completely new cognitive perspectives then appeared. Most of all, a number of concepts which make use of interpretative assumptions were created, which understand culture as a network of interactions and meanings. But the most rapid increase in the number of publications and research took place within the critical current, which as a scientific school is only two decades old. By contrast, postmodernism has by now lost its significance, although in the 1980s and 1990s it seemed to be the most important alternative to functionalism. Such rapid and profound changes in cognitive approaches to research into culture provoke reflection, and force one to adopt an open cognitive approach. This is why this monograph deals with different visions of culture in management, emphasising epistemological and methodological pluralism, and the need for the development of new, creative concepts of culture.

My interests in the epistemology and methodology of management science lead towards such non-orthodox areas of the theory of organisation as cultural processes. The research I carried out for the monograph entitled *Epistemology of Management* made me realise that reflection on the cultural processes of an organisation develops quickly and is source of a number of new approaches within the social sciences. Thus, making use of numerous threads and interpretations which appear as part of epistemological management projects, I decided to focus on the issue of cultural processes in management, and this monograph is the outcome.

This monograph contains an explication of several theses which place cultural analyses in management science on a very general plain of academic discourse.

1. The theory of culture in management science is a reflection of the theory of culture in science as such. This is why all deliberations on organisational culture and intercultural comparative studies of organisations should be carried out in the context of the development of cultural discourse in social and humanist sciences.
2. The basis for the reflection on culture is a proposal for a division into paradigms, which means largely diverse ways of understanding culture that are rooted in science and have epistemological, methodological and pragmatic consequences.
3. The subject of research should be the dynamics of organisational culture, which means culture from the procedural perspective, undergoing constant transformation. This includes the issue of spontaneous transformation of culture and the processes of planned and controlled changes.

The problem of a research field determined in this way is its excess. Cultural processes in organisations include numerous social phenomena that are difficult to define and study. Organisational culture is an ambiguous notion, described within different paradigms. This is why the stand taken here is based on epistemological pluralism, meaning openness to research into cultural processes in organisations from many perspectives. Pluralism in cultural research has a long tradition, as it relates to consideration of the assumptions of cultural relativism and the limiting of ethnocentrism, as well as the tension between functionalist and interpretative approaches present in cultural research from the very beginning.

It also seems that it is worth looking for completely new inspiration in the research into organisational culture, as the most popular concepts are by now exhausting their cognitive and pragmatic potential. In my opinion, further exploitation of the already classic models of E. Schein and G. Hofstede contributes little to management, and so it is worth looking at new concepts of culture, many of which are offered by social and humanist sciences. This is why special emphasis has been placed on looking for new inspirations in poorly spread, yet valuable perspectives, such as the neoevolutionary understanding of organisational culture and a critical approach to cultural processes in management. First of all, this is especially important from epistemological, methodological and pragmatic points of view, and concerns mostly the better understanding of culture in management. Secondly, it is important to carry out a reliable analysis of the cognitive effectiveness of different methods of research into organisational culture and culture in management. Thirdly, it is worth drawing on the practical effectiveness of culture management, as we are dealing with growing scepticism about the possibility of managing culture at all. This is why it seems of key significance for researchers into management culture to think about the existing concepts and methods, but also to be open to new inspirations.

The pragmatic orientation of management science also encourages attempts to carry out analyses from the point of view of organisational culture's usefulness in the process of introducing changes. The prescriptive aspirations of our discipline are supposed to lead to the improvement of an organisation. In this sense, organisational culture is a tool for the introduction of positive changes. It seems, however, that many researchers, especially interpretativists and supporters of the critical current, do not agree with viewing organisational culture as a tool of optimisation changes. In consequence, we are faced with a research problem that will be analysed further in this monograph – the basic question about the relationships between the cultural processes of an organisation and change management.

This current monograph consists of seven chapters, and assumes a beginning from reflections on the most significant cognitive problems of cultural currents, through an analysis of well-known and popular functionalist concepts of culture in management, ending with a presentation of less popular perspectives.

The first chapter focuses on an analysis of the basic problems of the development of cultural reflection in management science. The starting point is the historical overview of the evolution of cultural discourse in our discipline, with reference to the idea of culture in social and humanist sciences. Then, there is a proposal for a pattern of the diversification of culture concepts in management, consisting in distinguishing four paradigms: functionalism, symbolic interactionism, critical current and postmodernism. Based on this, the following chapters analyse diverse concepts of cultural current in management. The subjects of the next subchapter are the different ways of defining organisational culture, resulting from the proposals of paradigms in management. The chapter ends with an analysis of cognitive problems faced by the cultural discourse in management. The following chapters of this work attempt to solve these dilemmas.

The second chapter focuses on the oldest paradigm of understanding culture, which is functionalism, called the neopositivist-functionalist-systemic paradigm. This current is related to the creation and rapid development of the issues of cultural research in management, and offers numerous theoretical, methodological and empirical works. The chapter starts with a description of a functionalist vision of organisational culture, and after that focuses on the essence of the functionalist understanding of organisational culture. It then discusses the diverse models, typologies and functions of organisational culture which are widespread in management. The chapter ends with an attempt to look critically at the paradigm, both from the point of view of different cognitive perspectives and the pragmatic usefulness of these theories. It is a rather extensive chapter, even though it only briefly discusses a number of functionalist concepts of organisational culture. Apart from the first and last subchapters, it is of a reconstructive character, and so it is an attempt to select and briefly discuss a number of functionalist concepts of culture that are rooted in the theory and practice of management.

The third chapter analyses the significance of the second perspective, also originating from the functionalist paradigm, which is the influence of a cultural context on management processes. The most important projects described here include intercultural comparative studies based on the models of cultural dimensions, conducted by, among others, G. Hofstede, A. Trompenaars and C. Hampden-Turner, R. Hous and R. Inglehart. After a brief presentation of the models and cultural dimensions assumed by these researchers, the concept of cultural circles is discussed, which is a result of the intercultural comparative studies conducted. The next subchapter analyses the most important – from the perspective of management – research issues, undertaken by researchers carrying out intercultural comparative projects, and which are cultural determinants of the competitiveness of companies and whole economies. After that, a presentation is made, using the example of Polish culture, of how ambiguous the results and interpretations of the results of intercultural comparative studies can be. The last two subchapters concern two fundamental processes which take place in modern culture. The first is cultural convergence, which occurs with the deepening of globalisation processes. The second is the development of modern consumer culture, which is becoming the dominant model of values of modern societies.

The fourth chapter focuses on the issues of culture and organisational culture described from a point of view which is completely new to social sciences: the neoevolutionary perspective. It shares some elements with the neopositivist and functionalist paradigm, but to a great extent it is a separate cognitive strand. Should neoevolutionism turn out to be a promising basis for epistemological and methodological analyses in social sciences in the future, it will probably crystallise into a fully separate paradigm. The beginning of the chapter discusses the issues of neoevolutionism from the perspective of management science, and then makes an attempt to formulate an overview of the neoevolutionary concept of culture. The following subchapter introduces a theoretical proposal for considering culture within a projected and a rather promising general theory of replication (memetics). Then, there is an attempt to apply neoevolutionism to the analysis of organisational culture, through an analogy with primitive hunter-gatherer communities.

The subject of the fifth chapter is an analysis of cultural processes in management from the perspective of symbolic interactionism. This is the paradigm that has gathered the greatest number of works in the world over the last thirty years among non-functionalist approaches and within the cultural discourse in management science. The chapter starts with a description of the symbolic-interpretative paradigm, oriented towards the presentation of an outline of different interactionist concepts in management. Then, there is an analysis of extensive applications of symbolic interactionism with regard to cultural research into management. The last issue discussed in this chapter is the concept of organisational identity, which is set within the interpretative paradigm and is a proposal for a new perspective on cultural issues in management.

The sixth chapter contains an analysis of culture from the perspective of a radical structuralism paradigm, which in our discipline took the institutional form of Critical Management Studies. The analysis starts with theoretical deliberations on the basic cognitive and methodological assumptions which underlie the critical current, and which lead to radical criticism of the previous, mostly functionalist, concepts of organisational culture and culture in management. Another issue is the deriving of the emancipation concept of organisational culture from criticism, which is based on the negation of the dominant paradigm. The position taken by the critical current is controversial, and so the subject of the last subchapter is a distanced view on Critical Management Studies and the interpretation of culture that they propose.

The last chapter focuses on a dynamic perspective on organisational culture, analysing the relationships between culture and changes in management. Here, organisational changes are understood both as spontaneous transformations of an organisation and planned changes, which, by definition, should be controlled. At the beginning of the chapter, an attempt was made to organise the relationships between culture and organisational changes with the use of the paradigm matrix of social sciences used throughout the work. After that, based on this pattern, functionalist, interpretative and emancipation concepts and methods of managing cultural changes were analysed. The last subchapter is a proposal for the application of a metaphorical approach to the analysis of organisational culture dynamics.

The summary of the work emphasises the need for a multi-paradigm perspective on organisational culture and the prospects for the development of reflection on culture in the social sciences. The postmodernist approach and its cognitive relativism occupy only a marginal position in my analyses of culture in management. I believe that practising science with extreme assumptions of epistemological relativism is actually impossible, and so despite its output in the cultural discourse, postmodernism should not be treated as a paradigm or a scientific approach *sensu stricto*, but as a source of inspiration, ideas and metaphors. I think that at least the radical version of postmodernism belongs to art, literature and essay writing, rather than science. It seems, too, that post-modern inspirations have been successfully used by representatives of other non-fundamentalist paradigms.

I hope that the concepts presented in this book will contribute to the broadening of our knowledge of cultural processes in organisations, and particularly that it will be used for the better understanding and further exploration of concepts, such as interpretative and critical perspectives on culture (e.g. sense-making) and the neoevolutionary approach. Finally, the proposed matrix of culture paradigms, drawn from G. Burrell and G. Morgan, is supposed to serve as a reference, but, of course, does not reflect the full complexity of reality. The book is based on Polish publications of Lukasz Sulkowski.*

---

* L. Sulkowski, Kulturowe procesy zarządzania, Difin, Warszawa 2012.
L. Sulkowski, Czy warto zajmować się kulturą organizacyjną, Zarządzanie Zasobami Ludzkimi, 2008, 6, 9–25.
L. Sulkowski, Społeczeństwo informacyjne a kultura konsumpcyjna, Prace Naukowe Akademii Ekonomicznej we Wrocławiu, 2006, 221–227.
L. Sulkowski, Czy kultury organizacyjne zmierzają do unifikacji? Zarządzanie zasobami ludzkimi, 2002, (3-4), 9–20.
L. Sulkowski, Kultura organizacyjna-próba oceny znaczenia nurtu kulturowego w zarządzaniu, Prace Naukowe Akademii Ekonomicznej we Wrocławiu, 2002, 157–161.
L. Sulkowski, Czy jest możliwe kształtowanie kultury organizacyjnej? Organizacja i Kierowanie, 2001, (4), 99–110.
L. Sulkowski, Organizacja w poszukiwaniu tożsamości, Przegląd Organizacji, 2005, (3), 7–10.
L. Sulkowski, Wieloznaczność kultury organizacyjnej, Przedsiębiorczość i Zarządzanie, 2012, 13(12).
L. Sulkowski, Kultura organizacyjna od podstaw, Wydawnictwo Społecznej Akademii Nauk, Łódź 2020.
L. Sulkowski, O związkach między kulturą organizacyjną a organizacją uczącą się, Przegląd Organizacji, 2003, (4), 9–11.
L. Sulkowski, Funkcjonalistyczna wizja kultury organizacyjnej w zarządzaniu-dominujący paradygmat i jego krytyka, Problemy Zarządzania, 2013, 20–32.

1 Cultural trend in management

1.1 The development of the cultural trend in management

When undertaking analysis of the development of the cultural trend in organisations and in management discourse, one has to make a few assumptions. First and foremost, the picture presented will be simplified, and thus will only include the dominant themes of the afterthought and ideas quickly gaining popularity in the management environment. For reasons of clarity, the less-known concepts which complicate the chronological sequence of successive stages in management of cultural afterthought will be omitted. This simplification results in the narrowness of the views of many researchers, who are known more for their most important works than for evolving any contemporary views. For example, E. Schein is usually associated with the birth and development of the concept of organisational culture, as based on functionalism, although his later views would evolve in the direction of the interpretative approach[1]. Furthermore, one has to bear in mind that the development of the cultural concepts of the organisation and management are a part of broader thinking on the study of culture in the social sciences and humanities. There are a lot of very complex interdependencies between management and other disciplines examining the culture. Research into organisations draws from the achievements of sociology, cultural anthropology, social psychology, history, development economics, as well as behavioural economics, cultural expertise, linguistics and many other disciplines. At the same time, representatives of other disciplines use the ideas and research which fall within the remit of cultural discourse in management. The picture is further complicated by the division into theoretical and practical topics of cultural afterthought. Theoreticians tend towards research on the complex primary issues of culture in management, such as paradigms and research methodology, while practitioners look for simple solutions which can be translated into managerial actions and organisational techniques. One of the proposed solutions to these issues is a simplified analysis of the development of the cultural trend in management, which can be linked to the development of cultural thought in general. On one hand, the historical background which is the subject of this subchapter will serve the purpose. On the other hand, the placement of the concept of culture in

1 E.H. Schein, Culture: The Missing Concept in Organization Studies, *Administrative Science Quarterly* 1996, 41 (2), 40th Anniversary Issue, pp. 229–240.

management in the broad scheme of social sciences paradigms is simultaneously developed in this monograph.

The cultural afterthought has its roots in the eighteenth century, when the philosophers of romanticism began to take an interest in the development of civilisation, national cultural ideas and the culture-nature antinomy. The catalyst for the development of the concept of culture was the controversial philosophy of J.J. Rousseau, who took a critical look at the Enlightenment's civilisation ideals glorifying the natural state. Rousseau's arguments were challenged by the representatives of German and British romanticism, such as J.G. Herder, W. von Humboldt and A. Bastian. The latter proposed understanding culture as the 'psychological unity of mankind', which grouped universal ideas (*Elementargedanken*) with local ludic ideas of national culture (*Yőlkergedanken*)[2]. M. Arnold defined culture in terms of the order of civilisation by contrasting it to anarchy, which was a reference to T. Hobbes' 'Leviathan'.[3] In the second half of the nineteenth century, the Social Darwinism approach dominated views on culture. The philosophy of H. Spencer and F. Galton and L.H. Morgan's idea of cultural evolution, as well as the evolution of religion, represented a distorted picture of the development of culture from primitive to sophisticated forms, an obvious example of which had to be the enlightened, white European belonging to the ruling elite[4]. In the twentieth century, the cultural topic becomes the core problem of the social sciences and humanities, which remains unchanged at the beginning of the twenty-first century.

The beginning of the twentieth century saw fast development of the cultural idea and, at the same time, the birth of the idea that management could be understood as a science. Cultural issues were not essential to management in the first stages of their development. Representatives of the schools of scientific management and administration neither studied culture nor theorised about it. Actually, both F.W. Taylor and H. Fayol adopted only some pre-suppositional cultural assumptions which, according to critics, included the consolidation of structure and social order (*status quo*) around a new ruling class, i.e. the technocratic stewards (supervisors, managers)[5]. It pointed towards the nineteenth-century

2 A. Bastian, *Today in Science History*, 27 Jan. 2009; A. Bastian, Encyclopaedia Britannica Online, 27 January 2009.

3 A. Matthew, *Culture and Anarchy*, Cambridge University Press, 1993.

4 W. Raymond, *Social Darwinism;* John Offer, *Herbert Spencer's Critical Assessment*, 2000, pp. 186–199.

5 N. Monin, D. Barry, D.J. Monin, Toggling with Taylor: A Different Approach to Reading a Management Text, *Journal of Management Studies* 2003, 40, pp. 377–401.

concept of elite culture, and contemporarily, it is often the subject of critical – but at the same time – not always balanced assessment[6]. F.W. Taylor, for that matter, began *The Principles of Scientific Management* with a patriotic appeal to work on 'national productivity', and thus indirectly associated management categories with the national community and its cultural values[7]. H. Fayol went even further in the direction of cultural variables, describing among his management principles the *esprit de corps* – the 'team spirit' – which was supposed to be a source of harmony and cooperation. It seems that the concept of *esprit de corps* can be regarded as the precursor of the organisational culture trend, and is therefore a pre-cultural idea in management[8].

Increased interest in the cultural processes came from the school of social relations, the creator of which, as is commonly believed, was E. Mayo. Using the results of the famous Hawthorne experiment, Mayo saw the importance of management: the staff team, understood as a group based on social relationships, the communication feedback between subordinates and superiors, effective and personalised leadership[9], sensitivity towards the emotions of employees and soft skills training[10]. A focus on the values in the social group and the social nature of the management process links Mayo's and Roethlisberger's concepts with the cultural trend. In the Hawthorne experiment, employees adapted their pace of work and dedication less to their individual remuneration, and more to mutual social relationships and professed values and norms. Mayo also noticed that management is not a purely technical process (social engineering), but above all, constitutes social and psychological interaction. This was a criticism of the tough school of scientific management which marginalised the social sphere of the organisation[11]. The school of social relations also covers more compromising positions. H.S. Dennison developed the concept of linking managerial control, drawn from scientific management, with the needs of employees and social group

6 E.A. Locke, The Ideas of Frederick W. Taylor: An Evaluation, *The Academy of Management Review*, Jan. 1982, 7 (1), pp. 14–24.

7 *F.W. Taylor, The Principles of Scientific Management, 1911.*

8 *H. Fayol, Administration industrielle et generale; prevoyance, organisation, commandement, coordination, controle*, H. Dunod et E. Pinat, Paris, 1917.

9 J.A. Sonnenfeld, Shedding Light on the Hawthorne Studies, *Journal of Occupational Behavior* 1985, 6, s. 125.

10 A.J. DuBrin, *Human Relations Interpersonal Job-Oriented Skills,* 9 ed., Pearson Prentice Hall, New Jersey 2007, p. 2.

11 M. Anteby, R. Khurana, *A New Vision, Harvard Business School,*www.library.hbs.edu (28.07.2012).

dynamics, which is the subject of the school of social relations. Ideas similar to those found in organisational culture began to appear in the interwar period in the works of psychologists and sociologists unrelated to the school of social relations[12], such as K. Lewin, R. Lippitt, and R.K. White (social climate)[13], suggesting that the issue was then mature enough for deeper analysis.

The maturation process of the cultural issue in management in the period before World War II took place against the rapid development of the functionalist and interpretative theory of culture. In the twentieth century, as a result of that second tragic historical experience, the simplified and racist vision of culture in the form of Social Darwinism, derived directly from the nineteenth century, was rejected. Cultural anthropology resulted from universalist perspectives in cultural studies, but gradually came around to cultural relativism. A similar process, sometimes called the 'linguistic breakthrough' or the Sapir-Whorf hypothesis, took place in linguistics and sociology[14]. The second epistemological axis of analysis was the problem of the universality of culture. Some researchers, mainly from the school of F. Boas, and then R. Benedict and M. Mead, supported the position of particularism, which was in line with the assumptions of symbolic interactionism, which argued that cultures form an entirety in themselves (*gestalt*[16]) and cannot be generalised in research[15]. The line of the cultural universalists was developed by the functionalist schools, and later by the schools of structuralism seeking universals of culture. The most important representatives of structural functionalism were B. Malinowski, A.R. Radcliffe-Brown and E.E. Evans-Pritchard[16]. Thus, in the social sciences, two opposing epistemological perspectives were formed before World War II: interpretivism, which postulated

---

12 B. Kyle, H.S. Dennison, E. Mayo, Human Relations Historiography, *Management & Organisational History* 2006, 1, pp. 177–199.

13 B. Kyle, H.S. Dennison, E. Mayo, Human Relations Historiography, *Management & Organisational History* 2006, 1, pp. 177–199.

14 Sapir, Edward. The status of linguistics as a science. *Language* 1929, pp. 207–214; B.L. Whorf, P. Lee, S.C. Levinson, & J.B. Carroll, *Language, thought, and reality: Selected writings of Benjamin Lee Whorf*, MIT press, 2012.

15 F. Boas, *Race, Language, and Culture,* University of Chicago Press, 1940; M. Mead, *Coming of Age in Samoa,* William Morrow and Company, 1928, s. 297; R. Benedict, *Patterns of Culture,* Houghton Mifflin, New York, 1934.

16 *B. Malinowski, A Scientific Theory of Culture and Others Essays*, Ch. Hill, N. Carolina, The University of North Carolina Press, 1944; A.R. Radcliffe-Brown, *Structure and Function in Primitive Society: Posthumously*, 1952; E.E. Evans-Pritchard, *A Description of the Modes of Livelihood and Political Institutions of a Nilotic People*, Clarendon Press, Oxford 1940.

relativism and cultural particularism, and functional structuralism based on universalism and cultural realism. This opposition lingered on in the antinomy of the following decades, taking the form of structuralism (C. Levi-Strauss, T. Parsons[17]) versus post-structuralism (R. Barthes, J. Lacan, and M. Foucault[18]). As the 1960s gave way to the 1970s, cultural anthropology was dominated by the paradigm of the interpretative-symbolic and post-structuralism perspective, reflected in the statement by C. Geertz that 'man is an animal entangled in a web of meanings he wove himself', and that the study of culture is 'an interpretive science involving the search for meaning'[19]. Relativism and particularism in the cultural sense take precisely the form of post-structuralism, and later on, postmodernism, finding expression in the development of cultural studies. In the 1970s, S. Hall[20] and R. Williams[21] crystallised a critical neo-Marxist approach to cultural studies, based on the assumptions of radical structuralism. It utilises the intellectual base of the Frankfurt School, P. Bourdieu's sociology, A. Gramsci and L. Althusser's Neo-Marxism and radical feminism, thus developing a method of critical cultural studies which involves the ardent analysis of culture as a source of inequality, violence and the means of preservation of an unjust status quo[22].

One of the key sources of development of the theory of culture was the increase in the importance of intercultural relationships that came with the development of communication technologies, as well as the ongoing process of globalisation. Many organisations, working on an international scale, were facing specific issues of intercultural management. The huge cultural challenges facing them in the second half of the twentieth century included decolonisation and globalisation. Therefore, even as far back as the 1930s, cross-cultural comparative studies were beginning to quickly develop for pragmatic purposes, namely

---

17 C. Levi-Strauss, *Anthropologie Structural,* Plon, Paris, 1958; T. Parsons, *Societies: Evolutionary and Comparative Perspectives,* 1st edition, Prentice-Hall, p. 120.

18 R. Barthes, *Elements of Semiology,* Hill and Wang, New York 1967; J. Lacan, *The Seminar XI, The Four Fundamental Concepts of Psychoanalysis,* (editor) J.A. Miller, (translation) A. Sheridan, W.W. Norton & Co., New York 1977; M. Foucault, *Surveiller et punir,* Gallimard, Paris, 1975.

19 C. Geertz, *The Interpretation of Cultures: Selected Essays,* 1973, p. 5.

20 S. Hall, P. Walton, *Situating Marx: Evaluations and Departures,* Human Context Books, London 1972.

21 R. Williams, *Problems in Materialism and Culture: Selected Essays,* Verso, London 1980, Schocken, New York 1981; R. Williams, *Reissued as Culture and Materialism,* Verso Radical Thinkers Series, 2005.

22 P. Bourdieu, *Language & Symbolic Power,* Harvard University Press, 1991; L. Althusser, E. Balibar, *Reading Capital,* New Left Books, 1965.

to reduce communication problems and conflicts in social communication. G.P. Murdock was the pioneer of cross-cultural research, carrying out the first comparative statistical study of cultural behaviour[23], while E.T. Hall was a key figure in the development of the pragmatic approach to cross-cultural studies, achieving his competencies while doing consulting work for the U.S. government[24]. The concepts of cultural dimensions and distances[25] became the subject of further study, leading to the fundamental projects in cultural trends in management directed by G. Hofstede and other researchers, who took the *cross-cultural* perspective into account[26].

Sensu stricto, the birth of the theory of organisational culture took place after World War II. E. Jacques used the term with reference primarily to analysis of atmosphere in the workplace ('organisational climate')[27]. In the 1950s and '60s, research on culture in management was far and few between, and constituted a rather marginal problem. Mainstream research relates to the relationship between a culture and the changes in organisational development, leadership and human resources management[28]. For example, while analysing this organisational change, A. Bavelas also relates it to 'culture-specific organisations', distinguished by other rituals that affect the process of adaptation of new employees[29]. For two decades, the cultural issue in management has thus developed in two separate ways. On the one hand, it has tended towards a functionalist, narrow understanding of culture as an organisational climate[30], and on the other, the comparative studies

---

23 G.P. Murdock, *Ethnographic Atlas: A Summary*, The University of Pittsburgh Press, Pittsburgh, 1967.

24 E.T. Hall, *The Silent Language*, New York, 1959.

25 E.T. Hall, *The Hidden Dimension*, Muza, p. 204; E.T. Hall, *Beyond Culture*, New York, 1976.

26 G. Hofstede, *Cultures and Organizations: Software of the Mind*, Fontana, London, 1994.

27 *E. Jaques, The Changing Culture of a Factory: A Study of Authority and Participation in an Industrial Setting*, Tavistock, London, 1951.

28 *F. Friedlander, N. Margulies*, Multiple Impacts of Organizational Climate and Individual Value Systems upon Job Satisfaction, *Personnel Psychology* 22, 1969; R.N. Adams, *Personnel in Culture Change: A Test of Hypothesis*, *Social Forces*, Dec. 1951, 30 (2), pp. 185–189.

29 A. Bavelas, Some Problems of Organizational Change, *Journal of Social Issues*, 1948, 4, pp. 48–52.

30 Ch. Argyris, Some Problems in Conceptualizing Organizational Climate: A Case Study of a Bank, *Administrative Science Quarterly*, Mar. 1958, 2 (4), pp. 501–520.

of cultures have developed[31]. Even at this stage, the epistemological afterthought on management emerges, which leads to the conclusion that there is a plurality and inconsistency in the theory of culture and organisation[32].

The development of comparative cross-cultural studies, which most significantly relate to management issues, began at the start of the 1970s. In particular, there was a rapid increase in the number of publications after 1980, which was the year the first book on the results of comparative studies of cultures by G. Hofstede was published. These results were then widely deployed in management practise[33]. There are a number of cross-cultural comparative studies projects that investigate various aspects of organisations, from the connection of culture with efficiency, through leadership, to change management. Started by E.T. Hall, the pragmatic approach to cross-cultural management results in a number of methods improving competences and training programmes[34]. In addition to research papers, there is an increase in the number of business guides which take cross-cultural issues into account[35]. All comparative studies are based on functionalist assumptions and use standardised and representative survey methods. Even today, this is a very important trend in cultural studies, both in management and other social sciences. The most important researchers in this area are G. Hofstede, A. Trompenaars, Ch. Hampden-Turner, R. House, and R. Inglehart. Currently, the key issues for cross-cultural comparative studies are globalisation and multiculturalism.

The beginning of the 1980s also saw a significant increase in the role of the concept of organisational culture. This was likely due to many reasons related both to the logic of the development of cultural discourse in management

31 W. Oberg, Cross-Cultural Perspectives on Management Principles, *The Academy of Management Journal*, Jun. 1963, 6(2), pp. 129–143; E.T. Hall, W.F. Whyte, Intercultural Communication: A Guide to Men of Action, *Human Organization*, pp. 5–12.

32 K.H. Roberts, On Looking at an Elephant: An Evaluation of Cross-Cultural Research Related to Organizations, *Psychological Bulletin*, Nov. 1970, 74 (5), pp. 327–350.

33 G. Hofstede, *Culture's Consequences: International Differences in Work-Related Values*, Newbury Park, Sage 1980.

34 F.E. Fiedler, M.R. Terence, T.C. Harry, The Culture Assimilator: An Approach to Cross-Cultural Training, *Journal of Applied Psychology*, April 1971, 55 (2); W.B. Gudykunst, M.R. Hammer, R.L. Wiseman, *An Analysis of an Integrated Approach to Cross-Cultural Training*, Analisis de un enfoque integral al entrenamineto transcultural, Une analyse d'une approche integree a l'environnement transculturel, *International Journal of Intercultural Relations*, Summer 1977, 1(2), pp. 99–110.

35 H.F. Van Zandt, *How to Negotiate in Japan*, Harvard Business Review, Business School Publication, 1970.

itself, and to external factors. The rapid growth of interest in cross-cultural comparative studies drew the attention of many management researchers and practitioners to the growing role of cross-cultural communication. Globalisation and the opening up of many national economies which so far had autarchic tendencies contributed to a great interest in cultural issues faced by managers. G. Hofstede recognises the confrontation of the American and Japanese models of conducting business – with all their cross-cultural consequences – as one of the causes of the huge expansion of interest in the issue of organisational culture[36]. An important experience for American business came in the shock caused by the competitiveness of Japanese products on the US market. Even though the Japanese had radically different management models, which were based on collectivism as opposite to the American individualism, they achieved spectacular success in business. Thus, the American myth of management understood as *one best way* collapsed, and was gradually replaced with the awareness that an organisation is culturally conditioned. Another reason for the interest in organisational culture was the growing popularity of cultural studies in the social sciences and humanities, which embraced new, sometimes radically different views on understanding the culture (e.g. post-modernism and sociobiology). The systemic view of organisation and management was slowly running out of options, as originally it did not include culture as a subsystem. Initially, many management specialists thought that culture would become a remedy for the issues of the theory and practice of management. Research and publications which assumed a broad functionalist understanding of organisational culture became very popular among both theorists and practitioners. Among the large number of authors taking this approach to organisational culture as an internal variable, one can name E. Schein, Ch. Handy, T. Deal, A. Kennedy, P. Bate and A. Pettigrey[37], with G. Hofstede as the key representative of the comparative cross-cultural studies approach. Some of the concepts of organisational culture, such as the 'iceberg model'[38] or G. Hofstede's 'onion model', became so popular

---

36 G. Hofstede, The Usefulness of the 'Organizational Culture' Concept, *Journal of Management Studies* 1986, 23, pp. 253–257.

37 T.E. Deal, A.A. Kennedy, *Corporate Cultures: The Rites and Rituals of Corporate Life,* Penguin, Harmondsworth 1982; C.B. Handy, *Understanding organizations,* Penguin, London, 1999.

38 R. Selfridge, S. Sokolik, A Comprehensive View of Organizational Management, *MSU Business Topics* 1975, 23 (1), s. 46–61; W.L. French, C.H. Bell, *Organization Development,* Prentice Hall, New Jersey 1979.

that they even permeated the general public via guides and textbooks[39]. T. Peters and P. Waterman's bestseller, which put the value of the organisation at the centre of the proposed 7S model, reached the heights of popularity[40]. The dominant functionalist perspective towards culture assumed that it could be radically changed by means of organising techniques, and in practice, this optimistic approach to cultural change was indeed verified. But many culture transformation programmes of the time gave unpredictable results. With time, even in the opinion of some of the functionalism researchers, culture had become too amorphous and too poorly understood to provide a basis for a theory of management understood in the neopositivist sense.

The development of the interpretative-symbolic view expressed the growing scepticism with regard to the functionalist approach to culture. Researchers such as G. Morgan, G. Burrell and L. Smircich offered a look at organisations through the lens of interpretively understood culture[41]. This approach made use of the achievements of the symbolic interactionism paradigm in sociology, cultural anthropology and other social sciences, to describe the phenomenon of organisational culture. It meant that the focus was on anthropologically understood, individual, non-generalised case studies, the aim of which was to capture the meaning of 'organisation'. Researchers utilizing the concepts of the interpretative understanding of cultural trends include L. Smircich[42], N. Brunsson, J. Van Maanen, M. Pacanowsky, G. Morgan, M.J. Hatch, I.L. Mangham, M.A. Overington, C. Eden, C. Ouellet, and P. Cossette[43]. Over time, the interpretative trend became very diverse in its interests, using the achievements of organisational researchers who had not focused on the theory of culture in management before, such as K. Weick[44].

39 *G. Hofstede, Cultures and Organizations: Software of the Mind,* Fontana, London 1994.

40 T.J. Peters, R.H. Waterman, *In Search of Excellence,* Harper and Row, New York 1982.

41 L. Smircich, Concepts of Culture and Organizational Analysis, *Administrative Science Quarterly*, September 1983, pp. 339–359; G. Morgan, *Images of organization,* updated edition, Sage, London, 2006.

42 L. Smircich, Concepts of Culture and Organizational Analysis, *Administrative Science Quarterly*, September 1983, pp. 339–359.

43 *C. Ouellet, P. Cossette, Les travaux des chercheurs utilisant le concept de cognition en sciences de l'administration: une etude exploratoire, Actes de la 8 Conference Internationale de Management Strategique,* Paris, 1999.

44 R.L. Daft, K.E. Weick, Toward a Model of Organizations as Interpretation Systems, '*The Academy of Management*, Apr. 1984, 9 (2), pp. 284–295.

Another cultural trend which appeared in management studies and was inspired by the humanities was postmodernism. Postmodernists took a far-reaching critical look at the functionalist, universalist and objectivist cultural approaches. They proposed the concept of non-fundamentalist discourse based on methodological anarchism. Flagship postmodern ideas, such as deconstruction, simulacrum and metanarration, have gained favour in management. Some authors also used strong metaphors from organisational culture, such as theatre, rhizome and the panopticon[45]. Following the precursors of postmodernism and postmodern philosophers such as M. Foucault, P. Feyerabend, R. Rorty and J.F. Lyotard, a critique of objectivist efforts at cultural research was undertaken and, simultaneously, the ideas of cultural imperialism of modern science were highlighted. Postmodernism is an anti-methodological trend and of the few attempts to use postmodern methods, deconstruction and gloss were found to be essay writings rather than works of science. Some authors, previously interested in anti-functionalist, non-fundamentalist approaches to organisational culture, became postmodernists, including S. Clegg, G. Burrell, R. Cooper, B. Czarniawska-Jorges, M. Kostera, M.J. Hatch, P. Engholm, D.M. Boje, R.P. Gephart Jr and T.J. Thatchenkery[46]. In addition, many researchers and practitioners used metaphors and other concepts embedded in postmodernism. From the point of view of management sciences, postmodernism as a whole has not become a major trend. Nonetheless, it is worth noting its presence in management's cultural trends. Postmodernism in management is often confused with the interpretative approach and the critical trend. However, the differences are very significant and affect both the epistemological and the methodological sphere, and there will be more discussion of the distinction between non-functional paradigms in cultural studies in subsequent chapters. Radical postmodernism has been sharply criticised, yet in most cases with a well-founded critique on the part of the scientific community of its irrationalism, epistemological relativism, lack of scientific

---

45 G. Deleuze, F. Guattari, *Anti-Oedipus,* Trans. R. Hurley, 1972; M. Foucault, *Discipline & Punish: The Birth of the Prison,* Vintage Books, New York, 1995.

46 P. Engholm, *The Controversy between Modernist and Postmodernist Views of Management Science: Is a Synergy Possible?,* Internet, Monash University, May 2001; D.M. Boje, R.P. Gephart Jr, T.J. Thatchenkery, *Postmodern Management and Organization Theory,* Sage Publications, Thousand Oaks, 1996; M.K. Welge, D. Holtbrugge, International Management under Postmodern Conditions, *Management International Review* 1999, 39 (4), pp. 305–322; G. Burrell, R. Cooper, Modernism, Postmodernism and Organizational Analysis: An Introduction, *Organization Studies* 1998, 9 (1), pp. 91–112.

rigour and vagueness of the concept[47]. The result of this is the slow fading away of postmodernism in science, including the cultural discourse. Some researchers believe that the loss of importance of post-modernism also marks an increase in the importance of the realistic approach to culture in management[48].

The most recent research approach to cultural processes in the organisation is the critical view (*Critical Management Studies* – CMS), although of course its roots can be traced back to the ancient past. In the nineteenth century, Karl Marx described the capitalist exploitation of workers in factories and the bourgeois culture created around it. CMS representatives derive the achievements of the Frankfurt School and radical feminism directly from neo-Marxism. When presenting the metaphor of organisation, G. Morgan interprets it as a 'mental prison' and mentions a number of topics critical to the dominant culture of business: opposition to dehumanisation, the lack of responsibility, the exploitation of poorer countries by richer countries, as well as the utilisation of natural resources in a predatory manner and the destruction of ecosystems[49]. According to the representatives of the critical trend, all these problematic cases of the exploitive culture of modern business are systemically conditioned and not purely pathological. Culture in the view of the radical trend is a tool for wielding power. The first author to write about the issue of organisational culture from the critical point of view was H. Willmott, who in 1993 described organisational culture as a kind of ideology, a 'false consciousness', psychomanipulation and social engineering aimed at maintaining the status quo in the form of the exploitation of workers[50]. Since then, publications by M. Alvesson, D. Knights, J. Brewis, J. Gavin and A. Prasad have further developed this critical look at culture in management[51].

---

47 N. Chomsky on Post-Modernism, http://www.cscs.umich.edu/~crshalizi/chomsky-on-post-modernism.html (10.08.2012); A. Sokal, J. Bricmont, *Fashionable Nonsense: Postmodern Intellectuals' Abuse of Science*, Prószyński i s-ka, Warsaw, 1998.

48 M. Reed, Reflections on the 'Realist Turn' in Organization and Management Studies, *Journal of Management Studies* 2005, 42, pp. 1621–1644.

49 G. Morgan, *Images of Organization*, updated edition, Sage, London, 2006.

50 H. Willmott, Strength Is Ignorance; Slavery Is Freedom: Managing Culture in Modern Organizations. *Journal of Management Studies* 1993, 30 (4), pp. 515–552.

51 M. Alvesson, H. Willmott, *Making Sense of Management: A Critical Introduction*, SAGE, 1996; D. Knights, H.C. Willmott, *Organizational Culture as Management Strategy: A Critique and Illustration from the Financial Services* Industry, *International Studies of Management & Organization* 1987, XVII, No. 3, pp. 40–63.
J. Brewis, J. Gavin, *Culture: Broadening the Critical Repertoire*, [in:] *The Oxford Handbook of Critical Management Studies*, (editors) M. Alvesson, T. Bridgman, H. Willmott,

Obviously, this analysis does not exhaust the richness of all schools and topics of cultural discourse in organisations and management. For example, the development of the concept of organisational identity, cognitive organisation, organisational learning and many other aspects of management which can be regarded as cultural has been omitted. They have been assigned to one of the schools by default – for example, organisational identity is an important element of the interpretative understanding of organisational culture. Nor has any analysis of the prospects for the development of the cultural trend been carried out, because it is going to be the subject of the next part of the monograph. Taking into account the simplified nature of the analysis presented, the development of cultural afterthought may still be sorted in the form of eight trends presented below:

1. Preculturalism, encompassing the period from the birth of the management sciences to the creation of the school of social relations, focusing on selected, narrowly understood cultural organisational processes (motivation, *esprit de corps*), not theorizing on the subject of culture in the strict sense.
2. The school of social relations, which was founded in the 1930s and developed over two decades, which put socio-cultural issues at the heart of the management sciences, yet at the same time did not include explicit afterthought on culture.
3. The work environment trend, developed in the 1950s and 1960s, which grew out of research at the Glacier factory operated by E. Jacques and proposed a narrow understanding of organisational culture in management as a specific 'organisational climate'.
4. Comparative and cross-cultural communication perspectives, developed in the 1960s, which are also an important area of research contemporarily. These analyse the influence of cultures of different societies on an organisation's management processes.
5. The universalist understanding of organisational cultural perspectives, related to the huge expansion of research, publications and popularisation of papers in the 1970s, and especially the 1980s, in which organisational culture is understood as an internal variable that affects the efficiency of the organisation and is subject to managerial control through the use of management tools (known as the functionalist paradigm).

Oxford University Press, Oxford 2009, pp. 234–235; A. Prasad, *Postcolonial Theory and Organizational Analysis: A Critical Engagement,* Palgrave Macmillan, New York 2003, p. 309.

Tab. 1: Mainstreams connected with the cultural discourse of organization in chronological order. Source: own work.

	Recognition of cultural processes	**Relationships with other disciplines**	**Representatives**
Preculturalism until 1930	1. No identification of culture as an area of research. 2. Analysis of selected cultural issues such as *esprit de corps* (team spirit) and motivation.	1. Technical Sciences – Algorithmic and bureaucratic approach to management. 2. Economy – economy as a fundamental criterion.	F.W. Taylor, H. Fayol and M.P. Follet
Social relations 1930–1950	1. No identification of culture as an area of research. 2. Focus on social and cultural management processes. 3. Problems key to management: values, norms, human relationships, social ties and communication.	1. Social psychology – research on psychological motivation to work. 2. Sociology – influence of social processes on people's actions within organisations.	E. Mayo, E. J. Roethlisberger and H.S. Dennison
Work environment 1950–1960	1. Organisational culture defined as work environment. 2. Main research trends study the relationship between the organisational climate and the development and organisational change and leadership and human resources management.	1. Social psychology – influence of leadership on organisational development. 2. Cultural anthropology – functionalist, but narrow understanding of the culture.	E. Jacąues, F. Friedlander, N. Margulies, A. Bavelas and D. McGregor
Comparative studies and cross-cultural communication 1960–present	1. The culture of societies (formerly known as national) as key external variable for the organisation and economies affecting the efficiency.	1. Cultural anthropology – functionalist analysis of the culture via dichotomous dimensions of values.	E.T. Hall, G. Hofstede, A. Trompenaars, Ch. Hampden-Turner and R. Haus

(*continued on next page*)

Tab. 1: Continued

	Recognition of cultural processes	Relationships with other disciplines	Representatives
	2. Issues of the relationship between the culture and work efficiency, dedication, leadership and change management.	2. Development economics – influence of local culture on economic development. 3. Sociology – analysis of cultural circles as interpenetrating cultural spheres.	
Organisational culture – universalism 1970–present	1. Organisational culture understood as internal variable affecting the efficiency that managers may manipulate using organising techniques. 2. Issues: models, typology, classification, changes and organisational culture efficiency.	1. Sociology – functionalist concept of the culture as an element of social system. 2. Cultural anthropology – functionalist structuralism, cultural models and typologies stemming from ethnological research.	E. Schein, Ch. Handy, T. Deal, A. Kennedy, P. Bate, A. Pettigrev, G. Hofstede, C. Sikorski, L. Zbiegień-Maciąg and B. Czerska
Cultural interpretivism 1980–present	1. Culture interpreted as core metaphor, i.e. organisation is the culture which is greatly not being made aware and difficult to shape. 2. Key management issues include: interaction, communication, subcultures and countercultures, language, organisational games, spontaneous transformation of the culture, organisational identity and cultural barrier of rationality.	1. Cultural anthropology – interpretative concept of the culture and the critique of functionalism, as well as fieldwork, linguistic and textual methodology. 2. Sociology – paradigm of symbolic interactionism and inspirations with the perspectives of drama, ethnomethodology and well-established theory.	G. Morgan, L. Smircich, M. J. Hatch, K. E. Weick, N. Brunsson, J. Van Maanen and M. Pacanowsky

Tab. 1: Continued

	Recognition of cultural processes	Relationships with other disciplines	Representatives
Postmodernism 1985–present	1. Culture understood purely in metaphorical and ambiguous ways as a game, discourse and text. 2. Key issues include critique of functionalism and imperialism of science, deconstruction of organisational culture, gloss and cultural studies based on cognitive relativism.	1. Cultural anthropology – postmodern understanding of the culture. 2. Postmodern philosophy – critique of objectivism and methodological anarchism, deconstruction in the form of textualism, metaphors of the culture as rhizome, text and temple.	S. Clegg, G. Burrell, R. Cooper, B. Czarniawska, M. Kostera and P. Boje
Critical view on culture 1993–present	1. Culture is a tool for wielding power and maintaining an unjust social structure through indoctrination and symbolic violence. 2. Issues of unmasking and denaturalizing and humanizing organisational culture using the methods of emancipation.	1. Philosophy – ideas of social control, domination, false consciousness taken from neo-Marxism, concept of cultural industry from the Frankfurt School. 2. Sociology – P. Bourdieu's concept of symbolic violence.	H. Willmott, M. Alvesson, D. Knights, J. Brewis, J. Gavin and A. Prasad

6. Cultural interpretivism, developed in the 1980s as a reaction to the universalist trend, which assumed an understanding of culture as a core metaphor.
7. The postmodernism which emerged in management in the mid-1980s, using the assumptions of radical epistemological relativism and cultural relativism.
8. The critical view of culture in management stemming from *CMS*, which emerged in organisational discourse due to the 1993 publication of H. Willmott's work and was focused on a critique of the instrumentalist understanding of organisational culture, at the same time proposing the creation of emancipating cultures.

A summary of all these trends is found in Tab. 1 above, while the presented cognitive perspectives shall be a subject of analysis in the following chapters.

Analysing the development of the cultural concepts in management sciences, several conclusions may be drawn. The increase in the complexity of the theory and methodology of research is a clear trend. Three identified historical trends (preculturalism, social relations and work environment) have treated the issues of cultural management very narrowly, whereas five of the modern trends have created a very complex and multi-faceted picture of cultural management processes. The increase in the number and complexity of theories is caused both by the ambivalent current results of cultural research in the management sciences, as well as by a rapid increase in the number of schools and paradigms of understanding of management culture in the humanities and social sciences. The cultural discourse in organisations and management draws primarily from other disciplines, which makes the research issue highly interdisciplinary. Currently, in the social sciences (management included), there is no single adopted position on understanding and studying culture. Thus, a reasonable position would be to assume an epistemological and methodological pluralism, which means that it is acceptable to understand the basic concepts in various ways and to use extremely different methods when undertaking cultural research into organisations. At the same time, it is necessary to explicitly define definitions and cognitive and methodological assumptions.

2 Paradigm of functionalism in organizational culture

2.1 The functionalist understanding of culture in management

Functionalism was born from the spirit of sociology, anthropology and management sciences that were busy building their own identities in the early twentieth century. Spencer used the analogy between society and living organism, underlining the harmoniousness of collaboration and the significance of social order. E. Durkheim, considered the "father" of contemporary sociology, postulated a distinction between mechanistic and organic types of social solidarity.[52]. The former were seen as characteristic of primitive communities, while the latter - of modern industrial societies. The functionalist concept of culture was first used in the late 19th century, and spread thanks to the research of the most eminent functionalists, such as B. Malinowski and A. R. Radcliffe-Brown. It then reached the peak of its popularity in the 1960s thanks to T. Parsons[53]..
Functionalism is still adominating orientation in the social sciences, although it has been criticised in sociology by representatives of conflict theory, and more generally within the symbolic interactionism paradigm of the social sciences since the 1960s. Defending functionalism, R. Merton suggested to modify some of its assumptions, but keeping to the postulates of homeostasis, social hierarchy and functional dependency[54]. Today, functionalism does no longer dominate in many social sciences, but it still has prominent advocates, including N. Luhmann and A. Giddens[55].

Many critics of functionalism are of the opinion that it is closely related to neopositivism and that the convergence in time related to the creation of both

---

52 C.J. Calhoun, *Classical Sociological Theory*, Wiley-Blackwell, 2002, p. 106.

53 T. Parsons, *The Social System*, Routledge, London, 1951; T. Parsons, *Theories of Society: fFoundations of mModern sSociological tTheory*, Free Press, New York, 1961.

54 R.K. Merton, Social Theory and Social Structure (1968 enlarged ed.), New York, NY, US: Free Press, 1968.

55 A. Giddens, *Central problems in Social Theory : Action, Structure and Contradiction in Social Analysis*, London, Macmillan, 1979; A. Giddens, *New rules of sociological method: A positive critique of interpretative sociologies*, John Wiley & Sons, 2013. A. Viskovatoff's, Foundations of Niklas Luhmann's Theory of Social Systems, *Philosophy of the Social Sciences* 1999, 29 (4), pp. 481–516.

these currents was not a coincidence. Z. Bauman believes that an obvious result of the application of the enlightenment's ideals in the cultural discourse was Social Darwinism and its mission to 'civilise savages'[56]. A functionalist view of culture is based on assumptions focused aroundthe neopositivist Vienna Circle. This signifies cognitive and political optimism, and a belief in the project of objectivist science, which again leads to human progress. The neopositivist concept of the cultural discourse within the functionalist current was related to a striving for the studies of culture based on models drawn from the natural sciences. Thus, they were attempting to build such a project in the social sciences that, apart from objectivism and axiological neutrality, would offer a determinist model of cultural processes. This utopia is rooted in the mechanistic physics of the Newtonian paradigm, together with its own characteristic elements such as time and space universalism, determinism and a mathematical perception of reality. They were also striving for a cleansing of scientific research of 'metaphysical' elements, which were, by definition, omni-present in cultural discourse. System and structure became popular notions describing culture, and were seen from the perspective of the social functions. In the functionalist, and then structural understanding, culture was a system and a structure, through which the coherence of societies and other human communities was developed and maintained. Thus, the integrational role of culture was of crucial significance, as it connected, provided identity, and – in consequence – shaped the scientific progress and development of humankind. Logical empiricism, including its scientism, offered an epistemological and methodological basis for the development of functionalism in the social sciences. The theories developed were supposed to be subject to empirical verification, as a result of the development of a reliable scientific method, which would be in accordance with the cognitive ideals of natural science. The proposed empirical research method was supposed to allow for mathematical formalisation and quantification of the results of scientific inquiries. The goal of the analysis of a social group was to find the causative relationships between functions, i.e. variables, in the model. Thus, it would be possible to generalise, which would allow creation of a more general, repeatable pattern, allowing for the description of all social processes in a standard way[57].

---

56 Z. Bauman, *Legislators and Interpreters - On Modernity, Post-Modernity, Intellectuals*, Ithaca, N. Y.: Cornell University Press, 1987.

57 A. Giddens, *New rules of sociological method: A positive critique of interpretative sociologies*, John Wiley & Sons, 2013.

Management science consolidated at the same time as neopositivism and functionalism, i.e. at the beginning of the 20th century. It does not come as a surprise that the creators of management science, such as F.W. Talor and H. Fayol, assumed neopositivism as the default, natural way of practising it. Functionalism also dominates in the social sciences, and is the fundamental approach to cultural processes. After the Second World War, the systemic approach go connected with functionalism and neopositivism, which led to a consolidation of the dominant paradigm in the social sciences[58].

A system is a whole, comprising functionally interconnected sub-systems. The general systems theory was created by L. Bertalanffy, who integrated previous concepts[59]. Similarly to functional structuralism, the basic assumptions include integration of the whole system, a striving for homeostasis and balance, and functional correlations between its elements and a hierarchical system structure. The systems theory postulates a differentiation between closed and open systems, which bears a similarity to the Durkheimian analogy between the mechanistic and the organic. Another important issue is the assumption of emergence, or the appearance of specific features of a system at subsequent levels of complexity. The general systems theory was one of the attempts at creating the most general theories integrating science. This generality is both a value and a limitation of the concept at the same time. Far-reaching generalisations would allow the integration of science, eliminating the dichotomy between the natural and social sciences, but on the other hand, generality results in a lack of possibility to falsify concepts. This places the general systems theory on the level of science philosophy, not an actual empirical science[60]..

The understanding of organisational culture in the neopositivist-functionalist current refers to the assumptions of nomothetic science, which strives for the generalisation of credible research results. Organisational culture is seen as being an entity of a systemic and holistic character that objectively exists. It consists of specific elements (subsystems) which function within cause and effect correlations. The most often mentioned elements of organisational culture include values, norms, basic assumptions, cultural patterns, heroes, stereotypes, myths, stories, rituals and taboos.

---

58 D. A. Wren, A. G. Bedeian, J. D. Breeze. "The foundations of Henri Fayol's administrative theory." *Management Decision* 40.9 (2002): 906-918.

59 L. von Bertalanffy, *General Systems Theory: Foundation, Development*, George Braziller, New York 1960.

60 P. Bénéton, Histoire de mots culture et civilisation, Paris, 1975, p. , p. 23. za: Z. Bauman, *K Liquid Modernity.* Cambridge: Polity Press, 2000.

The functionalist view of culture puts emphasis on balance, harmony and order, which are related to research into the problem of internal integration. Therefore, the subjects of interest are not subcultures or counter-cultures which, by definition, limit the internal integration of culture. According to E. Schein, organisational culture develops within two key orientations. The first is the need for internal integration, which is manifested in the strength or homogeneity of culture, and the other is the striving for the external adaptation, which is manifested in its competitiveness. A balance between these two dimensions results in creation of an effective, positive organisational culture[61]. Internal integration can be viewed at as coherence and the strength of internal relationships, determining the way organisation functions as a whole. The levels of internal integration of functioning organizations may differ. One can create a continuum from full integration to complete disintegration, using the criticism of functionalism made by representatives of the conflict theory, such as R. Dahrendorf and L. Coser[62] (Tab. 2). A fully integrated organisation is a hypothetical entity, which never occurs in reality. It is theoretically possible only in the context of a total institution, which is a very special, extreme case of organisation. Full disintegration means the breaking of the organisational whole into smaller entities, as a result of decentralist tendencies. A fully disintegrated organisation is of a transitory and temporary character, as after reaching the critical point of system disintegration it can no longer be perceived as a whole.

An organisation can be maintained as a whole (integrated) by external or internal factors. In order to maintain it as a whole, it has to be integrated externally, institutionally and legally. Organisational coherence can also be studied from the system and internal perspectives. This makes it possible to look for the sources and mechanisms of integration on all levels and in all sub-systems. Strategy can be an important factor uniting an organisation – if both individual members and social groups (colleagues, employees and interest groups) identify themselves with the aims of the organisation, then this facilitates the integration of the whole system. Another factor that strengthens this integration in the area of strategy further is support for the organisation's aims from broader social groups, and not only the organisation's own members. This takes place when the

61 E.H. Schein, *Organizational Culture and Leadership*, John Wiley & Sons, 2010; E.H. Schein, *Organization Development.: A Jossey-Bass Reader*, John Wiley & Sons, 2017.

62 L. Coser, *The Functions of Social Conflict*, Macmillan, New York, 1956; R. Dahrendorf, *Class and Class Conflict in Industrial Society*, London 1969.

Tab. 2: Integrational and coercive concepts of an organisational system. Source: Own work based on R. Dahrendorf, *Class and Class Conflict*.

Integrational concept	Coercive concept
Organisation is permanent and stable	Organisation undergoes permanent changes
Organisation is a system of functionally integrated elements	Organisation is a system of random, temporary relationships between its elements
Organisation functions in the context of social order	Organisation functions in the context of a social conflict
Organisation elements contribute to maintaining the system as a whole	Organisation elements contribute to the disintegration and the change of the whole system
All existing organisations are based on a sharing of their common values by their members	All organisations are based on coercion of some members by others
Organisation is a whole	Organisation may be perceived as a whole

organisation's mission meets the conditions of social responsibility. An organisation is more integrated structurally when individuals approve and understand their place within the organisational structure and power relationships accompanying it, and when the structure is a reflection of the internal social diversification of the organisation and the external social structure.

Naturally, just as the areas of strategy, structure and culture can be treated as elements creating integration in situations when the aims, power structure or system of values at the level of individuals, social groups and organisations within a society are coherent, one can also see a contrary tendency (Tab. 3). An organisation's disintegration arises from the lack of strategic, structural or cultural coherence. However, it has to be understood that both integrational and disintegrational forces can contribute to an organisation's development.

The extent of an organisation's integration can change considerably with time. Internal reasons for these changes are usually difficult to foresee and are of a revolutionary character. They include, among others, the processes of takeovers and mergers, which happen in many globalised economic sectors. It is usually easier to diagnose the internal factors behind changes in an organisation's integration level.

In conclusion, the functionalist view of organisational culture, being the oldest, classical and most popular cognitive perspective in the social sciences, has a number of characteristic features.

1.

Tab. 3: Levels and areas of the internal integration of an organisation. Source: Own work.

	Strategy	Structure	Culture
Individuals	Convergence of individual aims with the aims of the organisation	Acceptance of one's own place within the structure	Identification of individuals and similar values within the organisation
Social groups	Convergence of group aims and interests with the aims of the organisation	Internal coherence of the formal structure (e. g. the division into groups in an organisation)	Identification of groups with an organisation, groups' acceptance of the organisational values
Whole organisation	Convergence of the organisation's aims with the aims of society	Coherence of the organisation's internal structure and the social structure of the environment	Social values consolidate the organisation's coherence

2.2 Elements of organisational culture

The differently interpreted models, elements and types of culture remain of key significance to the functionalist understanding of organisational culture. Thus, for the purpose of the conducted analysis, I propose to assume that the elements of a functionalist organisational culture are not other organisational sub-systems, such as strategy or organisational structure, but the strictly cultural variables, including values, basic assumptions, norms, artefacts and so on. A model could include those correlations between important variables describing organisational culture allowing us to predict the states of culture. This would fulfil the neopositivist postulates of causative relationships between variables and verifiability. This means that the model would offer the possibility of generating hypotheses concerning culture, and then, with the use of research methods, to reliably verify or at least potentially falsify them. Another consequence of creating a cultural model would be the generation of typologies (classifications) of the types of organisational culture, distinguished by significant criteria. Having made these assumptions, one can begin with the analysis of elements, move on to models and finish with the types of organisational culture and the methodology of studying them.

Values, norms and cultural models that are developed and spread in a given social group can be considered the fundamental elements of culture.

In the case of organisational culture, the group which is based on the community of values, norms and cultural patterns is organisation. The elements of organisational culture were first distinguished by E. Schein, P. Bate, A. Pettigrew and other authors in the 1970s. Culture elements are of key importance to the neopositivist-functionalist-systemic paradigm because their assumptions are of a systemic and analytical nature. Naturally, this does not mean that the elements of culture are not used in other paradigms. Interpretative, critical and even postmodern cultural studies selectively include cultural elements. As certain divisions have been established in the subject literature, and cultural analysis has been adapted to business practice, it is worth pointing to the 'canonical' elements of organisational cultures, including:

- Cultural values,
- Basic assumptions,
- Social and organisational norms,
- Ways of communication, stories, narratives, myths and metaphors,
- An organisational stereotypes,
- Rituals,
- Symbols,
- Customs, traditions,
- Organisational heroes,
- Taboos,
- Cultural patterns,
- Cultural artefacts,
- Subcultures.

In most cases, a culture's essence is formed by values or basic assumptions which include fundamental questions concerning the attitude towards an organisation (identity), the people in an organisation, the nature of the environment and other existential questions. Values give rise to social norms, understood as the rules of shaping an organisation's members' behaviour, which take the form of orders or prohibitions. An important element of organisational culture is the means of communication, which can be described with the use of stories, narratives, myths and metaphors. The first three of these are spread by employees, and are informal, oral descriptions of real – in the case of myths – unreal realities of the organisation from the past, rendering its 'spirit' (esprit de corps). Well-documented research shows that the human cognitive apparatus is well prepared to absorb, remember and even intuitively value narratives, especially those that are highly emotional[63]. Probably this is why stories about the unusual activities of an organisation's leaders, important events or dramatic situations are so well-rooted in the organisation's 'collective awareness'. The rhetorical construction of these stories is usually simple, although they often make use of paradoxes, antimonies and metaphors. The humorous elements are also of importance, and are often reflected in suspense and original punch lines.

The fourth important element of communication in organisational culture is metaphor, which also reflects the organisation's essence. Metaphors are deeply rooted in the minds of managers and other employees, and so influence the way the whole organisation, its social relationships and relations with its environment are perceived. For example, the use of the mechanistic or organic metaphor by managers should have an effect on the number of manifestations of organisational life[64]. The situation is similar to using war metaphors in relation to the free market and competitors.

Analyses of the next element of organisational culture – rituals, have been taken directly from cultural anthropology and sociology. Rituals are routine, ossified ways of action established in an organisation. Rituals are the carriers of the cultural tradition, which is manifested by the symbolic, repeatable activities of people[65]. The most important rituals include initiation rites (the way new employees are treated), rites of passage (action in the face of changing roles), integration (actions supporting employees' identification with their organisation) and degradation (the ways a loss of prestige is manifested). Rituals serve very important social functions, as on one hand they are statements, and on the other they establish behavioural norms. Regulation is a very significant aspect, as it provides employees with 'correct' actions, without the need to think and make decisions in every situation. An organisational behaviour that is not in accordance with the established rituals can be a source of cultural confusion and lead to disintegration of the organisational routine.

Stereotypes are simplified, evaluative images of reality which function in the social awareness[66]. Social actions are to a large extent carried out thanks

---

63 A. Norenzayan, S. Atran, J. Faulkner, M. Schaller, *Memory and Mystery: The Cultural Selection of Minimally Counterintuitive Narratives*, Cognitive Science, 2006, 30: 531–553.

64 G. Morgan, *Images of Organization*. Thousand Oaks, CA: Sage Publications. Walker Management Library, 1998

65 A.M. Pettigrew, On Studying Organizational Culture, *Administrative Science Quarterly*, No. 12, 1979.

66 PWN Dictionary, Internet, 2014.

to stereotypes, as they respond to the elementary rule of economy in the decision-making process. Most human perceptions and interpretations are made with the use of assimilated stereotypes, the medium for which is culture. These offer simple, normative regulations concerning all elements of the social reality, and are stereotypical answers to questions related to identity, employee relationships and cooperation with the environment, reflected in other elements of the organisational culture (stories, rituals, language, etc.) and the whole organisation (mission, vision, strategic goals and organisational structure). Leaving functionalism aside, stereotypes in organisational culture can be compared to the patterns proposed by S. G. Harris. He defines patterns as knowledge structures drawn from experience and used in order to act in analogous situations. Harris describes several types of such patterns rooted in organisational culture. For example, 'me in an organisation' determines the relationships between individual and collective identities, while 'personality in an organisation' integrates personal ideas and memories with the expectations of the other organisation's members[67].

A symbol is a thing, person, object or image being a sign of something, associated with a notion and bringing to mind certain – usually deep – meanings. In the case of organisational culture, symbols are signs that reflect cultural values. Functionalism is dominated by a narrowed understanding of symbols as logos, trademarks or colour patterns, while in interpretivism, this understanding is very broad, as actually everything in an organisation can have a symbolic meaning (words, events, situations, figures etc.).

Customs, similarly to traditions, include behaviour, actions and the ways of doing certain things established in a given society. In organisational cultures, customs and traditions are a kind of repeatable and ossified social practice, similar to rituals. The difference is that the usefulness of a given social action is maintained in the collective awareness. For example, an organisational custom could be the 'group coffee' shared by employees in the mornings. This has some ritual aspects because it is ossified, but on the other hand, employees correctly recognise its meaning and purpose. Contrary to rituals, customs are usually not as ossified and are more oriented towards individuals.

Organisational heroes are important figures who have left their mark on the organisation. Organisational heroes always include the founders, whose personality, ideas and creativity are usually the original source of the organisation's

67 S.G. Harris, Organizational Culture and Individual Sensemaking: A Schema-Based Perspective, *Organization Science* 1994, 5 (3), pp. 309–321.

culture. Other heroes may be managers, directors and charismatic employees. Narratives about heroes and the customs and symbols they created can have a large influence on the directions of an organisational culture's development. The subject literature offers many publications about 'organisational personality' and the link between organisational culture and the people who create it[68].

A taboo is a notion drawn from depth psychology, and earlier from Freud's psychoanalysis and cultural anthropology. It is a topic or social activity which is on the one hand hidden and unmentioned, and on the other, important to an organisation – it can even be a time-honoured custom[69]. Taboos are located within the interests of functionalists[70] and the representatives of alternative paradigms[71]. For example, they are often used in relation to the issues of discrimination and stigmatisation of disadvantaged groups in organisations[72].

Cultural patterns are most often interpreted from the perspective of one of the most popular anthropological books, R. Benedict's *Patterns of Culture*[73]. In the case of organisational culture, these are relatively well-established ways of action, common to all of an organisation's members, being a manifestation of its configuration of values. Cultural patterns concern all activities, including both the ways of proper behaviour in the organisation and the ways of communication.

Artefacts are notions drawn from anthropology and archaeology, which in the case of organisational culture, mean visible manifestations of the organisational culture's functioning. These can be physical (spaces, buildings, architecture), behavioural (greeting gestures, non-verbal communication) and lingual (language conventions, forms of addressing each other). The notion of artefacts was popularised in organisational culture by E. Schein, but it entails a

---

68 A.J. Chatman, S.G. Barsade, Personality, Organizational Culture, and Cooperation: Evidence from a Business Simulation, *Administrative Science Quarterly*, Sep., 1995, 40 (3), pp. 423–443; F. Manfred, R. Kets de Vries, D. Miller, Personality, Culture, and Organization, *The Academy of Management Review*, Apr., 1986, 11 (2), pp. 266–279.

69 Totem and Taboo, *Some Points of Agreement between the Mental Lives of Savages and By Freud, Sigmund*. Published, Routledge, 23rd June, 1999.

70 A.E.M. van Vianen, A.H. Fischer, *Illuminating the Glass Ceiling*: The Role of Organizational Culture Preferences, *Journal of Occupational and Organizational Psychology*, 2002.

71 J. Martin, Deconstructing Organizational Taboos: The Suppression of Gender Conflict in Organizations, *Organization Science*, Nov. 1990, 1 (4), pp. 339–359.

72 E. Wilson, *Inclusion, Exclusion and Ambiguity – The Role of Organisational Culture*, *Personnel Review* 2000, 29(3), pp. 274–303.

73 R. Benedict, *Patterns of Culture, Introduction* F. Boas, New York: Houghton Mifflin, 1934.

large degree of ambiguity. On the one hand, similarly to archaeology, its understanding seems to be limited to the visible, mostly material manifestations of culture, but on the other, following the example of cultural anthropology, artefacts can be understood as all manifestations of the basic assumptions and values of organisational culture. An additional challenge is the use of artefacts both in functionalist and interpretative paradigms[74].

Subcultures are social groups within organisational culture, which build their integration upon opposition to the dominant organisational culture (counter-cultures), or upon looking for autonomy. Subcultures usually crystallise around values that are not thoroughly consistent with the culture of the whole organisation[75]. Examples include the professional subcultures in hospitals, amongst doctors, nurses, managers and others. Subcultures and counter-cultures are key notions for the understanding of culture in the symbolic-interpretative paradigm[76].

It is easy to see that even a superficial analysis of culture elements reveals they are inseparable. For example, the meanings of norms, cultural patterns, and artefacts to a large extent overlap. All elements of organisational culture described are systemically interdependent, but hierarchically ordered. The reasons and original constituents of culture are values and basic assumptions. Other elements of organisational culture are often considered to be the only manifestations of these deeper elements.

An advantage of this canon of elements is the analytical approach, allowing us to operationalise and study organisational practices and make a consistent division, according to which cultural elements can be separated from other organisational subsystems, such as organisational strategy and structure. A disadvantage of this functionalist division is its incompleteness and the overlapping of culture elements. It seems quite obvious that a mission or structures of power are of a cultural character. Mission reflects values and organisational identity, while the structure of power is the dominant cultural pattern. However, in the case of the functionalist-systemic approach, these two elements should be ascribed to organisational strategy and structure, respectively.

---

74 P. Gagliardi, *Symbols and Artefacts: Views of the Corporate Landscape Communication and Social Order*, Transaction Publishers, 1990.

75 G. Hofstede, Identifying Organizational Subcultures: An Empirical Approach, *Journal of Management Studies*, 1998, 35: 1–12.

76 J.M. Jermier, J.W. Slocum, Jr., L.W. Fry, J. Gaines, Organizational Subcultures in a Soft Bureaucracy: Resistance behind the Myth and Facade of an Official Culture, *Organization Science, May, 1991*, 2 (2), pp. 170–194.

Some proposals for the analysis of culture elements, trying to omit these disadvantages of the 'canon' of culture elements, are based on an understanding located on the borderline between functionalism and interpretivism. In response, G. Johnson proposed a division into culture elements which is not disjunctive and which places the elements of strategy and structure among culture's constituent parts. This proposal includes the following elements of organisational culture:

- Paradigm: what the organisation is, its mission and values.
- Control system: processes aimed at monitoring activities.
- Organisational structures: hierarchies and the division of work.
- Structures of power: who makes decisions, using what prerogatives.
- Symbols: logos and utility models, as well as status symbols indicating power.
- Rituals and procedures: meetings, reports, consolidated more than necessary.
- Stories and myths: narratives about people and events, the aim of which is to spread information about what is valued in the organisation[77].

However, it seems that such broadening of the way culture is understood is quite risky in the case of the neopositivist-functionalist-systemic paradigm. Including organisational strategy and structure in culture means that they cannot be treated as subsystems that are organisationally equal to culture. In this case, studying the relationships between subsystems becomes pointless, while the concept moves closer to understanding culture as a 'root metaphor', which is characteristic of non-functionalist paradigms.

2.3 Models of organisational culture

Assuming the analytical perspective on the elements of organisational culture, it is worth considering the relationships between them too. The key to understanding culture is answering the question about the cognitive model, with the use of which we can formulate hypotheses concerning the state of culture. Organisational culture models, based on the neopositivist-functionalist-systemic paradigm, are characterised by:

- Systemic nature,
- Analytical nature,
- Reification,
- A striving for statistical balance.

---

77 G. Johnson, Rethinking Incrementalism, *Strategic Management Journal* Vol. 9, 1988, pp. 75–91.

A systemic nature is one in which elements of organisational culture, between which causative relationships in a model are described, form subsystems, and so a change in the state of one entails a change in the state of the whole system. An analytical nature is one in which the assumed model of culture can be divided into elements both theoretically and empirically. Thus, the elements of organisational culture described in the previous subchapter are not only a list of elements, but also constituents of a model. Reification means that organisational culture is treated as an extant, real entity, almost an object that can be studied. Understanding of organisational culture as a process is much rarer. And finally, the striving for balance means that functionalist models usually describe the status quo, so they are static.

The subject literature offers a large number of models that have often been used to build typologies, and have been tested with the use of empirical research. The most important, even canonical culture models are those of E. Schein and G. Hofstede, while the most popular modern models were created by K. Cameron and R. Quinn, as well as R. Goffee and G. Jones. Later on, I will present my own 3D model of organisational culture, based on G. Hofstede's model of dimensions, which I used for research in 2000.

E. Schein emphasises that organisational culture exists to some extent in order to answer two kinds of problems, concerning each organisation: problems with adjusting to the organisation's environment and problems related to its internal integration[78]. His model consists of three elements called culture levels, which were distinguished because of their permanence and visibility. This author perceives organisational culture as a collection of dominant values and norms of conduct that are characteristic of a given organisation, supported by assumptions as to the nature of reality and manifested in the form of artefacts – external and artificial products of the given culture[79]. According to the concept of this author, culture functions on three levels: artefacts can be found on the surface, below which are the values and norms of behaviour, with the lowest level occupied by the main, basic assumptions.

78 E.H. Schein, The Role of the Founder in Creating Organizational Culture, *Organizational Dynamics* 1983, pp. 13–28; E.H. Schein, Coming to a New Awareness of Organizational Culture, *Sloan Management Review* 1984, pp. 3–16; E.H. Schein, How Culture Forms, Develops and Changes, [in:] R.H. Kilmann, *Gaining Control of the Corporate Culture*, pp. 17–43; E.H. Schein, *Organizational Culture and Leadership*, John Wiley & Sons, 2004.

79 E.H. Schein, *Organizational Culture and Leadership*, John Wiley & Sons, 2004.

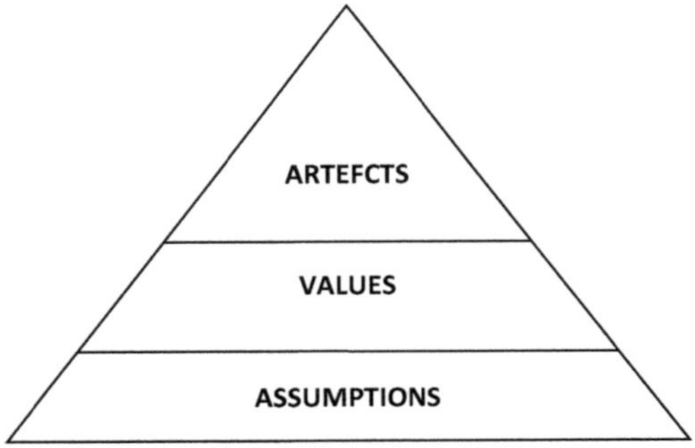

Fig. 1: An organisational culture model according to E. Schein. Source: Schein E. H., Organizational culture and leadership. A dynamic view, op. cit., p. 14.

Artefacts include logos, the appearance and design of buildings, dress code, status indication, common phrases and mental shortcuts, jargon, mottos, myths, legends, ceremonies and rituals. Norms and values can be divided into the declarative (which declare what is good for the organisation, what is praiseworthy and what is bad and reprehensible), and the followed (which we know about thanks to all kinds of informal conversations and behaviour). The basis and essence of organisational culture are assumptions, or collections of the basic patterns of orientation and ideas, as well as philosophical and worldview assumptions which influence perception and actions.

G. Hofstede proposed a model of organisational culture which orders the elements of culture hierarchically, comparing them metaphorically with onion layers:

Values are located at the core of the onion, rituals and heroes form the middle layers, while symbols form the outermost layer of the model. The last three elements of culture together form a broader category of practices. Symbols include words, gestures, objects and images, which are recognised by the members of a given culture. Heroes are people who symbolise the features most valued in a given culture, becoming role models in the process. Rituals are repetitive activities which express and emphasise the basic values of an organisation. They can be found in gestures, ways of greeting, religious and social ceremonies. Symbols, heroes and rituals form practices, which are clear only to the members of a given culture, while values are the ideas of what is important in a given environment and society. These are often called moral codes. They point to what should be, not to what actually is. The assumed system of values gives rise to an organisation's cultural norms, which determine what is permissible

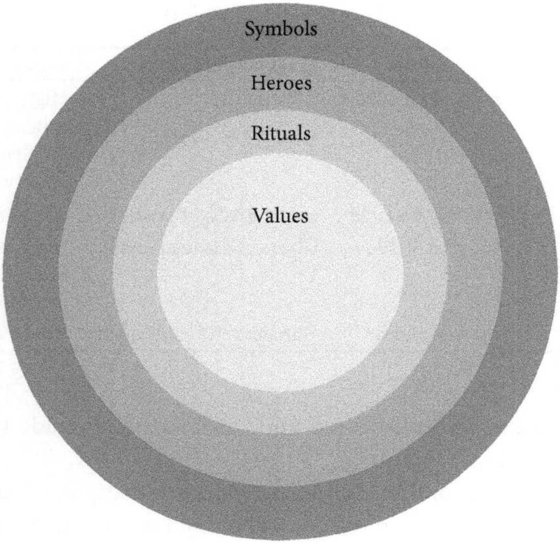

Fig. 2: G. Hofstede's 'onion diagram'. Source: G. Hofstede, *Cultures and Organizations: Software of the Mind*, New York: McGraw-Hill, 1991.

and what is prohibited. These indicate the kinds of behaviour we can expect of the members of a given organisational culture. As G. Hofstede emphasises, the presented structure of culture refers to national and organisational cultures, but in both cases individual elements play different roles. Members of different organisations differ mostly in terms of practices, and not in terms of values. On the national level, differences mainly concern values. As Hofstede claims, the core of organisational culture is the sense of community of practice, which is not common to all values. The values of an organisation's members depend mostly on external factors, such as nationality and age, and not just membership in the organisation.

A different model of culture, quite often used for the purpose of empirical research, was proposed by K. Cameron and R. Quinn, based on the distinction between two dichotomous dimensions: flexibility vs. stability and internal vs. external orientation. The combination of these dimensions results in four types of ideal organisational culture:

1. Clan culture is inwardly oriented and flexible, and often conditions paternalist management styles.

Tab. 4: Cameron\Quinn model of organisational culture. Source: Own work.

Ideal culture type	Dimensions	Ideal leadership type	Effectiveness
Clan	Internal Flexible	Paternalistic	High, especially in the sphere of employee involvement and quality
Adhocracy	External Flexible	Innovative leadership	Moderate or low
Market	External Stable	Charismatic leadership	High, especially in economic and innovative terms
Bureaucracy	Internal Stable	Bureaucratic leadership	Moderate or low

2. Adhocracy is outwardly oriented and flexible, which leads to innovation-oriented leadership.
3. Market culture is a combination of outward orientation and stability, which leads to strong leadership in the context of high competitiveness.
4. Bureaucratic culture is inwardly oriented and strongly structured, the consequences of which are highly formalised management patterns.

Cameron and Quinn proposed linking organisational culture with leadership and effectiveness, and developed a method and a tool for cultural diagnosis they call an Organisational Culture Assessment Instrument, which allows us to identify cultural gaps[80]. The clan culture is characterised by friendly professional relationships, with the organisation's members thinking they are part of one huge family. Leaders in this case are perceived as mentors. There is a high level of involvement in the tasks received, as loyalty and tradition bond the organisation's members together. Emphasis is put on long-term benefits, the organisation is characterised by a striving for agreement, and it is oriented towards interpersonal relationships. The decisive factors are managerial skills in managing teams and developing employees. The culture of adhocracy favours creativity and dynamic development. An organisation's employees are not afraid to take risks, and they like experimenting. A typical organisation's leader is an innovator, a visionary.

80 Cameron, Kim S. and Ettington, Deborah R. (1988) The Conceptual Foundations of Organizational Culture. *Higher Education: Handbook of Theory and Research*, pp. 356–396. New York: Agathon.
Cameron, Kim S. and Freeman, Sarah J. (1991) Cultural Congruence, Strength, and Type: Relationships to Effectiveness. *Research in Organizational Change and Development*, 5:23–58.

The decisive elements include managerial skills related to innovation management, orientation towards the future and managing constant improvement. A culture of hierarchy is typical of formalised organisations. In this case, a typical leader is a coordinator, organiser and observer. Work has to go uninterrupted and has to be done on time. There is a rule, according to which control improves effectiveness. The decisive elements are managerial skills related to assimilation management (clear indication of expectations and standards), a control system and coordination. In the case of a market culture, a typical leader is a supervisor, competitor and producer. A characteristic feature of such organisational culture is achievement of aims and beating the competition. It is important to fulfil the tasks, achieve results and succeed. The decisive factors are managerial skills related to motivating employees and propagating a customer-oriented approach. While the clan culture and adhocracy are flexible and allow freedom of action, the cultures of market and hierarchy value stability and control. The first two cultures are oriented towards internal issues and integration, while the other two are oriented towards the environment and diversity[81].

R. Goffee and G. Jones assume that cultural patterns in an organisation can be successfully explained with the use of the dimensions of sociability and solidarity[82]. In this case, sociability is understood as honest liking between the members of a given community, while solidarity is understood as the ability of an employee group to achieve common goals. Goffee and Jones's model allows us to distinguish four types of organisational cultures. The combination of a high level of solidarity with an equally high level of sociability results in a community culture. Its characteristic features include maintaining friendly relationships at work and outside work, justice and a reduction of fear in uncertain situations, sharing clearly determined, deeply rooted values, a fair distribution of risk and reward, clearly indicated competencies and a balanced assessment system. An important role is played by social events, which means the culture includes strong rituals. The meeting of a high level of solidarity and a low level of sociability gives rise to a mercenary culture, which is characterised by the seizing of opportunities, quickly and effectively, and effectively dealing with threats. Mistakes and shortcomings are unwelcome in this environment. An important role is played by reports containing specific data. All tasks are a result of top-down decisions,

81 K.S. Cameron, P.E. Quinn, *Diagnosing and Changing Organizational Culture, Based on The Competing Values Framework*, Addison Wesley.

82 R. Goffee, G. Jones, *What Holds the Modern Company Together?*, Harvard Business Review, November-December 1996, p. 134.

and their fulfilment is unquestionable. The personal interests of subordinates often coincide with the organisation's assumptions. However, in many cases employees are not loyal. Usually they stay in an organisation only as long as it suits their interests. Another kind of culture, distinguished by the above authors, is the network culture. This appears when a low level of solidarity and a high level of sociability are combined. This culture is oriented towards strong personal relations, deepening these relations and omitting formal procedures. Meetings in the office, gossiping and friendly chats are typical of this culture. Unlike the mercenary culture, in this case numerous informal meetings are organised at work, birthdays and Christmas are celebrated together and an important role is played by rituals. The last type of culture, created by a combination of a low level of solidarity and a low level of sociability, is the inconsistent culture. Its characteristic feature is the striving for the achievement of personal goals; it does not include the identification by employees with the goals of the organisation. There is no agreement between the managers on different levels as to strategic aims and development standards. In organisations of this type, showing emotions and attempts at friendly behaviour are unwelcome. Professional life is separate from personal issues. This kind of organisation's members assumes that all rituals are a waste of time. Resistance to changes and development is emphasised, while people are distrustful and unwilling to share information[83].

2.4 One-dimensional typologies of organisational culture

The distinction between models and typologies of organisational culture is quite fluid. However, based on the subject literature, a number of typologies and classifications of organisational culture can be proposed, which can then be divided into the one-dimensional and the multidimensional. Some of these are based on simple dichotomies, which locate organisational culture within the intensity scale of one feature. Others are more complex, two-dimensional or multidimensional classifications. One-dimensional models are presented for example by E. T. Hall, who distinguished high- and low-context cultures[84] because of the situational conditions of a communication process (context); R. R. Gesteland, who divided cultures according to the level of transaction concentration (pro-partner and pro-transactional cultures), according to the forms of desired and inappropriate behaviour (ceremonial and un-ceremonial

---

83 R. Goffee, G. Jones, *The Character of a Corporation*, Harper Business, Harper-Collins Publishers, New York 1998, pp. 21–43.

84 E.T. Hall, *Beyond Culture*, New York: Doubleday, 1976

cultures), according to the forms of behaviour applied (verbal, non-verbal and para-verbal – expressive and reserved cultures), and according to the approach to time (monochronic and polychronic cultures). It has to be emphasised that using one-dimensional classifications oversimplifies and limits typologies to only two types of culture. On the other hand, multidimensional classifications, which distinguish many types of culture, lead to the blurring of boundaries and the overlapping of descriptions of different cultures. The most popular typologies are two-dimensional, distinguishing four types of culture. Apart from R. E. Quinn's model, described previously, it is worth paying attention to the characteristics of the cultures of R. Harrison and C. Handy, T. E. Deal and A. A. Kennedy, N. H. Snyder, T. J. Peters, as well as R. Goffee and G. Jones.

The analysis can begin with one-dimensional classifications. Those most often found in the subject literature include the following dichotomies:

1) Weak culture – strong culture.
2) Positive culture – negative culture.
3) Pragmatic culture – bureaucratic culture.
4) Introvert culture – extrovert culture.
5) Conservative culture – innovative culture.
6) Hierarchical culture – egalitarian culture.
7) Individualist culture – collectivist culture.

1 Weak culture – strong culture

The typology of weak and strong cultures is one of the most-often analysed issues of the cultural current in management. The subject literature is dominated by the belief that strong organisational culture prevails. Strong organisational culture is characterised by homogeneity, which means uniformity and common agreement among employees as to key assumptions, values and norms. Strong identification with organisational values is supposed to lead to the greater involvement of employees and, in consequence, to greater effectiveness[85]. Internal cultural incoherence, the manifestation of which is the emergence of subcultures or even counter-cultures, could lead to a disintegration of the organisation (Tab. 5).

Still, the homogeneity of organisational culture has its drawbacks. V. Sathe, accepting the superiority of strong organisational cultures, proposes to assess them in organisational terms, taking into consideration their distinctiveness

---

85 T.J. Peters, R.H. Waterman, Jr., *In Search of Excellence: Lessons from America's Best--Run Companies*, New York: Harper, 1982

Tab. 5: Strong vs. weak cultures. Source: Own work.

Features	Strong culture	Weak culture
Degree of acceptance of organisational values and norms.	Agreement as to organisational values and norms.	Conflicts regarding organisational values and norms.
Sense of community among employees.	A strong sense of community among employees.	A sense of conflict of interests and striving for confrontation.
Degree of formalisation of norms.	Unwritten, commonly respected norms.	Formalised rules, which are often eluded.
Employees' involvement in their organisation's issues.	A high level of employees' involvement.	A low level of employees' involvement.
Degree of employee loyalty to the organisation.	A high level of employees' loyalty to the organisation.	A low level of employees' loyalty to the organisation.
Emotions related to being an organisation member – pride or shame.	Pride in being a part of the organisation.	Feeling ashamed of being a part of the organisation.
Emotions of the employees – a sense of being appreciated or humiliated.	Employees feel appreciated in the organisation.	Employees feel humiliated in the organisation.

and the extent to which they are spread and rooted[86]. However, there are also numerous researchers pointing to the disadvantages of strong organisational cultures. I. Janis described the dangerous phenomenon of 'group thinking', which is a social mechanism of group integration, coercing conformity[87]. A culture which is strong, or homogenous, distinct, spread-out and rooted in an organisation can limit the innovativeness and rationality of the decisions made, as well as hinder the process of introducing changes. The focus on the community of values obscures the views of non-conformists and provokes schematic thinking, which is shared by the majority. The unique, individual knowledge of some organisation members remains hidden, although it is often of key importance to the process of innovation. A different type of criticism is made by the researchers of the critical current (CMS), who believe that the issue of strong culture is a

86 V. Sathe, Implications of Corporate Culture, *Organizational Dynamics*, No. 12, 1983.

87 J.L., Irving, *Victims of Groupthink*, New York: Houghton Mifflin., 1972, p. 9; J.L., Irving, (1982). *Groupthink: Psychological Studies of Policy Decisions and Fiascos.* Second Edition. New York: Houghton Mifflin, 1982.

typical example of the instrumentalisation of organisational culture, which was called 'organisational culturism' by H. Willmot, and the 'pigeonhole problem' by L. Smircich[88]. Strong organisational culture means striving for the creation of an oppressive mechanism for employees, the aim of which is to coerce even greater involvement and loyalty, which is supposed to increase effectiveness. In this sense, strengthening the organisational culture is a kind of social engineering and psychomanipulation, leading to higher indoctrination and in consequence, to exploitation of the employees.

2 Positive culture – negative culture

The criterion for distinguishing positive and negative cultures is mostly their long-term influence on the effectiveness of organisational activities. Positive cultures should support the achievement of goals indicated by managers, while negative cultures can hinder the achievement of these goals. Based on research, P. Bate described a syndrome of negative organisational culture that can be juxtaposed with a positive culture (Tab. 6)[89].

Manifestations of 'negative cultures' are related to the risk of passivity (subordination) and conservatism. Passivity can result from the fact that the paternalistic management style prevails. Thanks to the sense of security resulting from the subordination to organisational power, employees no longer have to make decisions. Conservatism is related to a striving for the maintenance of the known, safe, status quo. Nevertheless, in the case of turbulence in the organisation's environment, both passivity and conservatism contribute to lowering the enterprise's competitiveness.

3 Bureaucratic culture – pragmatic culture

There is much research concerning the problems of the bureaucratisation of organisational cultures, which has led to the creation of this typology[90].

---

88 H.C. Willmott, Strength Is Ignorance; Slavery Is Freedom: Managing Culture in Modern Organizations. *Journal of Management Studies*, 1993, Nr 30/4, pp. 515–552; L. Smircich, Concepts of Culture and Organizational Analysis, *Administrative Science Quarterly*, 28 (3).

89 P. Bate, The Impact of Organisational Culture on Approaches to Organisational Problem Solving, *Organisational Studies*, no. 5, 1984.

90 Ch. Grey, *Trust, Control and Post-Bureaucracy*, Judge Institute of Management Studies, University of Cambridge, UK, Ch. Garsten, Organization Studies **March 2001** vol. 22 no. 2 **229–250**; J.Q. Wilson, *Bureaucracy: What Government Agencies*

Tab. 6: Negative vs. positive cultures. Source: Own work, based on P. Bate, 1984.

Features	Negative culture	Positive culture
Emotionality	Emotional coldness – avoiding expression and feelings.	Moderate or strong emotionality – sharing emotions with others.
Personalisation of organisational bonds	Depersonalisation of interpersonal relationships – a high level of formalisation.	Personalisation of relationships in the organisation – personal, direct statements, a lower level of formalisation.
Employee activity	Subordination – expecting guidelines from superiors in order to solve problems.	Activeness – employees strive for making decisions and solving problems by themselves.
Approach to changes	Conservatism – lack of flexibility in new situations.	Flexibility – openness to changes and readiness to implement them.
Isolation	Focus on one's own duties, specialisation.	A wider perspective on the enterprise's functioning, attempts at generalisations.
Approach to other organisations	Antipathy – people are opponents, rather than supporters (individualism).	Friendliness – people are more often supporters than opponents (collectivism).

Bureaucratic cultures are bound by a number of formalised rules, orders and prohibitions, which standardise an organisation's life in every detail. These are cultures of the written word, with limited and routine interpersonal contact. Pragmatic cultures are characterised by a lack of detailed organisational regulations (Tab. 7). There is a clear orientation towards verbal communication of an interpersonal character. The dichotomy between bureaucratic and pragmatic

Do And Why They Do It, Basic Books, 1989; J.M. Jermier, J.W. Slocum, Jr., L.W. Fry, J. Gaines, Organizational Subcultures in a Soft Bureaucracy: Resistance behind the Myth and Facade of an Official Culture, *Organization Science,* Vol. 2, No. 2 (May, 1991), pp. 170–194; P. Lok, J. Crawford, The effect of organisational culture and leadership style on job satisfaction and organisational commitment: A cross-national comparison, *Journal of Management Development*, Vol. 23 Iss: 4, 2004, pp. 321 – 338; M. Handman, The Bureaucratic Culture Pattern and Political Revolutions, *American Journal of Sociology,* Vol. 39, No. 3 (Nov., 1933), pp. 301–313;R. Deshpandé, J.U. Farley, Corporate Culture and Market Orientation: Comparing Indian and Japanese Firms, *Journal of International Marketing,* Vol. 7, No. 4 (1999), pp. 111–127; J.H. Astrachan, Family Firm and Community Culture, *Family Business Review*, 1988, 1: 165–189.

Tab. 7: Bureaucratic vs. pragmatic cultures. Source: Own work.

Features	Bureaucratic culture	Pragmatic culture
Formalisation	High; written communication and documentation prevail.	Low; verbal communication prevails.
Approach to changes	Careful, sceptical; changes entail the creation of new regulations.	Positive; changes are related to striving for the improvement of the organisation.
Basis for organisational power	Formal, impersonal, described and precisely indicated prerogatives.	Prerogatives of formal and informal sources of power, personal power, often unspecified.
Integration	Around formalised rules determined in documents, i.e. mission statements. Striving for homogenisation.	Around people or problems. Heterogeneity, changeability and a conflict of interests of subcultures are allowed.
Values	Order, unity, clarity.	Effectiveness, speed of action, flexibility.

cultures is deeply rooted in social values, which then spread to organisational cultures[91].

4 Introvert culture – extrovert culture

The analogy of introvert vs. extrovert cultures was transferred from the level of personality to the level of organisations[92]. To make it simple, we can say that an introvert personality is focused on itself and closed to other people, while an extrovert personality is oriented towards others, which means it is open. Translating it into the classification of organisational culture, introvert cultures can be described as closed, and extrovert as open (Tab. 8).

In the dichotomy between extrovert and introvert cultures, especially important research problems include linking the personality profiles of the management with the type of organisational culture[93], the relationships between

91 R.D. Hisrich, B. Bucar, S. Oztark, A Cross-Cultural Comparison of Business Ethics: Cases of Russia, Slovenia, Turkey, and United States, *Cross Cultural Management: An International Journal*, Vol. 10 Iss: 1, 2003, pp. 3 – 28.

92 C. Sikorski, *Kultura organizacyjna w instytucji*, UL, Lodz 1990.

93 J.A. Chatman, Improving Interactional Organizational Research: A Model of Person-Organization Fit, *The Academy of Management Review*, Vol. 14, No. 3 (Jul., 1989),

Tab. 8: Introvert vs. extrovert cultures and the organisational culture. Source: Own work, based on: C. Sikorski, 1990.

Features	Introvert culture	Extrovert culture
Tolerance for others	Low tolerance for other views and values.	High tolerance for other views and values.
Knowledge of the problems of other employees	Good knowledge of the problems of other employees.	Poor knowledge of the problems of other employees.
Sensitivity to the feelings of other employees	High sensitivity to the problems of other employees.	Low sensitivity to the problems of other employees.
Suspicion of new employees in an organisation	High level of suspicion of new employees.	Conventional confidence in new employees.
Approach to the change of a job	Employees do not plan to, or imagine changing jobs.	Employees can plan to change job, depending on the market offers.

teamwork, leadership and extroversion[94], and extroversion's influence on relationships between interested parties[95].

5 Conservative culture – innovative culture

The influence of organisational culture on innovation is one of the most significant subjects of cultural research. Most researchers believe that culture, reflected in mentality, is of key significance to shaping the level of innovation, enterprise, flexibility and creativity. Thus, all these notions form the basis for the classification of cultures. Innovative cultures are also known in the subject literature as entrepreneurial, flexible or creative cultures. The main problems

pp. 333–349; J. Ch. White, P.R. Varadarajan, P.A. Dacin, Market Situation Interpretation and Response: The Role of Cognitive Style, Organizational Culture, and Information Use, *Journal of Marketing*, Vol. 67, No. 3 (Jul., 2003), pp. 63–79

94 P. Castka, C.J. Bamber, J.M. Sharp, Measuring teamwork culture: the use of a modified EFQM model, *Journal of Management Development*, Vol. 22 Iss: 2, 2003, pp. 149 – 170; D.G. Kolb, D.M. Shepherd, Concept mapping organizational cultures, *Journal of Management Inquiry*, Sage, vol 6, No. 4, 1997, pp. 282–295

95 D. Gary; Ch. Rosa; da Silva, R. Vinhas, R. Stuart, A Corporate Character Scale to Assess Employee and Customer Views of Organization Reputation, *Corporate Reputation Review*, Volume 7, Number 2, 1 July 2004, pp. 125–146

of research into such types of culture are enhancing innovation[96], relationships between innovative culture and competitiveness[97], relationships between the degree of sector innovation and culture[98], links between innovative culture and organisational learning[99], and many others. Entrepreneurial organisational cultures have been researched by S. McGuire, who proposed the addition of creativity and readiness to undertaking challenges in the cultural model. Important characteristics of entrepreneurial cultures are an orientation towards people, empowerment, and the creation of values through innovation and changes[100].

An organisational culture is oriented towards changes and the readiness to act in a situation where there is not enough information, as well as a tendency to take risks. Organisations with high tolerance for uncertainty do not strive to maintain the status quo, but are ready to accept internal changes and to make transformations. Usually, they adapt to changes in the environment more easily and are flexible. They attach greater significance to the openness of organisation, and not its stability.

Conservative culture usually involves striving for a reduction of uncertainty, functioning in a context of low risk, supporting the maintenance of the status quo and emphasising the organisation's stabilising role. The role of tradition is also stressed at the enterprise level. The variants of action and scenarios developed are of a determinist character; they assume avoiding risks, maximum limitation of the information deficit and one-option planning. In most cases, changes are treated as threats (Tab. 9).

---

96 E.C. Martins, F. Terblanche, Building Organisational Culture that Stimulates Creativity and Innovation, *European Journal of Innovation Management*, Vol. 6 Iss: 1, 2003, pp. 64 – 74; G.N. Chandler, Ch. Keller, D.W. Lyon, Unravelling the Determinants and Consequences of an Inn Ovation-Supportive Organizational Culture, *Entrepreneurship: Theory and Practice*, Vol. 25, 2000.

97 G.A. Knight, S.T. Cavusgil, Innovation, Organizational Capabilities, and the Born-Global Firm, Palgrave Macmillan Journals, *Journal of International Business Studies*, Vol. 35, No. 2 (Mar., 2004), pp. 124–141.

98 J.A. Chatman, K.A. Jehn, Assessing the Relationship between Industry Characteristics and Organizational Culture: How Different Can You Be?, *The Academy of Management Journal*, Vol. 37, No. 3 (Jun., 1994), pp. 522–553.

99 R.F. Hurley, G.T.M. Hult, Innovation, Market Orientation, and Organizational Learning: An Integration and Empirical Examination, *Journal of Marketing*, Vol. 62, No. 3 (Jul., 1998), pp. 42–54.

100 S. McGuire, *Entrepreneurial Organizational Culture: Construct Definition and Instrument Development and Validation*, Dissertation Submitted to the Faculty of the School of Business and Public Management of the George Washington University, 2003.

Tab. 9: Innovative vs. conservative cultures. Source: Own work.

Features	**Innovative culture**	**Conservative culture**
Orientation towards changes	Orientation towards changes in the organisation.	Orientation towards maintaining status quo in the organisation.
Entrepreneurship	High entrepreneurship.	Low entrepreneurship and innovation.
Approach to tradition	Distance, tradition is treated as a burden.	Respect, tradition is treated as a model.
Respect for authorities	Undermining the value of the authorities, counting on 'fresh blood'.	High respect for the experienced employees of the organisation.
Approach to information	Accepting activities in the face of an information deficit.	Striving for action only when there is all information available.

The danger of conservatism is one of the key cultural threats in modern organisations that function in environments undergoing constant change. The most important elements in this case include maintaining and transferring the same values, cultivating tradition and striving for action without any change to the status quo. Although a conservative orientation supports the enterprise's stability, too much conservatism can be dangerous to each business entity. Conservative enterprises isolate themselves from information, resist changes and can be effective only if their sector is very stable, which is found less and less often.

6 Hierarchical culture – egalitarian culture

The division according to the hierarchic criterion combines cultural and structural problems with issues of organisational power. This classification is sometimes used in analyses of bureaucratic or power-oriented organisational cultures, for example in the public sector[101]. Another area of research includes the attempts to build systemic relationships between a hierarchic culture and organisational strategy and structure[102], as well as organisational learning[103].

101 R. Parker, L. Bradley, Organizational Culture in the Public Sector: Evidence from Six Organizations, *International Journal of Public Sector Management*, Vol. 13 Iss: 2, 2000, pp. 125–141

102 K.A. Bates, S.D. Amundson, R.G. Schroeder, W.T. Morris, The Crucial Interrelationship between Manufacturing Strategy and Organizational Culture, *Management Science*, Vol. 41, No. 10 (Oct., 1995), pp. 1565–1580

103 C.P. Ruppel, S.J. Harrington, Professional Communication, *IEEE Journals & Magazines*, **Volume:** 44, 2001, **pp.:** 37–52.

The favouring of hierarchisation is linked with a belief that people differ, and an organisation reflects this diversity. Thus, organisations should include a number of management levels, and there should be a significant diversification of rights, privileges and benefits among different groups of employees. Special significance should be attached to maintaining discipline and strengthening the authority of power. Hierarchic organisations are dominated by the acceptance of a strong diversity of employees. They clearly prefer elitist thinking, and emphasise the significance of the discipline and order created by the power structure.

The striving for equality is a consequence of the belief that people deserve similar rights, and that an organisation is a reflection of such fundamental equality. Thus, organisations should have a flat structure and limit the number of management levels as much as possible – broad diversification of employees' rights, privileges and benefits is unwelcome. Equality gives rise to the following attitudes in organisations: emphasising similarities between employees, favouring egalitarian thinking, orientation towards spontaneity, and the flexibility of structures and power relationships.

The dimension of hierarchy vs. equality is primal with regard to the dimension defined as authoritarianism vs. democracy (participation). Authoritarianism means striving for a one-person, unquestioned decision-making process in an organisation, while democracy means striving for a group (fully participatory) decision-making process. The dimension of hierarchy vs. equality is also primal in relation to the dimension of power centralisation[104].

7 Individualist culture – collectivist culture

The dimension of individualism vs. collectivism was popularised in the cultural research into organisations conducted by G. Hofstede, and is also used as an axis for the analysis of organisational cultures. This typology is most often used to indicate the relationships between a type of culture and a type of manager's personality[105], but it is also linked with the level of entrepreneurship[106],

---

104 R. Harrison, Understanding Your Organisation Character, *Harvard Business Review*, 1972, May-June.

105 J.A. Chatman, S.G. Barsade, Personality, Organizational Culture, and Cooperation: Evidence from a Business Simulation, *Administrative Science Quarterly*, Vol. 40, No. 3 (Sep., 1995), pp. 423–443; J.A. Chatman, J.T. Polzer, S G. Barsade, M.A. Neale, Vol. 43, No. 4 (Dec., 1998), pp. 749–780.

106 M.H. Morris, D.L. Davis, J.W. Allen, Fostering Corporate Entrepreneurship: Cross-Cultural Comparisons of the Importance of Individualism versus Collectivism, *Journal of International Business Studies*, Vol. 25, No. 1 (1st Qtr., 1994), pp. 65–89.

Tab. 10: Hierarchic vs. egalitarian cultures. Source: Own work.

Features	**Hierarchic culture**	**Egalitarian culture**
Inequalities between positions	Striving for the consolidation of inequalities between different positions in an enterprise.	Striving for the levelling of differences between different positions.
Wage differential	Accepting large differences between the wages for different positions.	Striving for the limitation of differences in wages.
Management style	Autocratic	Participatory
Level of centralisation of decisions	Centralisation of decisions	Decentralisation of decisions
The source of organisational hierarchy	Natural and objective; a belief that employees occupying lower positions in an organisation usually have fewer skills than employees on higher levels.	Social, conventional; hierarchy is related to different roles, determined for pragmatic purposes.
Stability of the power hierarchy	Hierarchy should be stable.	Hierarchy should be flexible and undergo changes.
Relationships between employees	Subordinates are dependent on their superiors.	Superiors and subordinates are interdependent.
Privileged position of employees on higher levels	Employees at higher levels of the organisation should have privileges.	Everyone in the organisation should have equal rights.
Concept for exercising power	The dominant concepts emphasise the significance of the superiors and the process of managing employees.	The dominant concepts emphasise the significance of employees and their involvement and participation in the managerial process.

involvement[107], the level of confidence and social capital[108], as well as many other variables.

Individualism means putting the value of an individual before the interests of a social group. This is related to a striving for the freedom of individuals and a

107 R.H. Moorman, G.L. Blakely, Individualism-Collectivism as an Individual Difference Predictor of Organizational Citizenship Behavior, *Journal of Organizational Behavior*, 1995, 16: 127–142.

108 L. Huff, L. Kelley, Levels of Organizational Trust in Individualist versus Collectivist Societies: A Seven-Nation Study, *Organization Science*, Vol. 14, No. 1 (Jan.–Feb., 2003), pp. 81–90.

belief that individual interests are the most important. According to this belief, organisations should focus on the motives and competences of individuals, rather than teams. Fulfilling individual interests can lead to success at the level of the whole organisation, as it favours rivalries and competitive attitudes, as well as nonconformist behaviour. An organisation is perceived as a group of individuals who have conflicting interests. The community approach (or in other words, collectivism) is the belief that the interest of a social group is more important than individual interests, and in an organisation this is manifested by an orientation towards group goals, even against individuals, while the preferred attitudes are conformism and collaboration.

The dichotomous typologies of organisational cultures described here are only the examples which most often appear in literature. In reality, there are many more typologies, based on more dichotomies than just these. Other examples include a culture of risk vs. avoiding uncertainty[109], flexible vs. inflexible cultures, changes vs. status quo. However, it seems that many of these dichotomies share common elements, which is why the analysis included seven classifications of organisational culture that are quite often used in one-dimensional research.

2.5 Multidimensional typologies of organisational culture

A consequence-modelled culture is another, different type of classification, and includes multidimensional typologies. The best known classifications of this type are by R. Harrison and C. Handy, T. E. Deal and A. A. Kennedy, T. J. Peters, O'Reilly, Chatman and Caldwell. These are mostly models which use the functionalist approach, oriented towards research into the relationships between an organisation's effectiveness and other internal variables. Another important issue concerns the strength of organisational culture and its influence on the integration of the system and its employees. One advantage of many Polish cultural analyses is the adjustment of concepts and methods of managing organisational culture to local specifics, an example of which is the large body of comparative research into organisations in Poland, as well as the descriptions of practical methods for managing organisational culture, given by the researchers mentioned.

The divisions proposed by R. Harrison and C. Handy are one of the earliest and, at the same time, the most popular multidimensional typologies of culture. The concepts of both authors were created separately but cover very similar values. R. Harrison listed four types of organisations, which form specific

109 S. Rayner, R. Cantor, *How Fair Is Safe Enough? The Cultural Approach to Societal Technology Choice*, Risk Analysis, 1987, 7: 3–9

Tab. 11: Individualist vs. collectivist cultures. Source: Own work.

Features	Individualist culture	Collectivist culture
Priority of interests in an organisation	Individuals' interests are more important than the organisation's interests.	An organisation's interests are more important than individual interests.
An organisation's essence	An organisation is a group of individuals who have different interests.	An organisation is a group of collaborating people.
Work relationships	Rivalry between employees is necessary.	Cooperation between people is necessary for the organisation.
Perspective on the significance of individuals	An organisation is based on eminent individuals.	An organisation is based on teams.
Coincidence of the interests of an organisation and of its employees	Interests of the organisation and individuals are divergent.	The interests of the organisation and individuals coincide.
Approach to the freedom of individuals	An organisation functions thanks to the freedom of individuals.	An organisation functions thanks to group solidarity.
Degree of conformity	People in an organisation should have their own opinions and express them (non-conformism).	In an organisation, one should adjust to the opinion of the community (conformism).
Approach to conflict	Conflicts can contribute to the organisation's development.	In an organisation, one has to strive for harmony and avoid conflicts.
Approach to familism	Ideal interpersonal relationships in an organisation are different from the relationships in a family, as they are based on a contract guaranteeing mutual benefits.	Ideal interpersonal relationships in an organisation should remind of a family.
Significance of private life in an organisation	Professional and private lives of employees should be strictly separated in an organisation.	Professional and private lives of employees merge in an organisation.

cultures. These are organisations oriented towards power, roles, tasks and people. Each of them prefers a specific normative system related to the core value. The system of values shared by employees determines the convergence between the interests of the organisation and its employees, and shapes the enterprise's ability to deal with the environment. Organisations rarely include all four types

Tab. 12: Types of culture according to R. Harrison and C. Handy. Source: Own work based on: Harrison R., *Understanding your organization's character*, Harvard Business Review 1972, pp. 119–128; C. Handy, *Understanding Organizations*, Penguin Books, Clays Ltd., Fourth Edition, Harmondsworth 1976.

Types of culture →	**Culture of power**	**Culture of roles**	**Culture of tasks**	**Culture of people**
Aspirations	Rivalry, attempts to dominate the environment	Order, stability	Orientation towards tasks, the achievement of goals, development	Satisfying the employees' needs, orientation towards personal success
Power and the system of work	Centralisation of power, a large degree of internal control, autocratic style, paternalism	A strong hierarchy, high formalisation, procedures	Cooperation, teamwork, distribution of power, based on experience, knowledge and competences; flexible organisation	A lack of hierarchy and control, specialists work independently of each other
Values shared	Rivalry, competitiveness	A sense of security, competences	Setting and achieving goals, cooperation, self-control	Self-reliance, individual skills, freedom of action

of culture in their pure form, but most enterprises have a tendency to focus on a given system of values. The description of the types of cultures proposed by R. Harrison and C. Handy is presented in Tab. 12.

Using the popular definition of corporate culture as the way people act within a company, T. E. Deal and A. A. Kennedy applied two criteria to the description of culture with reference to an organisation's functioning. These concern the risk level of the activity and how soon the results of its actions are visible. The combination of these two criteria allows us to distinguish four cultures[110].

1. The culture of the tough macho. Dominated by young, educated, brilliant heroes. They are dynamic and have lots of ideas. The atmosphere at work is youthful; there is a climate of quick action and risk-taking. The organisational culture is characterised by fighting and individualism. Success is what counts.

110 T.E. Deal, A.A. Kennedy, *Corporate Cultures: The Rites and Rituals of Corporate Life*, Perseus Publishing, Cambridge, Massachusetts 1982, pp. 107–127.

2. Culture focused on the company. The organisation's heroes are people who persistently fulfil their plans. They are mature and act calmly. They are a kind of mentor. They assume that the environment is a source of threat to the organisation, so it is better to make good, well-thought-out decisions. Orientation towards group actions and partnership. Hierarchy is of significance, and attention is paid to the order of meetings and speeches given during them. A scientific and technical atmosphere prevails.
3. 'Work hard, play hard' culture. The heroes are active people, devoted to work. They think one has to work hard and have some fun. In this case, personal contact is of great importance. Many meetings and events are held, and the people celebrate together. Many people believe that the organisation's environment is full of opportunities, which should be skilfully used.
4. A culture of process. An organisation is dominated by the subordination to rules, impersonality and minimalism. What counts at work is stability and fulfilling tasks based on rules and procedures. Heroes are hard-working people who appreciate stability and make no mistakes, even in difficult situations. The role of a hierarchical order and formal positions occupied by individual members is emphasised. In this case, interpersonal relationships are of an artificial character.

Because of the need to shape a pro-effective culture, it is necessary to examine the concepts distinguishing the types of cultures favouring changes. One of the models which allow us to analyse the convergence between culture and the possibilities of changing it is N. H. Snyder's model. It distinguishes two dimensions: (1) orientation towards the organisation and (2) orientation towards achievements. Thus, there are four types of organisational cultures: quality-oriented culture (which values effective planning, accepts changes and is oriented towards solving problems); creative culture (dominated by innovation, entrepreneurship, taking risks and initiating changes); productive culture (characterised by effectiveness, coherence, strict procedures, rituals in action and resistance to changes), and supportive culture (teamwork, cooperation, growth and responding to changes)[111]. The model by T. J. Peters is similar. It distinguishes four types of culture, depending on their influence on innovation, action, control and harmony of the culture in an organisation (Tab. 13).

O'Reilly, Chatman and Caldwell (1991) created *An organisational Profile Model*, which distinguished as many as seven dimensions: innovation, stability,

111 A.J. Rowe et al, *Strategic Management: A Methodological Approach*, Addison-Wesley Pub. Co., Reading, MA, 1990.

Tab. 13: Types of culture according to T. J. Peters. Source: Own work based on: Zbiegień-Maciąg L., *Kultura w organizacji: Identyfikacja kultur znanych firm,* op. cit, pp. 72–75 [based on:] Peters T. J., *Management decision,* Business Policy in Action, 1993, vol. 31, no. 6.

	Orientation towards employees	Orientation towards work
External orientation	**Culture of innovation** An organisational culture oriented towards innovative change, which has a tendency to take risks. Informal, direct contacts prevail. Can be chaotic.	**Culture of action** An organisational culture oriented towards action, achievements, and results. Initiative is what counts the most. Perfect, professional actions are rewarded. An organisation is characterised by the acceptance of changes. There may be problems with delegating responsibilities.
Internal orientation	**Culture of harmony** An organisational culture dominated by deliberation. People and teamwork are most important. External values are accepted only when they correspond to those shared within the organisation. The priorities are cultural values, which influence strategic decisions. Insusceptibility to changes.	**Culture of control** An organisational culture oriented towards strong control. Conservatism and bureaucracy prevail. A very hierarchical structure. Formal contacts and written communication dominate. Reluctance to taking risks. Subordinates strongly oppose all changes. A closed organisation.

respect for people, orientation towards effects, accuracy, orientation towards teamwork, aggressiveness. An organisational profile is a diagnostic tool, which allows one to correlate organisational culture with the personality traits of leaders, management and employees of the given organisation. This makes it possible to define and measure employees' involvement and loyalty, which then allows for assessment of the effectiveness of the culture[112].

The cultural model which is used to diagnose problems and allows for planning of intervention was designed by D. Denison. It is based on the assumption of coherence between organisational culture and strategy and distinguishes four dimensions, each divided into three operational dimensions:

112 A. Charles, O'Reilly III, J. Chatman, D.F. Caldwell, People and Organizational Culture: A Profile Comparison Approach to Assessing Person-Organization Fit, *The Academy of Management Journal,* Vol. 34, No. 3 (Sep., 1991), pp. 487–516.

1. Mission is divided into the parameters of strategic direction, strategic aims and the organisation's vision.
2. The ability to adapt was described with the use of the creation of changes, orientation towards customers and organisational learning.
3. Involvement was analysed with the use of empowerment, orientation towards teams and the development of skills.
4. Coherence consists of the basic values, consistency and integration.

Diagnosis of a culture leads to the description of a culture model from the point of view of its flexibility, stability and openness, which in turn allows us to foresee its effectiveness.

For the purpose of his own research, R. A. Cooke devised *An Organisational Culture Inventory*, which makes it possible to measure the intensity of 12 norms of organisational behaviour, located within three areas: 1) cultural constructivism, 2) passivity and defensiveness, and 3) aggression and defensiveness. This model makes use of normative assumptions and a constructive culture, accepting it as positive and effectiveness-oriented, while the other two types of culture are just the opposite. Constructive cultures are oriented towards social relationships and satisfying the higher needs of the organisation's members. They value working in groups, which is especially important in the case of complex, creative work. The norms of conservative cultures include achievements, self-fulfilment, encouragement to develop, as well as a sense of belonging and cooperation. Passive and defensive cultures are oriented towards tasks and cooperation with people who do not pose a potential threat to professional status or position. The key element is the defence of one's position in an organisation with the use of a network of influences, satisfying superiors' needs, as well as avoiding confrontation and conflict. This type of culture results in lower motivation and a drop in the effectiveness of employees. Norms, with the use of which the passive and defensive culture is operationalised, include striving for approval, conventionalism, dependence and avoidance.

Aggressive and defensive cultures are oriented towards tasks, competition and individual needs. The key value is power, which can lead to entanglement in internal status conflicts, which results in lower effectiveness. Employees are encouraged to compete, and they strive to strengthen their influence. The most important norms include opposition and criticism of others, fights over power and influence, competitiveness (the aim of which is to defend one's own position), and perfectionism leading to attachment to the process and details.

G. Hofstede proposed typical models of organisational culture, characteristic of chosen cultural circles. The two key dimensions in this case are power

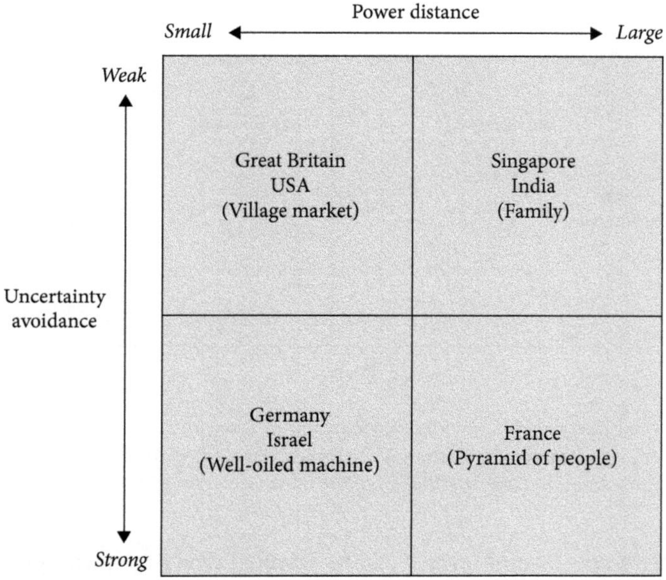

Fig. 3: Cultural models of organisation. Source: G. Hofstede, *Cultures and Organizations: Software of the Mind*, New York: McGraw-Hill, 1991.

distance and uncertainty avoidance, the combination of which gives rise to a typology of four models of ideal organisational cultures, characteristic of five cultural circles[113]:

A two-dimensional typology of organisational cultures, which draws on G. Hofstede's concept, was proposed by C. Hampden-Turner and F. Trompenaars. The combination of these dimensions created four ideal models, described metaphorically as: Incubator, Guided missile, Family and the Eiffel Tower, which are references to the types of organisational culture characteristic of different cultural circles:

One of the oldest concepts of cultural management includes the notion of *organisational climate*. A climate is what the employees of a given organisation believe to exist, but is not necessarily what actually is. The author lists four types of organisational climate: autocratic, bureaucratic, innovative and informal. The climate of a given organisation is the result of the dominant form of its

113 G. Hofstede, *Kultury i organizacje. Zaprogramowanie umysłu*, PWE, Warszawa 2000.

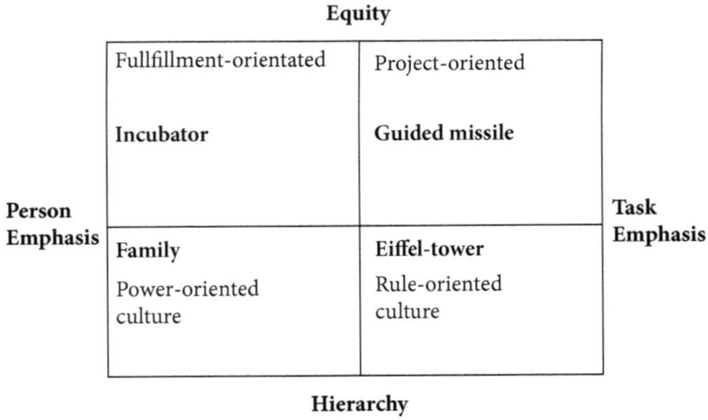

Fig. 4: Types of organisational culture according to Trompenaars and Hampden-Turner. Source: C. Hampden-Turner, A. Trompenaars, *Riding the Waves of Culture: Understanding Diversity in Global Business*, McGraw-Hill, 1997.

management's motivation, which can be oriented to achievement, power, security or a sense of belonging. In consequence, the motivation of power, resulting from the need to exercise influence and to control others, leads to the creation of an autocratic climate, dominated by power and influence, as in the case of R. Harrison's culture of power. Interpersonal relationships include, on the one hand, domination, and on the other, submission. Promotion is related to fulfilling superiors' orders without any mistakes. Organisational power focuses on controlling the information flow and increasing the extent of the subordination of others. The motivation of achievements contributes to the creation of an innovative climate. This type of culture is dominated by creativity, the broadening of knowledge and the development of the skills and qualifications which are most useful to the fulfilment of its tasks. Management focuses on achieving the best results possible, encouraging its employees to be active and creative. Organisations of this type adjust flexibly to the different tasks and requirements of their environment. With the motivation of security, the striving for minimising physical and social threats creates a bureaucratic climate. This is clearly oriented towards stability, based on norms, rules and procedures. The management protect themselves by avoiding unforeseen events and risky ventures. Hierarchy plays an important role here, and internal organisation is formalised. Employees are passively subject to strict rules of action, which they have no influence on, while their development consists mainly in the assimilation of rules, regulations and skills that are formally certified. From the point of view of an informal climate, being part of a group is of key importance. This climate favours the ability to establish relationships and work in a team, while employees are equal partners who shape their activities together. The dominant value in an organisation is being accepted by the environment. Management focuses on the smoothing out of the influences of different employees, the development of social sensitivity, and the habit of helping and supporting others.

C. Sikorski divides organisational cultures by the attitude of the organisation's members to cultural dissonance. Cultural dissonance is related to the existing differences between the ways employees think and behave in organisations, which are the most common reasons for conflict and misunderstanding. Cultural dissonance hinders the organisation's functioning, especially in the case of multicultural organisations, international corporations and organisations including a number of different subcultures. The attitude towards this phenomenon is an important feature of organisational culture, which should be treated as a separate criterion for the typology of organisational cultures.

2.6 A 3D model and typology of organisational culture

The proposed model of organisational cultures I used in my research is based on three dichotomous dimensions borrowed from G. Hofstede and other researchers. Although Hofstede proposed studying organisational cultures according to other dimensions of values than in cultures of whole societies, there are numerous authors who think his model is more general, and so apply it to organisational cultures too. It seems that three out of five dimensions proposed by Hofstede can be used as a basis for such multidimensional models and typology. I am also in favour of this approach, as I believe that three of the dimensions included in Hofstede's model are of a universal character, whether they concern individuals, organisational cultures or social cultures. The model, based on the combination of the dimensions of individualism/collectivism, power distance and tolerance for uncertainty, sets these three dimensions in the area of fundamental, 'existential' assumptions of individuals and human communities (Tab. 15). The dimension of individualism/collectivism determines the basic assumptions about the degree of attachment to a social group[114]. The dimension of power distance reflects a universal feature of human nature that can be found in all communities in the form of the attitude towards power in a

114 J.A. Chatman, S.G. Barsade, Personality, Organizational Culture, and Cooperation: Evidence from a Business Simulation, *Administrative Science Quarterly*, Vol. 40, No. 3 (Sep., 1995), pp. 423–443

Tab. 14: The division of cultures according to C. Sikorski. Source: Based on C. Sikorski, *Kultura organizacyjna*, C. H. Beck, Warszawa 2002, pp. 51–154.

	Acceptance of cultural dissonance	**Lack of acceptance of cultural dissonance**
Antagonistic relations	**Culture of rivalry** An organisational culture characterised by strong rivalry. Its members believe that it is necessary to prove their superiority. There is a need to participate and have team achievements. A collectivist culture, focusing on the roles played by people. A heterogenic culture. There is a clash of different cultural patterns. Presence-oriented.	**Culture of dominance** A characteristic feature of this culture is its members' belief that they are superior. It is a homogenous culture, which includes models of behaviour in accordance with tradition. There is a tendency to subordinate the organisation's activity to models of national culture and a strong need for security, and in consequence, avoiding uncertainty. A collectivist culture. A paternalist management style. Past-oriented.
Non-antagonistic relations	**Culture of cooperation** This culture is characterised by routine activities in a competitive environment, focusing on the quality of bonds and dialogue between people. A heterogenic culture. The rules of autonomy, equality, respect for differences. The rule of harmony with the environment. In the case of activities, a larger emphasis is placed on the customers' needs than on the competition. Identification with culture. A feminine culture – avoiding conflicts and rivalry. Democratic management style.	**Culture of adaptation** A culture oriented towards non-routine activities in a competitive environment, focusing on the quality of bonds and dialogue between people. This culture is homogenous in the area of values. Subordination to the formal aims of the organisation. Emphasis on the customers' needs and one's own professional development. A strong need for achievements and internal motivation. A large tolerance for uncertainty. Short power distance (a partner-like nature of relationships). Individualist orientation towards achievements, combined with an objective assessment of everyone's needs and aims. Future-oriented.

social structure. And finally, the tolerance for uncertainty can be derived from a skill characteristic only of people, which is planning for the future, together with an intuitive evaluation of the probability of their success. There is no agreement among researchers as to the dimensions of organisational culture, but regardless of their opinions, most can see the relationships between the dimensions of

Tab. 15: Three dimensions of G. Hofstede, on the level of individuals, organisational culture and social culture. Source: Own work.

The dimension of values	Individuals	An organisational culture	Social culture
Individualism/ collectivism (community)	An attitude of an individual towards the community. Attachment to a group.	Values and norms, enhancing the status of individuals or organisational bonds.	Values and norms, enhancing the status of individuals or social bonds, such as national, civic.
Hierarchy – equality (power distance)	An attitude of individuals towards power. An attitude to inequality.	Tendency to interpret the organisation in the categories of structuration and an increase in status differences, or the opposite.	Striving for the enhancement of structuration and an increase in status differences, or the opposite.
Tolerance for uncertainty	Tendency to take risks and open planning. Lower stress related to planning.	Readiness to develop and carry less probable and riskier variants of plans.	Valuation of the readiness to take risks. A lower level of autonomy and social frustration caused by uncertainty.

culture proposed by G. Hofstede, such as individualism vs. collectivism, power distance, and corporate culture[115].

From among the many dimensions of values, I distinguished three which appear in numerous concepts and research into the influence of culture on organisation (proposed by G. Hofstede, A. A. Trompenaars and C. Hampden-Turner, R. D. Lewis, and E. Marx). Together, they form consistent configurations of cultures, and are linked with other subsystems (strategy and structure). All values studied largely diversify organisational cultures. The model of organisational culture developed includes as few of the most important diversifying values (dimensions) as possible. Naturally, it is possible to create typologies of other dimensions, including (more or less) values. Some of the dimensions of values assumed by other concepts were not included in this model at all. It was therefore assumed that they do not concern the level of culture or are of a secondary

115 Z. Aycan, R. Kanungo, M. Mendonca,, K. Yu, J. Deller, G. Stahl, A. Kurshid, Impact of Culture on Human Resource Management Practices: A 10–Country Comparison, *Applied Psychology*, 2000, 49: 192–221.

character. Dimensions distinguished here were recognised as primary, so it is also possible to derive secondary dimensions from them, used in other concepts and research. In most cases, secondary dimensions can be derived from the primary with an analysis of the given dimension's semantic contents. The three distinguished values are as follows bellow.

1 Hierarchy – equality

The favouring of hierarchisation is linked with a belief that people differ, and that an organisation should reflect this diversity. Thus, organisations should include a number of management levels, and there should be a significant diversification of rights, privileges and benefits among different groups of employees. Special significance should be attached to maintaining discipline and strengthening the authority of power. Hierarchical organisations are dominated by the following attitudes: (1) acceptance of a strong diversity of employees, (2) a preference for elitist thinking, (3) emphasis on the significance of order which gives rise to the structure of power. Hierarchisation in an organisation is reflected in the employees' beliefs and can be identified with the use of the following methodological indicators[116]:

- Structure should be steep,
- Inequalities between positions are indispensable,
- There should be a large wage differential,
- An organisation needs an authoritarian management style,
- An organisation needs centralisation,
- Hierarchy reflects very significant individual differences between employees in lower and higher positions in an organisation; employees in lower organisational positions usually have lower skills and abilities than the employees at higher levels,
- Hierarchy should be stable,
- Subordinates are dependent on their superiors,
- Employees at higher levels in an organisation should receive privileges,
- An organisation is dominated by concepts emphasising the significance of superiors and the process of managing employees.

The drive for equality results from the belief that people deserve similar rights and an organisation is a reflection of such fundamental equality. Thus,

116 Compare: G. Hofstede, *Cultures and Organizations: Software of the Mind*, New York: McGraw-Hill, 1991

organisations should have a flat structure and limit the number of management levels as much as possible. Large diversification of employees' rights, privileges and benefits is unwelcome. Equality gives rise to the following attitudes in organisations: (1) emphasising similarities between employees, (2) favouring egalitarian thinking, (3) orientation towards spontaneity, flexibility of structures and power relationships.

Hierarchy is juxtaposed with equality, which can be described with the use of the following methodological indicators:

- Structure should be flat,
- An organisation should strive for equality between different positions,
- The wage differential should be limited,
- An organisation needs a participatory management style,
- An organisation needs decentralisation,
- Hierarchy is related to playing different roles, for pragmatic purposes,
- Hierarchy should be flexible and undergo changes,
- Superiors and subordinates are interdependent,
- Everyone in an organisation should have equal rights,
- The dominant concepts in an organisation emphasise the significance of employees and their involvement and participation in the managerial process.

The dimension of hierarchy vs. equality is primal in relation to the dimension of authoritarianism vs. democracy (participation). Authoritarianism means striving for a one-person, unquestionable way of making decisions in an organisation, while democracy means striving for a group (fully participatory) decision-making process. The dimension of hierarchy vs. equality is also primal in relation to the dimension of power centralisation[117]. In G. Hofstede's concept, the dimension of hierarchy-equality corresponds to the distance in power relations. A large distance means orientation towards hierarchy, while a small distance means equality[118].

2 Individualism – community

Individualism means putting the value of an individual before the interests of a social group. This is related to striving for the freedom of individuals and a

117 C. f. R. Harrison, *Understanding Your Organization's Character*, Harvard Business Review, 1972, May-June.

118 G. Hofstede, *Cultures and Organizations: Software of the Mind*, New York: McGraw-Hill, 1991

belief that individual interests are most important. According to this belief, organisations should focus on the motives and competences of individuals, rather than teams. Fulfilling individual interests can lead to organisational success, as this favours rivalries and competitive attitudes, as well as nonconformist behaviour. An organisation is perceived as a group of individuals who have conflicting interests. S. Lukes emphasises the following basic elements of individualism: human dignity, self-determination and the autonomy of individuals, respect for privacy and the possibility to fulfil oneself[119]. In organisations, individualism is manifested by: (1) treating individual freedom as the priority value, (2) the acceptance of individual attempts at independence, (3) a preference for individual interests, (4) orientation towards rivalries and (5) creating the cult of personality (lone heroes or charismatic leaders). Individualism in an organisation may be determined with the use of the following methodological indicators[120]:

- Individual interests are more important than the interests of the organisation,
- The organisation is a group of individuals who have different interests,
- Rivalry between employees is indispensable,
- The organisation is based on eminent individuals,
- Interests of the organisation and individuals diverge,
- The organisation functions thanks to the freedom of individuals,
- People in an organisation should have their own opinions and be allowed to express them (non-conformism),
- Conflict can contribute to the organisation's development,
- Perfect interpersonal relationships in an organisation differ from the relations in a family, as they are based on a contract guaranteeing mutual benefits,
- An organisation requires the strict separation of the professional and private lives of its employees.

The community approach (or, in other words, collectivism) is a the belief that the interests of a social group are more important than individual interests, and in the case of organisations this is manifested by the orientation towards group goals, even against individuals, while the preferred attitudes are conformism and collaboration. Emphasising the value of group solidarity, organisations are often perceived as social groups or teams. They achieve success thanks to

---

119 S. Lukes, *Individualism*, Oxford University Press, Oxford 1973.

120 C. f. G. Hofstede, *Cultures and Organizations: Software of the Mind*, New York: McGraw-Hill, 1991

cooperation and unanimity, which is why individuals should identify themselves with a group. Mostly, it is the teams that are motivated, and only then the individuals. The community approach is manifested by: (1) accepting the idea that the common good is the superior value, (2) emphasising the significance of cooperation in a social group, (3) emphasising the importance of community, (4) orientation towards cooperation and unity in an organisation and (5) creating a cult of group-work.

The community approach is linked with familiarism[121]. Familiarism is the strength of relationships between individuals and their families, which is reflected in the organisational sphere. A high level of familiarism supports the development of family entities, but can cause problems when creating organisations managed in a different way (separation of ownership and management). A low level of familiarism more often accompanies the creation of larger, bureaucratic organisations, which limit the significance of family enterprises in business. The community approach is juxtaposed with individualism, and can be recognised with the use of the following indicators:

- The interest of an organisation is more important than individual interests,
- An organisation is a group of collaborating people,
- Cooperation between people is indispensable in an organisation,
- An organisation is based on teams,
- An organisation and its employees have common interests,
- An organisation functions thanks to group solidarity,
- People in an organisation should adjust to the opinion of the majority (conformism),
- An organisation should strive for harmony and the avoidance of conflicts,
- Perfect interpersonal relations in an organisation should be reminiscent of a family,
- The personal and professional lives of the employees merge in an organisation.

3 A high tolerance for uncertainty – a low tolerance for uncertainty

A high tolerance for uncertainty is related to the readiness to act in situations when there is not enough information. In the case of organisations, this means a tendency to take risks and an orientation towards changes[122]. Organisations

121 F. Fukuyama, *Trust: The Social Virtues and the Creation of Prosperity*. Free Press, 1995.

122 C. f. C. Sikorski, *Zachowania ludzi w organizacji*, Warszawa, Wydaw. Naukowe PWN, 1999, pp. 43–55.

with a high tolerance for uncertainty do not strive to maintain the status quo, but are ready to accept external changes and make transformations[123]. Usually, they adapt to changes in the environment more easily and are more flexible. Their variants of action and scenarios developed are of a rather indeterminist character. Information deficits and multiple variants are assumed, and rapid changes are treated as opportunities. Greater attention is paid to the organisation's openness, rather than its stability. A high tolerance for uncertainty means: (1) orientation towards changes in the organisation, (2) the acceptance of action in case there is not enough information and (3) a multi-variant game model in the decision-making process. A high tolerance for uncertainty can be presented with the use of the following indicators[124]:

- Employees should be provided with challenges at work,
- Employees are motivated mostly by achievements and praise,
- Uncertainty is an indispensable element of the organisation's life,
- The organisation should allow for multiple variants of action,
- Quick changes are opportunities for the organisation,
- The organisational reality cannot be expressed by strict rules, and so it is necessary to limit their number.

A low tolerance for uncertainty combines the striving for the reduction of uncertainty, functioning in the context of low risk, maintenance of the status quo, and an emphasis on the organisation's stabilising role[125]. The variants of action and scenarios the organisation develops are of a determinist character; they assume avoiding risks, a maximum limitation of the information deficit and one-option planning. In most cases, changes are treated as threats. A low tolerance for uncertainty means: (1) orientation towards maintaining the status quo in an organisation, (2) striving for action only when all information is available and (3) assuming a one-variant, determinist model of decision-making. The dimension of low uncertainty tolerance can be presented by the following indicators:

---

123 The juxtaposition of change and status quo in an organisation is not invalidated by the approach of 'dynamic stability', which is currently being developed, and which tries to weaken the destructive consequences of rapid internal changes by strengthening employees' sense of stability – E. Abrahamson, *Change Without Pain*.

124 C. f. G. Hofstede, *Cultures and Organizations: Software of the Mind*, New York: McGraw-Hill, 1991

125 C. f. Z. Jasiński, *Czynniki warunkujące gotowość pracowników do zmian w organizacji*, pp. 104–107.

- Employees should be provided with high stability at work,
- Employees are motivated mostly by security and the organisational status quo,
- The organisation's development is possible only in the context of reduced uncertainty,
- The organisation acts in accordance with a single, unifying plan,
- Quick changes are a threat to the organisation,
- The organisational reality has to be ordered with the use of both general and detailed organisational rules.

The presented primary dimensions can correlate with other values too. For example, to a certain extent hierarchisation conditions formalism, or ceremonialism of culture, and the existence of autocratic management styles[126]. The proposed configuration of primary values can be compared with the proposals contained in several significant projects of intercultural research by R. House, C. Hampden-Turner, as well as A.A. Trompenaars and G. Hofstede. The GLOBE project by R. House included nine dimensions of culture influencing leadership in organisations, similar to those described here. These are: collectivism vs. individualism, power distance (corresponding to the dimension of hierarchy), and avoidance of uncertainty vs. tolerance for uncertainty. Other cultural dimensions studied in the GLOBE project are probably of a secondary character in relation to the three assumed primary dimensions. These dimensions include: orientation towards achievements, which is secondary to individualism; the equal rights of men and women, probably related to equality; orientation towards the future vs. the present, which probably correlates with the tolerance for uncertainty; family community, which is a special type of community approach; assertiveness, related to individualism and hierarchisation, and the humanist vs. impersonal orientation, which correlates with equality.

Trompenaars' and Hampden-Turner's model and research distinguish seven elementary dimensions of values[127]. Two of these, *individualism/collectivism* and *equality – hierarchy*, overlap with the dimensions presented in this monograph. G. Hofstede's research project led to the distinguishing of four dimensions of culture: *hierarchy – equality*; *individualism/collectivism*; *uncertainty avoidance*,

126 R.R. Gesteland, *Cross-Cultural Business Behavior*, Copenhagen: Copenhagen Business School Press, 1999

127 C. Hampden-Turner, A. Trompenaars, *Riding the Waves of Culture: Understanding Diversity in Global Business*, McGraw-Hill, 1997

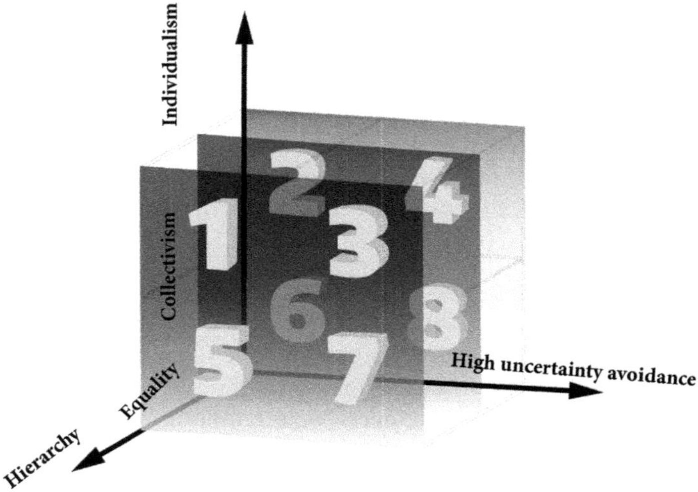

Fig. 5: A three-dimensional typology of organisational culture. Source: Own work.

and *masculinity – femininity*[128]. The first three dimensions can be found, albeit in a slightly different form, in the model of organisational culture presented in this work. The dimension of *masculinity – femininity* does not seem completely clear and is defined in different ways (for example, it is defined differently in the GLOBE project). This dimension is secondary, as it correlates with the dimension of *hierarchy – equality*. The model was further developed by Hofstede with the addition of a fifth dimension called 'Confucian dynamism'.

Naturally, it is debatable whether the model of organisational culture presented here includes all the most important dimensions of culture, but the three chosen dimensions form a good basis for the development of diverse types of organisational cultures.

The values presented above can be found together in organisations, wherein they form certain configurations of values, constituting a typology of organisational cultures which can be reflected with the use of a three-dimensional model:

By comparing the three basic dimensions, one can build a classification covering eight types of perfect organisational cultures[129].

---

128 G. Hofstede, *Cultures and Organizations: Software of the Mind*, New York: McGraw-Hill, 1991

129 M. Weber, *The Methodology of the Social Sciences*.

Type 1 – Organisations of ossified management

This is a configuration combining individualism, hierarchism and a low tolerance for uncertainty. The values of the organisation justify the fact that the managerial positions in the structure are occupied by privileged people. The significance of managers is emphasised, and myths are created about them (especially about those on higher levels). They are made organisational heroes. Emphasis is put on stability and discipline, which is supported by an autocratic management style that, at lower levels, often takes the form of despotism, and paternalism on higher levels. There is formalism in the organisation, assuming a ceremonial and ritual form, which includes its internal communications. The centralised information flow is fully consistent with the organisational structure and takes the form of a pyramid (messages come from top to bottom). Type 1 is a conservative, traditional organisation, in which changes take place as a response to the pressure of the environment, and are of a top-down character. A moderately competitive orientation prevails, as conflicts are suppressed by formalism, while personal changes are delayed because of conservatism. Power is strong and concentrated at the top of the hierarchy. There is no familism in such organisations, and all indications of nepotism and cliques are officially and unofficially condemned. There is no atmosphere that would support the creation of subcultures, much less counter-cultures.

Type 1 organisations are characterised by a complex, formalised organisational structure. Strategy can be formally extended and documented, but it is quite reactive and inflexible. Usually, the orientation towards operational activities prevails, although strategic orientation is also possible. However, in such cases strategies only include one variant and are not very detailed. Type 1 organisations are adjusted to functioning in stable sectors, which develop slowly and require the centralisation of activities and specialisations (because of the economy of scale). In the case of rapid changes in the environment, they can prove ineffective.

Type 2 – Organisations of personal benefits

Orientation towards individualism, equality and a low tolerance for uncertainty: Values indicate that all employees have a right to decide and benefit from staying in the organisation. The significance of the employees' ethos is often emphasised. There is a common belief that ordinary workers are exploited by those in charge. Mythology is of an unofficial character and is created based on stories about opportunities the organisation missed because of the managers. Managerial positions are treated with mistrust and envy. On the other hand, promotions are perceived in terms of power usurpation. Social relationships in such organisations are reminiscent of a war between everybody, where employees have professional ambitions but others bring them down to mediocrity. Managers have limited power and a sense that their positions are under constant threat. This is why, believing that the autocratic management style is superior, they are forced to play a complex game of manipulation and negotiation between different organisational actors. The level of formalism is moderate. Communication is not largely centralised and formalised. The information flow is open, which gives employees access to the managers. To sum up, it can be said that Type 2 is to a certain extent similar to Type 1 – it is a conservative organisation, which makes changes as a response to the pressure of the environment of a top-down character; also the level of familism is rather low. However, in organisations of this type, two hostile counter-cultures are often created, including performance workers and the management. Such organisations often have a flattened organisational structure. Strategy is usually limited, tends to be reactive and oriented towards operational activities. Type 2 organisations can be most often found in stable economic sectors which change slowly. In the case of this culture, changes are unwelcome.

Type 3 – Organisations of transformational leadership

An orientation towards individualism, hierarchism and a high tolerance for uncertainty: The organisation's values focus on charismatic leadership. Autocratic management styles prevail. The significance of leaders is emphasised and myths about them are created. They are made organisational heroes. Organisations of this type are not highly formalised – leaders contact all levels of the organisation, using both official and unofficial channels. The information flow remains open (there are no barriers), although communication is aimed at the main link – the leader. Type 3 organisations are oriented towards changes that are quickly implemented by transformational leaders, and so a Type 3's values include creativity and expansiveness. A moderately competitive orientation is typical, although conflicts are suppressed by leadership. Power is strong and concentrated at the top of the hierarchy, while organisation is supposed to be cohesive and centralised. In this case, the level of familism is relatively low, and nepotism and cliques are not tolerated. No subcultures or counter-cultures can be created.

In Type 3s, an orientation towards strategic activities usually prevails – the vision of the leader is the basis for the strategy. Organisations of this type usually allow the introduction of quick, deep organisational changes, although decisions about these are made top-down. Type 3s can be most often found in dynamic economic sectors, which develop rapidly or undergo transformation.

Type 4 – Organisations of adventurers

An orientation towards individualism, equality and a high tolerance for uncertainty: A Type 4 organisation values the focus on the rivalry between individuals in the context of a 'free internal labour market'. One of these values is ‘Change leading to the organisation’s development’. The leaders have strong personalities and similar rights. Organisational mythology emphasises the role of individuality, autonomy and creativity. Participatory management styles dominate. Type 4 organisations are quite informal, and internal communication is fully open and dispersed. Motives and concepts of changes are created by individuals. Employees are oriented towards rivalry, both within and between teams. Power is distributed among individuals who manage their teams. The level of familism is relatively low. Subcultures are formed around individualities, but they are not very strong, are of a fluid character and do not transform into counter-cultures.

Type 4 organisations often have a flattened and informal organisational structure, while their strategies are multi-variant and expansive. Orientation towards strategic activities prevails. Changes are implemented quickly, in an anticipatory way, and can be initiated by many centres (they are decentralised), which allows for deep transformation, strongly involving employees. Problems and complications result from the multiplicity and changeability of influences, which may lead to anarchy.

Type 4s are most often found in dynamic, rapidly developing and dispersed economic sectors (a lower level of capital concentration).

Type 5 – Organisations of stabilisers

An orientation towards community, hierarchism and a low tolerance for uncertainty: the values of the organisation justify the maintenance of the status quo. Mythology is created around a ‘golden age’ of no changes and complete security and stability, both for managers and workers. Type 5s value tradition, and their organisational heroes are long-standing managers who strive for the maintenance of stability. An autocratic management style, close to paternalism, prevails. The level of formality is high, and often takes a ceremonial, or even ritual form. Excessive bureaucracy is common. Communication is formalised and centralised. Conservatism dominates – changes are implemented slowly and are coerced by the environment. Decisions about changes are made top-down, and are often resisted by employees at lower levels. There is a moderate orientation towards cooperation. On the one hand, power is concentrated at the top of the hierarchy, while on the other, there is a strong influence from employee lobbies (unions, councils etc.) and sometimes from other interested parties (for example, political elements). Familism is moderate, nepotism is officially condemned, but unofficially it is present in the organisation. Even cliques are common. Strong subcultures appear, and sometimes counter-cultures, usually based on the juxtaposition of workers with management, and the antagonisms between different employee groups.

Type 5 organisations are characterised by a complex, formalised organisational structure. Strategy is single-variant and highly reactive. An orientation towards operational activities prevails. Special emphasis is placed on maintaining the cohesion of the organisation. It is difficult to introduce changes, and they are of a reactive character when they are introduced. Type 5s are most often found in stable, slowly changing economic sectors with strong employee lobby groups.

Type 6 – Organisations with conservative communities

An orientation towards the community, equality and a low tolerance for uncertainty: a Type 6 organisation's values are oriented towards the employees' sense of security. Similarly to type 5, the value is tradition, but in this case organisational heroes are employees who strive for the social security of employees (for example, leaders of trade unions) and performance workers who have a sense of injustice and feel undervalued. Participative management styles dominate, sometimes using populist motifs. Decisions are usually made jointly. Professional career paths are open, and there is a fairly high rotation of managerial positions. Communication is informal, open and decentralised. Type 6 includes highly conservative organisations, which implement changes very slowly and only as a result of pressure from the environment. Decisions about changes can be top-down or as an initiative by one of the power centres. Type 6 organisations are oriented towards cooperation and satisfying the needs of numerous organisational groups. Power is distributed among different centres of influence – employees and managers, individual departments, branches, units and sections. The level of familism is high and individual centres form cliques and can support the promotion of family members. Strong subcultures, or even counter-cultures appear.

Type 6 organisations are characterised by a flattened, decentralised organisational structure. Strategy is usually limited and reactive, and is oriented towards operational activities. It is very difficult to introduce changes, as they are hindered by dispersed power. Type 6s can be most often found in stable, slowly changing economic sectors.

Type 7 – Organisations of thriving teams

An orientation towards the community, hierarchism and a high tolerance for uncertainty: this type of organisation's values are oriented towards organised, dynamic teams. Myths concern the quick, bold, successful actions of teams (organisational units). The organisation's heroes are the leaders who know how to make use of teamwork. Participative management styles dominate. Communication is informal, decentralised and completely open. The dominant value is change. Type 7 includes dynamic organisations, oriented towards quick changes, often of an anticipative character. Changes can be planned top-down or result from grassroots initiatives. There is a moderate orientation towards cooperation. On the one hand, power is concentrated at the top of the hierarchy, but on the other, the influence of the teams of employees can be very strong. The level of familism is quite high, and there are clear cliques. Strong subcultures appear, and even counter-cultures, but are eliminated by managers.

Type 7 organisations are characterised by a fairly extended organisational structure, which doesn't lend itself to limitations on communication. Strategic orientation prevails, but strategy itself is understood as a multi-variant game. There are no complex, long-term planning procedures. Type 7s can be most often found in young, dynamic, rapidly developing economic sectors.

Type 8 – Organisations with dynamic communities

Orientation towards the community, equality and a high tolerance for uncertainty: Type 8 organisations' values are oriented towards flexible community. Mythology is created around spontaneous, bold activities and decisions made by teams (groups of employees). A Type 8 organisation's heroes are team members who take part in successful activities. Participatory management styles dominate, often taking the form of democracy. The level of formalism in the organisation is low. Communication is informal, decentralised and completely open. Values include community and change. Type 8 organisations are dynamic and oriented towards quick changes which anticipate trends. Changes are often the results of grassroots initiatives. A strong orientation towards cooperation is typical of these organisations. Power is distributed among teams of employees. In most cases, the level of familism is high and there are clear cliques, although no strong subcultures are created, as they are quickly eliminated. There are no counter-cultures.

Type 8 organisations are characterised by a flattened and decentralised organisational structure. Strategy is complex and quite expansive. An orientation towards strategic activities prevails, which are understood as multi-variant organisational games. Orientation towards operational activities is also possible, which results from the sense of a lack of possibilities to create a strategy in such a changeable sector. This type of organisational culture allows quick, anticipatory and grassroots organisational changes. Type 8s are most often found in dynamic, quickly-developing economic sectors.

It is important to note that the values studied for organisational indicators are not dependent only on culture. The type of strategy, structure or degree of familism can be also conditioned by the type of ownership, market position or the enterprise's financial situation, which is why the descriptions of the types of organisational culture have to be treated as having been conditioned by many factors.

As one can see in the presented description of culture types, the configuration of values has an influence on most areas of an organisation's management, including the methods of managing human resources. To put it simply, types of armies have been used to describe the individual types of organisational cultures (Tab. 16):

Tab. 16: Types of organisational cultures and examples of human resource management. Source: Own work.

	Recruitment	Motivation	Development
1. Army of knights	Looking for qualified individuals, only management.	Managers reward individual employees.	Training of management, on detailed issues.
2. Mercenaries	Recruiting qualified and strongly competitive individuals.	Mechanisms of rewarding the best (rules of awarding bonuses).	Self-improvement, limited internal training on detailed issues.
3. Conquistador army	A leader looks for potential supporters – determination and motivation to work are the key elements.	Involvement and loyalty to the leader are rewarded.	Education is a process of integration around the leader.
4. Levy in mass	Self-recruitment – most of those who are interested can get the job.	Mechanisms of rewarding and, in consequence, selection (the weakest do not gain).	Self-education, limited specialist training.
5. Army of janissaries	Recruits are loyal and susceptible to discipline.	Rewards follow bureaucratic regulations.	Strong indoctrination training, which enhances loyalty.
6. Revolutionists	Recruits are susceptible to missionary activities.	Self-rewards and, in consequence, selection (the weakest do not gain).	Indoctrination training, network mechanisms of promotion.
7. Duke's squad	Recruits want to function in a strong and loyal team.	Involvement and loyalty to the group are rewarded.	Integration training, focused on the management.
8. Partisans	People who have ideas and want to implement them in a team are recruited.	Involvement and loyalty to the group and ideas are rewarded.	Integration and indoctrination training. Includes managers and specialists.

Type 1 – Army of knights
Type 2 – Mercenaries
Type 3 – Conquistador army
Type 4 – Levy in mass
Type 5 – Army of janissaries
Type 6 – Revolutionaries
Type 7 – Duke's squad
Type 8 – Partisans

Naturally, the influence of organisational culture on the human resources (HR) function as presented here is slightly exaggerated, and in some cases, largely simplified. The patterns of human resources management, resulting from the configuration of organisational values, can be different, but there is no doubt that the type of organisational culture has a significant influence on the system of managing human resources. Of course, organisational culture is one of the reasons for the creation of human resources management, but other variables are also important, such as the specificity of a given activity and enterprise. From the point of view of managers, there is a need for an awareness of what values are functioning in the organisation and what their influence on human resources management is. The selection, motivation and education of employees, oriented towards the reproduction of the same type of organisational culture, can be limited by change and the effectiveness of the organisation.

The model of organisational culture presented herein, and the typology of organisational cultures resulting from it, are mostly a theoretical concept and require in-depth verification by empirical research in the future. What is needed now is research into organisations' members' value systems, together with an analysis of the type of HR management, strategy, structure and power in the given organisation.

2.7 Functions of organisational culture

An organisational culture serves five functions, related to (1) integration, (2) perception, (3) adaptation, (4) granting identity and (5) stimulating organisational changes. According to P. Bate, it is a social 'adhesive' which keeps organisations together[130]. This 'adhesive' is participation in the organisation, manifested by the acceptance of common goals, values, norms and views. The perceptual function

130 P. Bate, The Impact of Organisational Culture on Approaches to Organisational Problem Solving, *Organisational Studies*, no. 5, 1984.

is related to the way organisation members perceive reality, environment, the organisation and themselves. In defining organisational culture, A.M. Pettigrew referred to the perceptual function as a system of jointly accepted meanings that are clear to a group at a given time[131]. To P. Bate, this includes meanings that people keep together, and which are defined as the 'organisational reality'[132]. The perceptual function of organisational culture can be manifested in the perception of the organisational reality and the environment from the perspectives of cognitive filters and stereotypes common to the organisation's members.

The adaptive function of organisational culture is related to the possibility of developing patterns of action in specific situations, thanks to the perception of the organisational reality and environment as being relatively stable. Thus, organisational culture reduces this area of uncertainty, grants meaning to reality and points to patterns of behaviour in different situations. E. H. Schein perceives this from the perspective of the adaptive function, which makes it possible for a group to adapt to the environment, and which is related to the integration function, which further means holding an employee group together. The integration function of organisational culture is linked with the reaching of agreements on the attitude of group members to the organisation itself. Schein lists the following factors that allow us to assess the degree of cultural integration in an employee group: (1) development of a common language based on similarly understood notional categories, its own dictionary, and granting of common meanings to abstract terms related to the organisation's activity; (2) determination of the group boundaries separating it from the environment, including a determination of the criteria for this demarcation and the rules for excluding group members and accepting new ones (this contributes to the strengthening of the group identity); (3) creation of an internal hierarchy and the rules of social stratification within the group; (4) consolidation of rules, regulations and rituals which determine the relationships between group members; (5) determination of the criteria for rewards and punishments and (6) adoption of a common ideology, which allows for justification of the attitude of group members to the organisation itself and its rules[133].

---

131 A.M. Pettigrew, On Studying Organizational Culture, *Administrative Science Quarterly*, No. 12, 1979.

132 P. Bate, The Impact of Organisational Culture on Approaches to Organisational Problem Solving, *Organisational Studies*, no. 5, 1984.

133 E.H. Schein, *Organizational Culture and Leadership*, John Wiley & Sons, 200, p. 50.

Culture makes it possible for employees to identify themselves with the organisation, which takes place by building consensus. According to E.H. Schein, the elements forming a consensus subject to agreement are: (1) vision, mission and strategy; (2) the organisation's goals, which on the one hand lead to the fulfilment of the mission, and on the other, take into consideration the interests of subgroups which function within the employee group; (3) the means allowing for achievement of goals, such as the management system, decision-making procedures, work distribution, technology and others and (4) the criteria for the assessment of the organisation's activities, and the chosen strategies and methods of correcting activities in unforeseen situations. Providing an organisation with an identity entails the creation of a common, cohesive image of the organisation, and a sense of community for its members. When confrontations take place, different images of the organisation begin to resemble each other. Thus, a cohesive image of the organisation is created, which is clear to its employees and environment.

The role of organisational culture depends on the organisation's stage of development. E. Schein distinguished these as being the stages of birth, early growth, middle age and maturity[134]. At the stages of birth and early growth, organisational culture is shaped by the values and personality of the founder, and mainly serves an integrational function. At the middle-age stage, culture is usually diversified. An organisation is dominated by hired employees, who are not family members. Values, subcultures, and sometimes even counter-cultures appear. A crisis of organisational identity can appear and changes can take place. Culture becomes a source of organisational rules, and the functions of perception, adaptation and developing identity gain significance. When the organisation is mature, the most desirable function of culture is the catalysis of changes, otherwise the organisation can become dominated by the stabilising function and, in consequence, the organisational culture can ossify. As a result of petrifaction, culture limits the flexibility and competitiveness of the organisation. Naturally, the catalyst function of culture can be present, to a certain degree, at all stages of the organisation's development. When trying to create a classification of values and cultural patterns distinguishing organisations, one should take into account the necessity of including functions which stabilise and bond organisations, as well as those supporting changes.

---

134 E.H. Schein, *Organizational Culture and Leadership*, John Wiley & Sons, 2004, p. 283.

2.8 Critical opinions of the functionalist approach to culture in management

Criticism of functionalism and neopositivism is present in many works in social sciences, as the negation of the dominating paradigm was the foundation for alternative paradigms[135]. Several criticism points, including primarily issues of integration, stability, uniformity, reification and inadequacy of the methodology are worth considering from the point of view of the cognitive and pragmatic utility of cultural theory in management.

Due to integrational perspective, culture is seen as a relatively coherent and homogeneous value system, which is contrary to the image of organisation and culture, often including conflicting and mutually exclusive countercultures and subcultures. The assumption that an organisation needs to be integrated - at least to a minimum extent - should not be equated with the assumption that all elements of the organization contribute to its coherence, and the basis of its activity is harmony and unity. In the context of rapid changes in the environment, a radical, integrative and functionalist perspective cannot be defended. Conflicts, inconsistencies and contradictions can dynamise changes and development of an organisation, opening new perspectives and enabling selection of creative solutions[136].

This, however, does not change the fact that the organisation still maintains a minimum degree of consistency, so that it is still, despite regularly growing internal conflicts, one whole. Two issues should be noted regarding the integration of the organisation. Firstly, organisation management should not only strive to increase its consistency, because a perfectly coherent organization is hermetic and poorly adapted to internal and external changes. Secondly, the sources of integration are complicated, which means that the organisation is consistently increasing or decreasing, and requires strategic, structural and cultural factors to be taken into account on the level of individuals, social groups and organisation in the environment. Historically, as the criticism of the integrative approach grew, functionalists developed a concept that defends an integrative approach based on balance. T. Parsons introdcued the concept of punctuated equilibrium,

135 K. Davis, Mit analizy funkcjonalnej jako metoda specjalna w socjologii i antropologii, *Amerykańska Recenzja socjologiczna*, 1959, 24 (6), s. 757 – 772.

136 C. f. L. Coser, *Funkcje konfliktu społecznego*, Macmillan, Nowy Jork 1956; R. Dahrendorf, *Konflikt klas i klas w społeczeństwie przemysłowym*, London 1969.

assuming the possibility of change, and at the same time the system's tendency to regain balance in the transformation process[137].

Representatives of critical current (CMS) accuse functionalism creating a false conciliatory, cooperative vision of organisational culture, whereas is in fact ideological and hides the interests and strength of dominant groups. In this way, functionalism preserves the unjust status quo with the use of indoctrination and manipulative organizational culture[138].

The systematic approach entails the presentation of culture in the form of interrelated elements that can be described using variables, indicating that they are reliable objects that can be tested. Due to the reification of culture, functionalism has more problems with grasping the essence of procedural culture, which is transformation and flow, not an object that can be studied. According to representatives of alternative paradigms, the assumption of neopositivist cause and effect model to explain culture can lead to problems. They believe that cultural discourse deals with meanings in a complex network of relationships and that they call for the interpretation of correlations, rather than causal analysis of variables, derived from the scientific way of the natural sciences. Interpretivists have methodological reservations about functionalism related to lack of understanding and individual approach. According to representatives of interpretative-symbolic current, the use of objectivist and statistical methods, used primarily for the purpose of mass phenomena studies, does not allow to understand the essence and sense of organisation that can be found in deeply internalised meanings[139].

Another criticism of functionalism is its use of functions that determine its usefulness in explaining the existence of certain phenomena in culture. It seems that many cultural phenomena are non-functional and even anti-functional. It is difficult to find the advantages of creating, for example, certain destructive counter-cultures in organisations[140]. According to critics, the vision of functionalist culture is excessively rationalized, and closer to the idea of *homo*

---

137 T. Parsons, *Teorie społeczeństwa: Fw zakresie MSPÓŁCZESNE Sw przypadku Teoria*, Free Press, Nowy Jork, 1961, s. 68.

138 V. Fournier, C. szary, W krytycznym momencie: warunki i perspektywy dla krytycznych studiów zarządzania, Departament zarządzania, *Stosunki międzyludzkie* 2000 stycznia Vol. 53 Nr 1 7 – 32.

139 O.I. Vásquez-Rivera, "Organizational culture from its paradigms of study: an approach to the interpretative-symbolic perspective." *Entramado* 12.1 (2016): 66-80.

140 L. Coser, *Mistrzowie myśli socjologicznej: idee w kontekście historycznym i społecznym*, 2nd Ed., Fort Worth: Harcourt Brace Jovanovich, Inc., 1977, s. 140.

oeconomicus, and is consequently deceptive. In addition, interpretivists believe that functionalist explanations develop an overly deterministic vision of man and culture, which assumes that human behaviour follows the pattern. There is not much room for free will, while interpretivists believe that people are not cultural puppets. An overly optimistic approach is associated with both learning and improving culture. Research experience shows that many methods to learn and improve organisational culture are highly unreliable.

3 Culture of society in management

3.1 Comparative cross-cultural studies

The concept of comparative cross-cultural studies appeared in the social sciences as early as in the 1930s, thanks to the *Cross-Cultural Survey* conducted by G.P. Murdock[141]. This was a large comparative study, based on the quantitative methodology, which later on allowed for recording of data on 189 cultures in the form of over 2,000 variables[142]. With time, the method of cross-cultural studies became rooted in sociology[143], cultural anthropology[144], as well as psychology[145] and linguistics[146]. This led to the creation of valuable databases, making it possible to process information not only about modern societies, but also about communities which had undergone radical changes or had completely disappeared.

The methodology of cross-cultural studies is representative and includes mass sampling, allowing for conduct of statistical analysis. The data gathering techniques used are dominated by interrogative methods, such as structured questionnaires and interviews, but observational methods are also used. The methodology is quantitative and follows the assumptions of the functionalist canon, which means it includes a striving for objectivity, the researcher's

---

141 G.P. Murdock, *Ethnographic Atlas: A Summary*. Pittsburgh, The University of Pittsburgh Press, 1967.

142 J.W.M. Whiting (1986), G.P. Murdock, (1897–1985). *American Anthropologist* 88 (3) pp. 682–686.

143 E.K. Scheuch, Theoretical Implications of Comparative Survey Research: Why the Wheel of cross-cultural Methodology Keeps on Being Reinvented, *International Sociology* June 1989 vol. 4 no. 2 147–167.

144 J.A. Harkness, F.J. R Van de Vijver, P.P. Mohler, Cross-cultural Survey Methods, *Hoboken*, NJ: John Wiley & Sons, 2003.

145 F van de Vijver, K. Leung, *Methods and Data Analysis of Comparative Research*, [in:] J.W. Berry, Y.H. Poortinga, J. Pandey, *Handbook of Cross-Cultural Psychology*, Vol. 1: Theory and method (2nd ed). Handbook of cross-cultural psychology (2nd ed.), (pp. 257–300). Needham Heights, MA, US: Allyn & Bacon, xxv, 406 pp; R.W. Brislin, Comparative Research *Methodology:* Cross-Cultural *Studies*, International Journal of Psychology, Volume 11, Issue 3, 1976, pp. 215 -229; J.W. Berry, Y.H. Poortinga, J. Pandey, *Handbook of Cross-Cultural Psychology: Theory and Method*. Boston: Allyn & Bacon, 1997.

146 R.W. Brislin, *Back-Translation for Cross-Cultural Research*, *Journal of Cross-Cultural Psychology*, September 1970, vol. 1 no. 3, pp. 185–216.

axiological neutrality, lack of involvement in the research process and generation of explanations with the use of models that form causative links between variables.

Several of the existing cross-cultural studies projects are especially important from the point of view of management science. The reason for this is their usefulness in generating culture-conditioned explanations and for profiling the issues of research in accordance with the interests of organisation and management researchers. Today, significant concepts of intercultural diversification from the point of view of management can be found in studies by G. Hofstede, A. Trompenaars and C. Hampden-Turner, R. House and R. Inglehart and many more[147]. All models mentioned interpret culture from the perspective of the dichotomous dimensions of values, within the functionalist paradigm. This means understanding culture as an independent variable, which influences the activities of the people being members of the cultural community studied.

Naturally, these are not the only comparative projects in cross-cultural studies that are related to issues of management. The subject literature offers a whole range of such research, mostly concerning intercultural differences in human resources management[148], effectiveness[149], accounting systems[150], security policy[151] and many other problems[152]. However, as N. J. Adler noted, based on a review of

---

147 G. Hofstede, *Culture's Consequences*, Sage Publications, Beverly Hills 1984; R.J. House, P. Hanges, A. Ruiz-Quintanilla, *GLOBE. The Global Leadership and Organizational Behavior. Effectiveness: Research Program*, [in:] 'Polish Psychological Bulletin', 28 (3), 1997, pp. 215–254; R. Inglehart, *Modernization and Postmodernization. Cultural, Economic and Political Change in 43 Societies*, Princeton University Press, New Jersey 1997.

148 A. Laurent, *The Cross-Cultural Puzzle of International Human Resource Management.* Human. Resource. Management., 1986, 25: 91–102.

149 K.L. Newman, S.D. Nollen, *Culture and Congruence: The Fit between Management Practices and National Culture, Journal of International Business Studies,* Vol. 27, No. 4 (4th Qtr., 1996), pp. 753–779.

150 G. L Harrison, J. L McKinnon, *Cross-cultural research in management control systems design: a review of the current state,* Accounting, Organizations and Society, Volume 24, Issues 5–6, July 1999, Pages 483–506.

151 M. Janssens, J.M. Brett, F.J. Smith, *Confirmatory Cross-Cultural Research: Testing the Viability of a Corporation-Wide Safety Policy, The Academy of Management Journal,* Vol. 38, No. 2 (Apr., 1995), pp. 364–382

152 U. Sekaran, *Methodological and Theoretical Issues and Advancements in Cross-Cultural Research, Journal of International Business Studies,* Vol. 14, No. 2, Special Issue on Cross-Cultural Management (Autumn, 1983), pp. 61–73; M. Tayeb, *Organizations*

literature from the 1970s, comparative cross-cultural studies were only peripheral to the research published in the leading periodicals (1 %)[153]. At the moment, their number is much greater, although the scale of intercultural comparisons is problematic, because they are often limited to just a few cases, and are difficult to analyse with the use of statistical methods. Because of their popularity and significance in management, only several key projects will be analysed in more detail.

The cross-cultural studies by G. Hofstede form the concept of intercultural comparisons most often quoted in economic interpretations and management science[154]. Hofstede conducted a questionnaire of tens of thousands of IBM employees, and distinguished culture-related differences between them, which he divided into four elementary dimensions (and later five, including the Confucian dynamism – LTO):

- Individualism – collectivism (IND).
- Large power distance – small power distance (PDI).
- A large level of avoiding uncertainty – a low level of avoiding uncertainty (UAI).
- Masculinity – femininity (MAS).

The model and studies by A. Trompenaars and C. Hampden-Turner (conducted at the Centre for International Business Studies at Amstelveen in the Netherlands) distinguished seven elementary dimensions of values[155]. Two of these, *individualism – collectivism* and *equality – hierarchy*, overlap with the dimensions proposed by G. Hofstede. One of the dimensions, *inner-directed – outer-directed*, refers more to the level of purely individual orientations (characteristic only of individuals) and cannot be translated into the level of social groups and cultures. The dimension of *analysis – synthesis* refers to ways of thinking, and so is also located on the individual level. The dimension of *synchronisation – sequence*, which determines cultural orientation towards time, seems to be an apt reflection of the differences between societies. The remaining dimensions are probably of a

---

and National Culture: Methodology Considered, Organization Studies, May 1994; vol. 15, 3: pp. 429–445.

153 N.J. Adler, *Cross-Cultural Management Research: The Ostrich and the Trend, The Academy of Management Review*, Vol. 8, No. 2 (Apr., 1983), pp. 226–232.

154 M. Sondergaard, *Research Note: Hofstede's Consequences: A Study of Reviews*, Citations and Replications, *Organization Studies* May 1994 vol. 15 no. 3 447–456.

155 C. Hampden-Turner, A. Trompenaars, *Siedem kultur kapitalizmu. USA, Japonia, Niemcy, Wielka Brytania, Szwecja, Holandia*, Dom Wydawniczy ABC, Warszawa 1998, pp. 20–21.

secondary character, and correlated with the primary dimensions. For example, the dimension of *achieving a position – maintaining a position* correlates with the dimension of *equality – hierarchy*. The research by A. Trompenaars and C. Hampden-Turner is the continuation of G. Hofstede's model and research methodology.

R. House's GLOBE project includes nine dimensions of culture influencing leadership in organisations. The aim of the project is to create an intercultural theory of leadership, based on a multidimensional model. The dimensions include: *collectivism vs. individualism*; *power distance* (which corresponds to the dimension of *hierarchy*), and *uncertainty avoidance vs. tolerance for uncertainty*. The other cultural dimensions studied as part of the GLOBE project are of a secondary nature in relation to the three primary dimensions assumed, and include: *orientation towards achievements*, which is secondary in relation to *individualism*; *gender equality*, probably related to *equality*; *orientation towards the future vs. the present*, which probably correlates with the tolerance for uncertainty; *family community*, which is a special case of the dimension of community; *assertiveness*, linked with individualism and hierarchy; and *humanist vs. impersonal orientation*, correlated with *equality*. The GLOBE project was based on the methodology of representative mass survey and its sample included 17,000 middle-level managers.

R. Inglehart's project is based on the theory of social transition, together with economic and socio-cultural development from modernisation to post-modernisation. The dimensions of culture include traditional and religious vs. rational and secular values, as well as survival (material) vs. life quality (post-material)[156]. Inglehart's theory is based on empirical research conducted in 43 societies, expanded with the results of the Word Values Survey[157]. The project's results form a map covering two aggregated dimensions of values, in which all of the studied societies are located.

3.2 Significance of cultural circles

Some of the comparative cross-cultural studies give us a picture of similarities and differences between societies which is far from the interpretative concept of the uniqueness and individuality of each culture. Some studies have even focused

156 R. Inglehart, *Modernization and Postmodernization. Cultural, Economic and Political Change in 43 Societies*, Princeton University Press, New Jersey 1997.

157 R. Inglehart, M. Basanez, A. Moreno, *Human Values and Beliefs: A Cross-cultural Sourcebook*, University of Michigan Press, Ann Arbour 1998.

on cross-cultural universals. And so, D.E. Brown's comparative research led to the creation of a catalogue of over 500 cultural universals that can be found in all communities researched. These also include such cultural elements as language, beliefs, and customs[158]. Other examples include the comparative cross-cultural studies of emotions and facial expressions conducted by P. Ekman, which led to definition of a universal canon of human emotions and the facial expressions accompanying them[159].

Apart from the cross-cultural studies focused on similarities, there is more research emphasising intercultural differences, which are of importance from the point of view of research into organisations. Such studies include the previously mentioned projects by R. Inglehart, A. Trompenaars and C. Hampden-Turner, and G. Hofstede. Their authors do not deny that there is a more or less complex canon of cultural universal behaviour, but they focus on studying the differences. For example, in the case of G. Hofstede's research, cultures are created around the same universal values, but there are significant differences in the way they are expressed, which is reflected in different levels of individualism, power distance and the avoidance of uncertainty. In the case of all three research projects, cultures form a kind of cluster with overlapping values, at the same time forming clear cultural circles. This indicates that research on the level of the circles (being the broadest cultural communities showing diversity), should carry equal status in the analysis of culture on the level of society and organisation. The following level no longer concerns differences but universal similarities, rooted in human nature, which is shown in the figure below.

Thus, apart from comparative research into the cultures of societies and organisations, as well as cultural universals, there is another important level of analysis, which is often omitted in interpretations. An illustration of the significance of cultural circles, confirmed by the research conducted as part of the projects of R. Inglehart, S. Ronan, R. House, G. Hofstede, A. Trompenaars and C. Hampden-Turner, are the analyses of social cultural circles[160]. This is best shown on the map presenting the results of the research by R. Inglehart, which is an interpretation of the occurrence of cultural circles (Fig. 7).

---

158 D.E. Brown, *Human Universals*, McGraw-Hill, New York 1991.

159 P. Ekman, W.V. Friesen, *Unmasking the Face: A Guide to Recognizing Emotions from Facial Clues*, Malor Books, 2003.

160 Although the differences between many dimensions of values and the ranking of countries are significant.

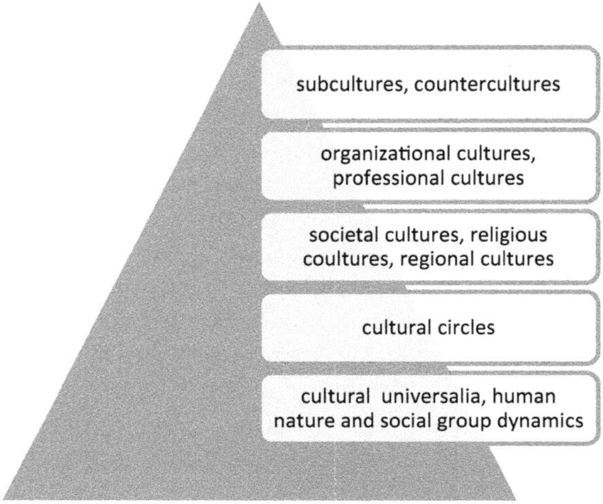

Fig. 6: Cultural analysis levels. Source: Own work.

A slightly simpler classification of cultural circles, but focused on organisational behaviour, was proposed by S. Ronan, who divided culture into nine circles:

1. Anglo-Saxon (USA, Canada, Australia, New Zealand, the United Kingdom, Ireland, RSA),
2. Arabic (United Arab Emirates, Kuwait, Qatar, Bahrain, Oman),
3. Middle Eastern (Turkey, Iran, Greece),
4. Far Eastern (Singapore, Malaysia, Hong Kong, Vietnam, Indonesia, Taiwan, Thailand),
5. Germanic (Germany, Austria, Switzerland),
6. Latin American (Columbia, Peru, Mexico, Chile, Venezuela, Argentina),
7. Latin European (France, Belgium, Italy, Spain, Portugal),
8. Nordic (Denmark, Norway, Sweden, Finland),
9. Untypical (such as Brazil, India, Israel, Japan)[161].

When looking at one's own culture, it is easy to see the simplifying, stereotyping, and even stigmatising character of the concept of cultural circles and social cultures. Ideal models of social culture and cultural circles are abstract, and do

161 S. Ronan, *Comparative and Multinational Management*, J. Wiley & Sons, New York, 1986

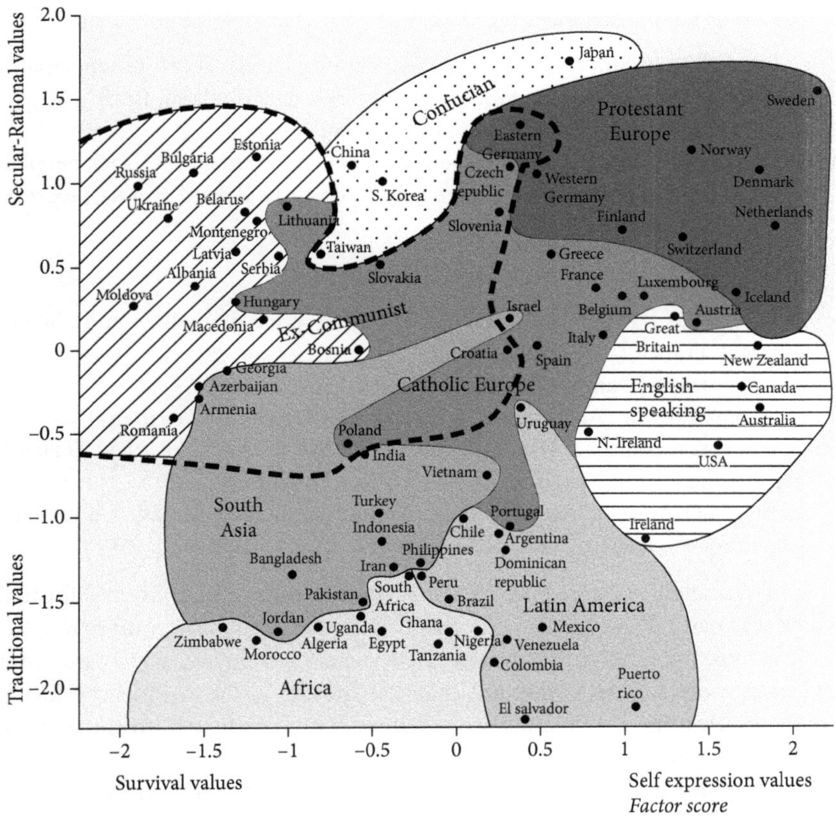

Fig. 7: Key cultural dimensions according to R. Inglehart. Source: R. Inglehart, *Modernization and Postmodernization. Cultural, Economic and Political Change in 43 Societies*, Princeton University Press, New Jersey 1997, p. 98.

not take into consideration the internal differentiation of culture in the form of subcultures and counter-cultures.

In the GLOBE research, R. House distinguished similar but not identical cultural circles[162], with the main axis of division being the distinction between Eastern and Western business cultures.

162 R. House, *Culture, Leadership, and Organizations*, GLOBE, Study of 62 Societies, Thousand Oaks, Sage Publications, 2004, pp. 179 – 183.

The Eastern cultural circles included:

1. Confucian Asia (Singapore, Hong Kong, Taiwan, China, South Korea, Japan),
2. South Asia (Philippines, Indonesia, Malaysia, India, Thailand, Iran),
3. Middle East (Turkey, Kuwait, Egypt, Morocco, Qatar),
4. Sub-Saharan Africa (Zimbabwe, Namibia, Zambia, Nigeria, RSA, black people),
5. Eastern Europe (Greece, Hungary, Albania, Slovenia, Poland, Russia, Georgia, Kazakhstan).

The Western cultural circles included:

1. Latin Europe (Israel, Italy, French-speaking part of Switzerland, Spain, Portugal, France),
2. Nordic Europe (Denmark, Finland, Sweden),
3. Germanic Europe (Austria, the Netherlands, Switzerland, Germany),
4. Anglo-Saxon countries (Canada, the United States, Australia, New Zealand, Ireland, the United Kingdom, RSA – white population),
5. Latin America (Ecuador, Salvador, Columbia, Bolivia, Brazil, Guatemala, Argentina, Costa Rica, Venezuela, Mexico).

These cultural circles were created by historical processes of cultural diffusion, which was naturally quicker in places where communication was more intense. It often took the form of expansion, imperialism or conquest, which are faster and more radical forms of cultural changes. The aim of the analysis conducted here is to illustrate the significance of the research conducted on the cultural circles level, which is why later on it will be limited to Europe.

The European cultural circle is based on common cultural roots, but is at the same time an internally diverse area. The cultural community is related to the influence of Christianity, the heritage of ancient Greece and Rome, and common history and cultural identity. The differences result from internal national, ethnic and religious divisions, which allow us to distinguish a continuum from regional cultures, through national cultures to cultural circles in Europe as a whole. Social culture shapes the mentality of a society's members. This is why it is worth examining cross-cultural studies more closely and resolving the problem of how social culture influences the competitiveness of the entire economy and enterprises of a given country.

Cultural diversity leads to a diagnosis of different levels of social capital in European countries[163]. Such diversity of social capital can hinder the processes

163 J.S. Coleman, Social Capital in the Creation of Human Capital, *American Journal of Sociology*, no. 94, 1988, pp. 95–120.

of cultural integration[164]. Thus, it is worth considering the problem of cultural convergence in the European Union. An equally interesting cultural phenomenon is the analysis of the sources of progress on our continent, which is traditionally related to modern science and technological development. For the last few centuries, Europe has been part of the main current of economic development and modernisation. However, it is not easy to explain this phenomenon, as it would require arguments based in history, geography, sociology, law and culture. According to D.S. Lande, the most important reasons for the development of Europe include the autonomy of the intellectual search, the creation of an institutionalised scientific method in the form of science, and the separation of Church and State[165]. The birth and development of a modernist society, driven by scientific progress and based on economic freedom and democracy, are also linked with cultural factors. Based on the intercultural research described above, one can analyse the degree of similarity or difference between different European countries.

Analysis of the results of the projects mentioned above in terms of cross-cultural studies points to a cultural diversification of European countries that allows us to distinguish several cultural circles. Each of these areas has developed a different kind of employee mentality in the European Union.

1. The Anglo-Saxon cultural circle is characterised by the highest rate of individualism in Europe, a low power distance, a low level of uncertainty avoidance and high masculinism. It includes the United Kingdom, Ireland and non-European countries: the USA, Canada, Australia and New Zealand. The key values which connect Anglo-Saxon cultures are the orientation towards rivalry and achievements, straightforwardness and lack of formalism, striving for equal opportunities, orientation towards changes and progress, an appreciation of professionalism and specialisation, as well as initiative and diligence[166]. Employees who come from Anglo-Saxon cultures do not have many problems on the labour market. They are flexible, ready to compete and communicate in the modern *lingua franca*. In the context of the integration of the European labour market, employees from countries other than Anglo-Saxon

164 R.D. Putnam, *Bowling Alone. The Collapse and Revival of American Community*, Simon&Schuster, New York 1999, pp. 15–30

165 D.S. Landes, *Wealth and Poverty of Nations*, Abacus, 1999 , p. 233

166 B. Bjerke, *Business Leadership and Culture*. Northampton, MA: Edward Elgar, 1999, pp. 118–119

often encounter certain cultural problems. With the English and Irish labour markets open to EU citizens, they face an influx of great masses of employees from countries of a lower standard of living. The English and Irish labour markets offer huge possibilities for cultural absorption and assimilation, but access to their most prestigious occupations is difficult for foreigners. Citizens of Western European countries used to the social labour market, such as Germany, Italy and Scandinavia, have problems adapting to the liberal model typical of the United Kingdom and Ireland.

2. The Scandinavian cultural circle is characterised by an average level of individualism, the lowest power distance in Europe, an average level of uncertainty avoidance and a feminist orientation. It includes Sweden, Norway, Finland and Denmark. Values which distinguish Scandinavian countries in Europe are egalitarianism, respect for democratic decision-making procedures, orientation towards maintaining continuity and a coalition nature. Employees are used to reducing statutory differences in gender equality, and different social and ethnic groups. The exercise of power is treated as a pragmatic organisational solution, not a permanent attribute of a superior. The coalition nature is related to avoiding conflicts and aggression, as well as striving for agreement on important decisions. In consequence, this leads to the enhancement of participatory methods of making organisational decisions[167]. Thanks to their pragmatism and the openness of their economies, Scandinavians integrate well with most employees from the European Union. Most enterprises and employees have vast international experience, and there are relatively few language problems, as knowledge of English is quite common in Scandinavian countries. Thus, in the case of Scandinavian enterprises, cultural barriers are not very significant in the process of internationalisation.
3. The cultural circle of francophone countries, including France, Belgium and Switzerland, is characterised by a high level of individualism, relatively large power distance, a relatively high level of uncertainty avoidance and a feminist orientation. Key values of the francophone culture include appreciation for individuality and creativity, awareness of the significance of freedom, subjection to the power authority, striving for the maintenance of status quo and resistance to changes, a demanding attitude towards the state and the significance of aesthetics in life[168]. Employees expect stability

167 Ibidem, pp. 220–242.

168 Lewis R.D., *When Cultures Collide. Managing Successfully Across Cultures*, Nicholas Brealey Publishing, London 1996, pp. 202–208.

and in many cases treat their professional lives as a necessity, allowing them to fully develop in their private lives. French employees encounter serious problems with integration in the European Union labour market. Most of all, there is the language barrier. Most Frenchmen do not speak any foreign language fluently, and few citizens of other EU countries speak French. French employees have a rather demanding attitude, both towards their employers and the state or the local government. French managers are usually quite ethnocentric and convinced of the universal effectiveness of the organisational solutions developed in their country. This leads to conflicts and problems with human resources management in French companies making investments in other EU countries. Additionally, there are cultural problems related to the integration of employees from other European countries in France. There is strong resistance to the employment of foreigners, and protectionism concerning French employees. Virtually all the most prestigious positions and occupations remain in the hands of native Frenchmen. Another serious problem is the assimilation of members of ethnic groups, who end up facing ostracism or at least a glass ceiling. The attitude of some, such as the Arabic minority, is hostile and confrontational towards the French state and society.

4. The circle of Mediterranean countries includes Italy, Spain and Portugal. Historically, they are Catholic countries and use languages coming from the same Roman root, which is why they are to a certain extent similar to countries from the francophone culture circle. Greece, which is the cradle of Mediterranean culture, is significantly different in terms of language, religion and key values, and so should be described separately. The Mediterranean countries are characterised by a moderate level of individualism, a relatively high power distance, a moderate level of uncertainty avoidance and masculinism. The key values of Mediterranean countries include emotionality, directness, a pro-partner orientation, synchronous approach to time, attachment to family and readiness to improvise. Employees from Mediterranean countries give priority to their family life. Organisations are based on complex informal and familial relationships. Conduct of business is related to personal bonds, far from the impersonal ideal of bureaucracy. Southerners do not pay much attention to punctuality or meticulous performance of their tasks. Representatives of many countries from the north of Europe think they are untidy and unable to conduct business effectively. However, they have a large dose of resourcefulness and innovativeness, and are ready to introduce changes and improvise. Employees from the Mediterranean countries have problems adapting to other labour markets, mostly because they are attached

to their local culture and personal relationships. Southerners are often associated with negative stereotypes, which hinder their adaptation. Another problem is their relatively poor knowledge of foreign languages.

5. The Germanic cultural circle, including Germany and Austria, is characterised by a moderate level of individualism, a moderate power distance, a relatively high level of uncertainty avoidance and a masculine orientation. Values typical of the Germanic culture include punctuality, meticulousness, formalism, respect for authority and order, an orientation towards the maintenance of status quo and a pro-transactional approach. German employees follow the stereotype – they are disciplined, competent and aware of their value. They require order and a stable environment. They have problems accepting improvisation, a lack of specialisation and rapid changes. Their favourite configuration is professional bureaucracy. Their respect for power and authority is reflected in formalism and ceremony. However, this circle also includes well-developed participatory procedures, thanks to which authoritarian power is not the ideal. German employees usually speak English relatively well, and only the Dutch and Scandinavians beat them in this respect. In their case, an intercultural problem can be their ethnocentrism, manifested in their belief that they have the perfect management model. They have often problems understanding other cultural patterns and so treat them as less effective.

The comparison of cultural circles is neither full, nor fully disjunctive, as it lacks such countries as Greece, the Netherlands, Estonia and countries from Central and Eastern Europe. Additionally, it is simplified, and could be accused of spreading national stereotypes and being based on empirically unconfirmed concepts of 'national character'. Each social culture is unique and leans towards different cultural circles. Greece is a traditional, family-oriented, agricultural culture, which leans towards Mediterranean and also Orthodox cultures. The Netherlands is characterised by the culture of European Protestant countries, but has also been influenced by Germanic, Scandinavian, Anglo-Saxon and francophone cultures. Estonia is located in the circles of Russian and Scandinavian cultures. The countries from Central and Eastern Europe are very diverse in terms of culture, because of their history, language, religion, national identity and ethnic structure. Poland is a Catholic country, strongly influenced by German and Russian cultures. The Czech Republic has a Protestant tradition, but has also been influenced by Germanic culture. Bulgaria clearly leans towards the Orthodox Russian culture. The presented cultural diversity of Europe shows that historical processes have shaped some cultural centres (French, English), and despite significant differences between European cultures, they are smaller than if we compare European countries to societies from other continents (except for North America and Australia).

3.3 The cultural conditions of competitiveness

Many works have been written on the problem of the cultural conditions of economic development, as it is a methodologically complex area of research. The issues most often analysed can be divided into four areas:

1. Cultural sources of the development of capitalism.
2. Cultural correction of the classical economic theory, taking into consideration the significance of social and cultural variables in the definition of economic development and wealth.
3. Cultural conditions of globalisation processes, concerning the issue of economic and cultural convergence of societies.
4. Comparative research into social cultures and interpretations of their influence on economic development.

Due to the extent of the issues and the research, it was necessary to make a selection of projects related to comparative cross-cultural studies. This list was limited to a description of the results of the three previously-mentioned, famous research projects, which provide diverse results from comparative research which should be discussed.

Cultural issues in the conditions of economic development go back to the deliberations on the Protestant roots of the capitalistic spirit described by Max Weber[169]. Culture influences the competitiveness of whole economies (macroeconomics) and individual business entities (microeconomics). This is an indirect influence, closely related to other factors. Culture is also closely linked with law and institutional order, as well as political, social, demographic and economic variables. It is difficult to separate the level of social culture from the organisational cultures of different enterprises. In fact, culture is a problematic variable to interpret, but it is very difficult to describe the existing diversity of societies' competitiveness without using cultural explanations.

Interpreting the results of the intercultural research projects described, I would like to focus on the micro scale, which means cultural determinants of the competitiveness of enterprises. To a large extent, these are linked with the dominant work patterns and are popularly referred to as 'employee mentality'.

---

169 M. Weber, *Economy and Society: An Outline of Interpretive Sociology*, University of California Press, London, 1978

Out of numerous existing and possible interpretations of the influence of employee mentality on the competitiveness of enterprises, I will focus on only a few: the work ethos, attitude towards power, tolerance of social inequalities, emotionality at work and action in a multicultural environment.

- Differences in the attitude towards work.

The work ethos differs depending on the society. Applying the interpretation of the dimensions of masculinism – feminism and individualism – collectivism, proposed by G. Hofstede, to Europe, we can identify a division into societies oriented towards professional work and individual success, and societies oriented towards the standard of living and sense of community. This division is consolidated by stereotypes. Greeks, Italians and Spaniards are often regarded by the citizens of Northern Europe as being less involved in their professional career. On the other hand, Germans, the Dutch and the British are stereotypically perceived as people oriented mostly towards professional success, neglecting local community bonds (family, neighbours).

Another differentiation between the work ethos in European societies can be described based on the research of A. Trompenaars and C. Hampden-Turner. Universalists, including Scandinavians, Germans and Anglo-Saxons, assume similar measures of involvement and effectiveness for everyone, while particularists, coming from Mediterranean cultures, give preferential treatment to family and friends.

This idea of division is laid over a differentiation of attitudes to work between Western Europe and East-Central Europe. Poland, Slovakia, Bulgaria and Romania, who spent half a century under the pressure of real communism, are only now building their work ethos and native enterprises. In the case of these countries, generational diversity of the approach to work is very clear. Generations brought up during Communism often reveal demanding attitudes towards the state, passivity and distrust towards enterprises (low tolerance for uncertainty). On the other hand, young people are more willing to take risks and create their own business entities (higher tolerance for uncertainty).

Differences in the approach to work give rise to much cultural confusion. When confronted with employees from the north of Europe, employees from the south of Europe perceive them as 'workaholics', while they themselves are perceived as 'layabouts'.

- Differences in the approach to power and management.

In G. Hofstede's concept, the dimension which describes cultural relations of power is power distance. Scandinavians are an example of a society of egalitarian orientation, who do not tolerate strong, autocratic power. Similarly, Englishmen, Scots and Irishmen treat power pragmatically, as a way of organisation, and not a personal attribute. On the other hand, the French, Belgians and Portuguese often accept and respect autocratic managers, following the concept of charisma or authority associated with a social position. This diversity is a reason for cultural conflicts. Managers from countries of large power distance treat employees from Scandinavian countries as utopianists or even anarchists, questioning managerial rights. On the other hand, a manager from a country of a high power distance, trying to gain strong authority, is perceived by employees from less hierarchical cultures as someone who terrorises their workers and supports authoritarian power.

The problem of different approaches to power in A. Trompenaars and C. Hampden-Turner's model is related to the dimension of status ascribed vs. status achieved. In francophone and Mediterranean countries, managers have an attributed, personal authority of a fairly permanent character. Promotion is clearly related to age and experience (seigniorial power). Achieving a given power position also means receiving higher social status and prestige. In Scandinavian and Anglo-Saxon cultures, managers wield task-related power and its exercising is not accompanied by a personal aura (charisma). Promotion and position depend on success, thanks to which the chances of promotion are less dependent on age or social class.

- Approach to social inequality.

The measures of power distance and status mentioned previously also relate to the degree of acceptance of social inequality. In this case, the level of individualism and masculinism plays a very significant role. Naturally, cultures of a large power distance are characterised by the logic of strong diversification of people, which is reflected in their social hierarchy. And so Italians, the Portuguese and Spaniards accept larger social inequalities. However, countries of a low power distance are far more interesting. In their case, there are two representative examples – the Anglo-Saxon cultural circle and the Scandinavian cultural circle. Anglo-Saxon culture has a low power distance, but this is accompanied by a high level of individualism and masculinism. This is an example of solutions of a configuration leading to the acceptance of competitive assumptions about the labour market. Social inequality is tolerated, because most people believe that social status is to a large extent the effect of personal achievements and work, so people owe their professional success or failure to themselves. The model of tolerance for high social and wage inequalities is enhanced by masculinism, an excellent example of which is the USA. However, one can clearly see that societies of high power distance mostly accept social class differences, which translate into differences in prestige and income, while cultures of low power distance tolerate only the differences in wages that result from individual success. The Scandinavian cultural circle is an example of a model society of 'social capitalism', the priority of which is to limit inequality. In their case, class, social and wage inequalities are not accepted. Society and the state strive for the creation of legal and cultural mechanisms which give equal opportunities and status. In the case of Scandinavian cultures, this egalitarian orientation is strengthened by feminism. A significant limitation on the model of 'social capitalism' is the process of globalisation and European integration, which may tempt those who earn the most to move their incomes to countries which are less burdened with redistribution. The clash between several legal and cultural models of the EU labour market is definitely slowing down the process of its integration. Many European countries, protecting their citizens as part of the model of 'social capitalism' and the welfare state, have introduced limitations on the integration of EU labour forces from countries which have recently joined the European Union.

- Emotionality at work.

In this case, there is a clear division between the north and the south. Stereotypically, people from the North of Europe are regarded as more reserved, while the southerners are often perceived as emotional and impulsive extroverts. To a great extent, the research by A. Trompenaars and C. Hampden-Turner confirms this distinction. Societies from the Mediterranean and francophone cultural circles are very emotional at work. The societies of Germanic and Scandinavian cultural circles prefer emotional neutrality at work, whereas Anglo-Saxon culture is located somewhere in between. Intercultural problems, resulting from the clash between affective cultures and cultures striving for affective neutrality, have been described by E. Hall. Numerous pragmatic problems in the processes of negotiation, management and social communication were described by R.R. Gesteland and R.D. Lewis[170]. Emotionality can disturb reserved employees, because it is believed to be a sign of feelings and private issues being mixed with professional activity. Affectation can also hinder communication and the process of making decisions, the results of

---

170 R.R. Gesteland, *Cross-Cultural Business Behavior*, Copenhagen: Copenhagen Business School Press, 1999.; R.D. Lewis, *When Cultures Collide. Managing Successfully Across Cultures*, Nicholas Brealey Publishing, London 1996.

which concern human resources. For many Europeans from the north, emotionality at work is an indication of a lack of professionalism. On the other hand, South Europeans need affectation in order to establish more honest and deeper communication. To them, the lack of emotional responses and expression of one's own feelings indicates indifference and a lack of involvement in the professional situation.

- Problems of contact with different ethnic, religious and cultural groups.

An intercultural matter of the utmost importance in the contact between representatives of difference societies is the fact that they build their identities upon different, sometimes even contradictory values and norms. As historical experience shows, cultural diversity contributes to social and economic development, while the striving for excessive cultural homogeneity hinders it. The European Union's labour market often sees clashes of cultural patterns, coming from very different contexts. In the ethnic sense, the European labour market is increasingly diverse. Over the last two decades, the number of foreign employees has significantly increased in EU countries, in terms of both the mixture of different EU citizens on the open labour market, and the influx of Asians (India, China, Pakistan, Indonesia), citizens of Arabic countries (e.g. Morocco, Algeria, Egypt), citizens of Eastern Europe (Ukrainians, Russians, people from former Soviet Union countries) and the citizens of South and Central Africa. The consequences of this ethnic diversity are extensive. On the one hand, we are dealing with the polarisation of opinions in West European countries, a manifestation of which can be seen in the increase in xenophobic feelings, but on the other, there is an escalation in conflicts with the growing ethnic minorities who are not assimilating well in their new host countries. In the case of the labour market, this often means discrimination against certain national groups of employees and creation of strong negative, ethnic stereotypes. Other reasons for internal tensions are religious, linguistic and other cultural differences between different social groups of EU employees. In this case, conflicts take place over the display of symbols of faith in the workplace and respect for religious holidays and customs. An extreme example of such tensions is the French fight with religious symbols and customs, in the name of the maintenance of the secular and neutral character of the state. In this author's opinion, such tensions have no universal, 'Solomon's solution', but should be resolved with the use of social and intercultural dialogue. Communication is here a method of bridging a gap between different cultures, religions and nations, and in this it seems that Europe has centuries-old experience in conducting such intercultural dialogues.

3.4 Convergence of cultures

Today, the evolution of social cultures, which also influences organisations, is closely related to the globalisation process. Globalisation means changes in the economic, technological and cultural spheres[171], and leads to the evolution of cultures towards common tendencies, related to the development of a consumerist culture, cultural syncretism (cultural supermarket, market place) and multiculturalism[172]. S. Huntington sees the globalisation process as a clash of civilisations, in which Western civilisation plays the most significant role. In the cultural sphere, a clash between civilisations can take the form of attempts at imposing the culture of one society on other countries[173]. S. Huntington believes that modern globalisation is just a version of cultural imperialism, based on economic and political power, which means this is an attempt at westernisation of the world. The opposition to this cultural imperialism can be seen as the spontaneous spreading of the most expansive patterns. Regardless of the assumptions of the way culture is distributed – be it cultural imperialism or spontaneous spreading – the globalisation of culture can be defined as a gradual unification of values, norms and cultural patterns in a number of countries.

Although most theoreticians agree that globalisation is the reason for the convergence of cultures, there are also works pointing more to cultural divergence, which can be caused by globalisation. A. Appadurai thinks that the globalisation of cultures does not lead to their homogenisation. As the influence of globalisation's elements is not uniform, new diverse cultural configurations are created, which do not result in the homogenisation of culture[174]. A.D. Smith believes that globalisation projects are a utopian goal, because competing national cultures use elements of globalisation in an instrumental way to improve their competitive position. This is why there is a growing aversion to globalisation, and this aversion can lead to national and international conflicts[175].

---

171 Cf.: L.C. Thurow, The Future of Capitalism. New York: William Morrow and Company, 1996, p. 157.

172 D.S. Grewal, Network Power: *The Social Dynamics of Globalization*, Yale University Press, 2008.

173 S.P. Huntington, *The Clash of Civilizations and the Remaking of World Order*, New York, Simon & Schuster, 1996, p. 310.

174 A. Appadurai, *Disjuncture and Difference in the Global Cultural Economy*, [in:] M.G. Durham, D.M. Kelner, Media and cultural studies, Blackwell Publishing, 2006, p. 307.

175 A.D. Smith, *Towards a Global Culture* [in:] M. Featherstone, Global Culture: Nationalism, Globalization and Modernity, Sage, 1991, p. 188.

In his trilogy *The Information Age: Economy, Society, and Culture*, M. Castells analyses the complex, multidimensional process of the development of a network society, which complicates the simple distinction between cultural convergence and divergence. On the one hand, the processes of economic and cultural globalisation deepen, and a network society develops based on the interactive communication technologies. But on the other, there is a growing significance to collective identities, which are not based on ethnic and national criteria. M. Castells describes complex and multi-directional cultural macro-trends of the modern world, such as:

- An increase in the significance of the network society, together with the increasing significance of economic globalisation processes,
- The development of networked forms of business, social and cultural activities,
- The increasing flexibility and instability of forms of employment,
- Deepening individualisation of work processes,
- Development of virtual, globalised, interactive and diversified media,
- The fall of traditional national and industrial countries, substituted by cross-national and post-industrial structures,
- A radical increase in collective identities, subcultures and counter-cultures, which are a challenge to globalisation processes[176].

Thus, an in-depth analysis of the complex processes in the creation of a network society at the turn of the 20th century shows that the processes of convergence related to globalisation and the spreading of consumerist cultures are accompanied by the deepening of differences based on the significance of new collective identities.

The mechanism of the globalisation of culture can be determined as a diffusion of different cultural elements, leading to cultural convergence[177]. The first rule of cultural diffusion, as defined by R. Linton, says that in the absence of other conditions, cultural elements are accepted mostly by societies coming into contact with the places where these elements were created, and then by more distant societies or societies having less direct contact with them. Today, unlike in the past, the development of communication technology, international trade and international contacts are why the condition for this diffusion is no

176 E. Castells, The Power of Identity: The Information Age: Economy, Society, and Culture, Viley – Blackwell, Tom 2, p. 2.

177 Linton, Ralph. 'SECTION OF ANTHROPOLOGY: THE TREE OF CULTURE.'*Transactions of the New York Academy of Sciences* 11.5 Series II (1949): 171–175.

longer geographical proximity between cultures. The cultures whose models dominate in international communication and exchange have a greater chance of spreading their values, patterns and norms worldwide. It is worth noting that the diffusion of cultural patterns takes place quicker than the diffusion of norms and values. Values are the core – and most permanent – elements of culture. The development and spreading of global culture lies mostly in cultural patterns, and only then norms and values. Local cultures do not assimilate global culture evenly. Potential communication and exchange centres are more likely to quickly adapt to the global culture, while the peripheries stick to the local culture longer.

The susceptibility of a given social culture to the assimilation of other cultural patterns differs depending on the strength, cohesion and differences between these patterns. Strong, cohesive, more isolated and different local cultures should be more resistant to the assimilation of foreign models. A.K. Kozminski points to three possible models of cross-cultural management: cultural domination, culture co-existence and cultural cooperation[178]. Furthermore, the reactions of local cultures to the expansion of global culture can differ. In extreme cases, these include quick and full assimilation or complete rejection. Between these extremes, there are a number of other reactions, including selective adaptation, hybridisation (a compromise between the models of global and local cultures) and cultural dualism (a split of cultural patterns)[179].

Research taking into consideration the age differences of the respondents shows that in the case of younger groups of respondents, the diversification of cultures in European societies is far lower than in the case of older groups. This indicates that we are facing the slow convergence of different cultural circles in Europe. It seems that this is a logical consequence of the processes of European integration and globalisation, together with their deepened contacts and intercultural communication. But there is still a question about the directions of this cultural integration. It seems that the values of Anglo-Saxon culture are gaining significance, including its high level of individualism, low level of the power distance, low level of uncertainty avoidance and quite high level of masculinism.

Today it seems that the United States, closest to the Anglo-Saxon cultural circle, has the greatest chance of dominating the global culture. American culture was not built upon strong ethnic national patterns, as happened in the

178 A.K. Kozminski, *Zarządzanie, teoria i praktyka*, PWN, Warszawa, 2010, pp. 217–218.
179 K. Krzysztofek, Global Governance, Global Culture, and Multiculturalism, Canadian Journal of Communication, vol. 27, 2002, pp. 74–76.

case of the cultures of other societies[180], but on the model of a multinational, mass, consumerist society. Its multi-nationality assumes the possibility of following the values of two cultures at the same time: the culture of the country of origin (ethnic) and the culture of country of residence (American). However, there is a gradual process of displacing or complementing the ethnic identity with American culture. American culture has assimilated the models of mass culture, which now contributes to its popularisation. In the future this should entail changes in the values of organisational cultures in many countries, leaning towards the American model of individualism, equality and high tolerance for uncertainty. Assuming that the expansion of models related to Anglo-Saxon cultural circles is very strong, one can see that they are being spread in many countries. The models of the consumerist behaviour of buyers disseminate, and there is the question of whether they are only American patterns, or patterns of modern free-market economies as such. Universal products and global brands are highly successful, which can be seen as a sign of American universalism[181]. Individual, charismatic styles of managing organisations develop and, at the same time, strong and involved teams supporting the decision-making process form around their leaders. The rules of enterprise spread, including the striving for success, initiative, self-confidence and individuals' ability to create a vision of an organisation, as well as models of bold, visionary and expansive organisations, adjusted to the rapid changes in the environment. American models of mass culture shape the global identity of employees and consumers, supplanting highly diverse configurations of local cultures[182]. Thanks to the development of the American management current, the ideas of analytical, individualist and egalitarian management of organisations are being popularised[183]. In the sphere of cultural rules of the American society, consumerist hedonism prevails over the rules of Protestant economic ethics, limiting consumption and accumulation for luxurious purposes[184]. The models of global culture spread mostly through

---

180 E. Dean, *Overview of Cultural Identity in United States*, w: INTERNET, http://ematusov.soe.udel.edu/final.paper.pub

181 Cf.: C. Hampden-Turner, A. Trompenaars, *Riding The Waves of Culture: Understanding Diversity in Global Business*, McGraw-Hill, 1997; G. Rizer, *Mcdonaldization*, Journal of American Culture, Volume 6, Issue 1, pp: 100–107

182 Cf.: G.S. Yip, **Total Global Strategy,** 2nd, Prentice Hall, NJ, USA, 2001, chapter 8.

183 It is worth noting that the American models of management are also influenced by other cultures (for example, the participatory management drawn from the culture of Japanese management).

184 D. Bell, *The Cultural Contradictions of Capitalism*, Basic Books, 1976, p. 56.

media, one consequence of which is a departure from the culture of the written word towards visualization. It can be forecasted that the models of national cultures will lean towards unification, based on American models.

The globalisation processes concern political and economic, as well as social and cultural spheres. Probably, in the long term, a new globally unified organisational culture will be created, characterised by: (1) relativisation of cultural values and norms (previously regarded as universal in local cultures), (2) unification of values and models, (3) national values' loss of significance and uniqueness, (4) unification of communication. Global culture is close to the models of consumerist culture, detached from national roots and oriented towards the satisfaction of economic needs. The mechanisms of spreading global culture include: (1) transnational corporations, (2) global financial markets, (3) unified mass communication, (4) *one best way* management models.

3.5 Modern consumerist culture

The direction of the cultural changes from the globalisation and westernization of lifestyles leads us to the issues of modern consumerist culture, which is subject to analyses within all paradigms, from functionalism to postmodernism.

Over the last few decades, the societies of Western Europe and the USA have faced a slow change in consumerist culture. The values of Protestant ethics, which determined the shape of early consumerist culture at the beginning of the 20th century, have gone out of date. For modern consumers, economy, restraint and rationalism are no longer virtues. The current ideal is based on ostentatious and excessive consumption, irrational in economic terms. On the one hand, this change is a result of the development of the free market and the activity of enterprises, but on the other, it presents significant challenges to management science.

The word 'consume' comes from the Latin *consumptio* for eating, using or even destroying goods. The sphere of consumption can be analysed from the perspective of human needs, the means of satisfying those needs (the objects of consumption, i.e. material and non-material goods), ways of satisfying needs (consumerist behaviour) and the effects of satisfying needs (results).

Consumerist foundations have always accompanied social groups, but before the industrial revolution they concerned only the elites. At the turn of the 19th and the 20th centuries, T. Veblen pointed to the aristocracy and bourgeoisie as 'leisure classes', concerned with ostentatious consumption of goods[185]. Nevertheless,

185 *T. Veblen, The Theory of the Leisure Class*, NY: McMillan, 1899

the economic and social changes taking place in developed countries led to the appearance of an entire consumerist class. Among the most important reasons for this change, D. Bell includes technological development and an increase in the standard of living, which led to a cultural transformation. Mass consumption became possible thanks to the use of electricity in households, the popularisation of production lines in industry and the appearance of mass media. A consumerist society is of a mass character – an idea supported by the rapid urbanisation processes taking place in the developed countries in the first half of the 20th century. Describing the departure from Protestant ethics to consumerist ethics in the United States, Bell also points to the popularisation of hire-purchase and the birth of marketing[186]. It seems that marketing is the perfect reflection of the consumerist civilisation and influences it to a great extent. The combination of the market power of money and the knowledge of how to wield social influence gave rise to the modern consumer. After all, consumerism is also related to other management aspects, such as strategic management and human resources management.

Consumption has become a root metaphor for modern culture, and is often perceived from the perspective of a binary opposition to several other processes, from both the economic and political spheres. These include consumption vs. production, consumption vs. investment, consumption vs. citizenship and consumption vs. ecology[187]. The processes of managing organisations are also determined by a consumptive nature, which is often interpreted as a cultural variable.

The culture of modernist consumers developed in free-market industrial societies in the second half of the 19th century and the first half of the 20th century. It reached its climax when scientific management was created, together with its ideology of Taylorism and Fordism – labels for the industrial modernisation of a mass society. The frameworks of these concepts are based on the assumptions of mass production, using the economy of scale, which is supported by uniform consumption[188]. Taylorism and Fordism stemmed from a spirit of capitalism, Protestant ethics, neopositivism and industrialisation. Scientific organisation of work needed a determinist work division, into elementary sequences and subject to detailed managerial supervision. Ideal, modernist consumers were rational,

186 D. Bell, *The Cultural Contradictions of Capitalism,* Basic Books, 1976, pp. 92–106.

187 A. Aldridge, Consumption. Polity, 2003, p. 16.

188 B. Jessop, Thatcherism and Flexibility: The White Heat of a Post-Fordist Revolution, in: *The Politics of Flexibility*, ed. B. Jessop, H. Kastendiek, K. Nielsen, O. Pedersen, UK: Edward Elgar, Aldershot, 1991, pp. 82–105.

they calculated costs, did not buy unnecessary or too-expensive things, made savings and tried to allocate their resources in an optimum way. Such consumers bought the things they really needed, which to a great extent were the products of technological and scientific development. They were treated in a unified, uniform and mass way, which lowered the unit costs of production. Modernist consumers belonged to the developing middle class, and the mass production of rapidly growing corporations was aimed at them.

With time, the aspirations of some members of the middle class increased. They started to expect that products would be distinctive, would grant them status and have a strong identity which would allow them to aspire to groups of a higher status. In the middle of the 20th century, the role of services in the economy also started to grow. Thus, changes towards the post-industrial economy led to the departure from Taylor and Ford's paradigm in management science. Writing about the birth of the post-industrial society, D. Bell drew attention to the transformation towards the information approach, oriented towards symbolic activities – services and consumption[189]. Among the significant trends of changes in modern society, A. Toffler includes:

- Creation of an indeterminist information society,
- An increase in the pace of living and the pressure of changes,
- Consumerism in a throw-away society,
- An increase in diversity and the possibility of individual and collective choices[190].

The processes mentioned give rise to a completely new, postmodern consumerist culture, which in the management sphere can be described as post-Taylorism or post-Fordism. This is characterised by the dominance of services in the economy, flexible production and distribution, decentralisation of management, individualisation of marketing and the organisational orientation towards knowledge.

Comparing modernist and postmodernist consumerism cultures, it is worth pointing out several key differences. Postmodernist culture departs from the assumption of consumer rationality, focusing on the manifestations of ostentatious, wasteful, irrational, and even exploratory and destructive consumption. The basis for making purchase decisions is no longer a modernist need, but an ephemeral whim. Modernist consumers were oriented towards permanent and

189 D. Bell, *The Cultural Contradictions of Capitalism,* Basic Books, 1976
190 A. Toffler, *Future Schock,* Random House, 1970.

measurable material goods while postmodern consumers are oriented towards services, often of an interpretative and symbolic character; modernist enterprises were oriented towards the production of goods, while today an orientation towards consumption prevails. Comparison of a larger number of features differentiating modernist and postmodernist consumer cultures can be found in Tab. 17.

The development of postmodern consumer culture has had significant consequences for management science. Adjusting an organisation to new cultural trends requires changes in the sphere of strategic management, marketing, and information management, and also leads to the need for reconstruction of other functional areas within organisations.

The strategy of organisations functioning in the culture of postmodern consumerism should be focused on flexibility, openness and quick decision-making. In consequence, organisations adjusted to the trends of globalising consumerist culture are multicultural, pluralist, networked, decentralised and heterarchical, and are based on symbolic goods[191]. Organisations functioning in an information society are based on self-directing, flexible employee teams.

Marketing, too, is undergoing deep transformations. The culture of modernist consumerism was oriented towards the economic rationalism of customers' activities and satisfaction of their clear needs. Modern consumerist culture is interpretative and symbolic, rather than rational and economic. Marketing is based on shaping the fluid identity of postmodernist consumers. The promoted brands mostly make use of the meanings ascribed to them, and not their material content. Mass culture sells meanings, and shapes and satisfies the fleeting whims of consumers. The ideology of 'McDonaldisation' and 'Disneyfication' leads to creation of a hyper-reality – utopian delusions of happy consumption. In order to face up to such deep changes, the marketing activities of organisations should be a subject of interest for most of their employees, not only those in specialised departments. For this purpose, one needs the employees to possess multidirectional qualifications, making them quickly adaptable to changing requirements. Multidirectional marketing has to take into consideration the fundamental significance of linguistic and cultural differences, developing multidimensional, network and interactive relationships with clients. Thus, it seems probable that in this situation, methods of partner and relational marketing would be developed, and then adjusted to the local cultural context. The assumption of social

191 P. Engholm, *The Controversy Between Modernist and Postmodernist Views of Management Science: Is a Synergy Possible?*, Internet, Monash University, May 2001.

Tab. 17: Modernist consumer culture vs. postmodernist consumer culture. Source: Own work.

Criterion	Modernist consumer	Postmodernist consumer
Consumer's rationalism	Economic rationalism	Limited rationalism in the economic sphere
The basis for purchase decisions	Necessity	Whim
Stability of aspirations	Consistent choices, consumer loyalty	Random choices, limited consumer loyalty
The basic consumer orientation	Material goods	Services
The perception of values	Materialism (striving for ownership, owning things)	Post-materialism (striving for using things)
The basic orientation of enterprises	Marginal role of consumption, central production role	Marginal role of production, central role of consumption
Consumer virtues	Economy, restraint	Prodigality, ostentatious consumption
Perception of the market reality	Real, measurable material goods	Immeasurable, non-material, virtual (e.g. brands)
Consumer motives	Accumulation of goods, economy, rationality of purchases	Interaction, satisfying whims and symbolic needs, following fashion
Model of communication with consumers	Sender – Channel – Recipient Linear model	Symbol – Interpreter Synchronous model
Aims of communication	Information and persuasion	Wielding influence Narration and continuation of discourse
Communication channel	Single, simple, one-directional, mass	Interactive, complex, feedback, individualised
Communication means	Text and images	Hypertext and interactive images
Communication subjects	Segments of customers with specific needs	Individuals of blurred identity, susceptible to the influence of communication
Dominant media	Mass media (television, press, radio)	Interactive media (Internet, interactive television)
Communication technologies	Sound and image transmission technologies	Web and computer technologies

constructionism and the significance of symbolic goods will make marketing specialists focus on the creation and promotion of meanings that have a greater chance of entering the cultural discourse. Reality is shaped by communication. Thus, the development of Internet communication, interactive television, telecommunications and videotelephony enhances the supremacy of symbols over the material aspects of the world.

Information management is becoming the key challenge for organisations submerged in the culture of modern consumption. Developing systems of network management and relational marketing requires extended communication with clients. Although it is difficult to find permanent strategic solutions on the turbulent global market, good contact with consumers, shaping their needs and satisfying their whims, remains the basis for the market success of an enterprise. The internet, an organisation's intranet, and the systems of gathering and processing information about customers, competitors and the entire sector, then become more and more important. Organisations create and develop units specialising in the management of internal and external information processes.

The currently dominant culture of postmodernist consumerism, created at the end of the 20th century in developed societies, is significantly different from the previous modernist culture. Most of all, this is due to the development of global markets, an increase in competitive intensity and a culture based on new communication forms. Consumers are under pressure from mass culture and the cultural industry, which actively seeks to shape their identity. Functioning in the context of new cultural systems poses new challenges for enterprises which manufacture and sell market goods to consumers. It changes their strategies, structures and organisational cultures, and in consequence, all other functional spheres. The deepest change is in the creation of flexible strategies oriented towards the positive market image of brands, the development of information management systems and the marketing of identities and relationships.

4 Culture and organisational culture from the neoevolutionary perspective

4.1 Neoevolutionism in management science

Today, the promising current of research into cultural processes seems to be the neoevolutionary perspective, which was initiated by socio-biology and creatively developed by evolutionary psychology. Evolutionary psychology, behavioural economics and – earlier – socio-biology introduced Darwinian inspirations to the social sciences, which shook the foundations of all science. It could be said to have been a kind of scientific revolution, and it once again dethroned man – the Copernican revolution had deprived us of the illusion that the Earth is the centre of the Universe, Darwin's theory of evolution negated the vision of man reigning in the world of nature and occupying the top rung of the ladder of creation. The development of the neoevolutionary perspective in the social sciences then eliminated the traditional division between 'matter' and 'spirit', pointing to the natural origins of consciousness and social life phenomena. It is also applicable to culture, the theory of which was created on the basis of the 'science of spirit', while in the neo-Darwinian interpretation it should be studied as a natural process.

Evolutionism, which explains a number of social life phenomena, can be used as a basis for the explanation of numerous cases of human collective behaviour forming the foundations of the processes of organisation and management. Thus, it is worth looking at the potential applications of this paradigm to determine further directions of research within management science. Over the last four decades, the neoevolutionary paradigm has spread to the social sciences, the first effect of which is the dynamic development of evolutionary psychology and socio-biology. The potential applications of this paradigm in management science cover a wide range of social problems based on evolutionary foundations, such as biological sources of organisation, natural sources of power structure, competition between individuals, conflicts and the fight for dominance, leadership in organisations, learning, group and organisational bonds, risk-taking, communication, sexual practices, and evolutionary conditions of social and organisational cultures:

- Biological foundations of organisation
  Organisational processes are rooted in human nature, as social activities are of an organised, social character. Most researchers believe that hominid evolution

sees positive feedback between brain size and the complexity of social life[192]. The proofs of the effectiveness of organisation can be seen in the startling effectiveness of primitive man's hunts for huge mammals, which required the coordination of group activities, and the finding and stigmatisation of 'evolutionary fraudsters' who faked their involvement[193]. This means that the evolutionary process includes the organisational function, which allows for and optimises group activities. Naturally, it covers both the conscious coordination of purposeful activities of social living, and the intuitive activities related to organisation and leadership.

- Leadership in a group
  The key existential problems connected with acquiring food, providing shelter, security and taking care of offspring and elders require cooperation, which in most cases is unstable. Individuals who have features allowing them to coordinate a group (such as intelligence, dominance, the ability to communicate and form coalitions), achieved the status of leader more often and the majority of the group submitted to them. Leadership, or the choice of an individual who makes decisions and imposes them upon the group, is not a feature characteristic only of homo sapiens[194]. As a solution enabling effective organisational functioning, it is necessary to create criteria for choosing the leader and maintaining the position, and these are usually based on authority. With men, authority, being a measure of social respect (status) and the readiness of group members to yield to the will of an individual, is not based on physical strength alone. Although physical dominance was of importance in the past – and in some cases today – it can still subconsciously help in acquiring authority. But the prevailing criterion is the ability to cooperate with a social group, based on communication and the influence of the social model (the ideal of a leader, image, reputation, respect etc.). Evolutionary research into leadership and power are still at the initial stage and are mostly concerned with the search for mental modules that interfere with these social processes.

192 D. Rendal, H. Notman, J.R. Vokey, *Homologizing the mind, [w:]*R.I.M. Dunbar, L. Barrett, *The Oxford Handbook of Evolutionary Psychology, Oxford University Press, 2007,* pp. *62–65*

193 E. Hoffman, K.A. McCabe, V.L. Smith, Behavioral Foundations of Reciprocity: Experimental Economics and Evolutionary Psychology, *Economic Inquiry*, 1998, pp. 335–352.

194 M. Van Vugt, *Evolutionary Origins of Leadership and Followership, Personality and Social Psychology Review,* November 2006 vol. 10 No. 4 354–371.

- Natural sources of the structure of power and hierarchy
  Social power and hierarchy are not solely the domain of humans, as they are also common in the world of animals. If we understand power as the possibility to impose one's will upon other individuals, then it is true for most primates and many other species. Power and hierarchy play an important role in the case of social species, because they place the leader not only in the position of dominator, but also a decision-maker who imposes his will upon both scattered individuals and the entire social group. The consequences of such decisions are far more significant because they concern all community members. The natural order assumes the domination of the strongest, but among chimpanzees coalitions are common, giving power to the most socially skilled, individual or even group. This has been confirmed by numerous observations of chimpanzees and bonobos, most famously by J. Goodall and F. de Waal[195]. In order to carry out long-term organisational projects, from the functional perspective it is necessary not only to appoint a centre of power, but to ensure its stability. Thus, one of the key problems in exercising power is its legitimization, which means accepting it as just.
- Rivalry between individuals, conflicts and the fight for dominance
  Rivalry, conflicts and fighting are inseparable attributes of the wielding of power, and take sophisticated forms among social species. Rivalry is related to limited access to resources and individuals' unlimited needs for survival and reproduction. Thus, fights and conflicts can be seen both on the individual level, and on the level of coalitions in the social groups of primates[196]. The complexity of competitive processes and conflicts requires effort in conducting analyses on multiple levels, and this is related to the problems of organisation and social games[197].
- Learning and creativity in a social group
  The organisational function mainly gains significance in situations where individuals and groups are faced with non-routine tasks, which do not offer ready-to-use solutions, available in the collection of standard cultural patterns.

---

195 B.M. Frans deWaal, The Brutal Elimination of a Rival among Captive Male Chimpanzees, *Ethology and Sociobiology*, Vol. 7, Issues 3–4, 1986, pp. 237–251; T. Dávid-Barrett, R.I.M. Dunbar, Cooperation, Behavioural Synchrony and Status in Social Networks, *Journal of Theoretical Biology*, Vol. 308, 7 September 2012, pp. 88–95

196 A. Campbell, A Few Good Men: Evolutionary Psychology and Female Adolescent Aggression, [in:] D.T. Kenrick, C.L. Luce (red.), *The Functional Mind. Readings in Evolutionary Psychology*, Pearson, Boston 2004

197 R. Axelrod, The Evolution of Cooperation, *Science* 27 March 1981: 1390–1396.

In such cases, creative mechanisms appear, the development of which entailed huge evolutionary costs. Thanks to flexible, non-routine organisations, leadership and creativity, a social group of *homo sapiens* is able to solve even the most complex problems related to survival, in the most difficult and even highly changeable conditions. From the point of view of management science, the processes of learning and getting to know the reality of a situation are of key importance. This is part of the creation of cognitive models which allow us to solve problems. As advanced research in evolutionary psychology into the processes of learning shows, people as a species have a cognitive apparatus which evolved for the purpose of solving specific, open problems related to survival and reproduction, while the theoretical mind is only a side-effect of living in a changeable environment requiring creativity. This turbulent environment is mostly one's own social group, which offers people huge possibilities but, at the same time, presents them with challenges related to changeability, unpredictability and creativity. Out of numerous interesting studies of human cognitive, evolution-determined processes, we can point to the syndrome of quick learning based on aversive experiences and the biological bases of conditioning, as well as the specificity of learning within the processes of primary and secondary socialisation[198].

- Group and organisational bonds: kin and non-kin altruism

  The explanation of the formation of group – and especially kin – bonds was one of the first problems of the modern applications of evolutionism in the social sciences. According to the research by Hamilton, Williams and Trivers, the reason for the development of kin bonds is genetic community. This also means that the strength of kin bonds is directly proportional to genetic proximity. In the case of the social sciences, it is a valuable explanation not only from the point of view of family sociology, but of the question of nepotism in a society. The interpretation of non-kin altruism if far more problematic: why are individuals ready to share with other, genetically alien individuals? In this case, explanations can be found in experiences drawn not only from research in evolutionary psychology, but also ethology. Vampire bats are ready to share blood with unrelated bats, in order to save their companions from death by starvation. They do it because of the promise of reciprocity[199] – social groups

198 M.E.P. Seligman, J.L. Hager, *Biological Boundaries of Learning: The Sauce-Bernaise Syndrome* [in:] D.T. Kenrick, C.L. Luce (ed.), *The Functional Mind. Readings in Evolutionary Psychology*, Pearson, Boston 2004.

199 R. Axelrod, *The Evolution of Cooperation*, Basic Books, New York 1984.

expect reciprocity from individuals who receive help. Social species also have complex mind modules, the aim of which is to find and punish fraudsters who do not want to return the favour. In the case of management, exploring the specificity of social bonds is very important, as they are reflected in the organisational relationships. Nepotism is a culturally universal mechanism that can be manifested in the development of family businesses, and in the creation of family cliques in enterprises and public organisations. Non-kin altruism can also be found in organisations and serves as a basis for cooperation between people.

The mechanisms of finding and punishing social fraudsters form the basis of a social game in all types of organisations. Thus, in order to model organisational processes correctly, it is necessary to refer to the evolutionary interpretation of social relationships.

- Risk-taking in social groups

The tendency to take risks seems a bit paradoxical from the perspective of evolution, but only because of individual survival. But if we look at it from the perspective of reproduction, then the evolutionary explanations become justified. Risk-taking, especially by males, is a method of ensuring reproductive success, especially in the case of non-dominant individuals. When the alpha male achieves his best reproductive effects, the determination of the remaining males to take risks increases. In the case of social species, such as people and apes, this risk does not necessarily have to be related to physical, individual confrontation, as it can encompass the forming of coalitions. In human groups, it is part of the possibility of physical or symbolic confrontation, which manifests advantage[200]. Taking risks also often has demonstrational purposes, the aim of which is to show advantage and discourage others from confrontation in case of sexual rivalry or attack[201]. The tendency to take risks in management is one of the most significant features of the dynamics of the world of organisation. Entrepreneurship is the readiness to take risks in the development of new undertakings. Financial and life risks are inseparably connected with the activities of managers and entrepreneurs. It is interesting to note that the tendency to take risks is deeply rooted in human nature.

---

200 M. Wilson, M. Daly, *Competitiveness, Risk Taking, and Violence: The Young Male Syndrome* [in:] D.T. Kenrick, C.L. Luce (ed.), *The Functional Mind. Readings in Evolutionary Psychology*, Pearson, Boston 2004.

201 J. Diamond, *The Third Chimpanzee. The Evolution and the Future of the Human Animal*, Harper, New York 1992, pp. 192–215.

- Group and organisational communication
  One prerequisite for permanent change and the development of a human community is the accumulation of knowledge and its output. On a larger scale, this is possible thanks to communication processes. The beginnings of these processes can be seen in birds, mammals, and particularly apes, but a language able to transmit complex and abstract ideas is probably characteristic only of people, and is a result of feedback between social development and brain specialization. The creator of the nativist concept of language, developed today by evolutionary psychology[202], is N. Chomsky[203]. The human ability to learn a language and use it probably evolved from a simple system of vocal signals, which later on began to be used to communicate emotions and ideas, and to describe reality. A little earlier, separately from the system of verbal communication, the module of quick non-verbal communication also evolved. This includes, for example, facial expressions and gestures[204]. Language, a sophisticated symbolic system, is also positive feedback between the integration of social groups and change, and the creation of more complex groups and societies. As there is no material evidence of the development of speech, it is difficult to analyse the evolutionary influence of the development of language on people, but undoubtedly language could be one of the reasons for the great leap which led to the shaping of the current form of *Homo sapiens*[205]. Language is the key bond of all social groups and organisations, and the basis for the development of culture. It is often taken for granted, which is why management science noticed its role only in relation to comparative cross-cultural studies[206].
- Masculinity and femininity
  Evolutionary psychology has explicitly proved that there are differences between the cognitive and emotional apparatus of men and women,

---

202 S. Pinker, Language as an Adaptation on the Cognitive Niche [in:] D.T. Kenrick, C.L. Luce (ed.), *The Functional Mind. Readings in Evolutionary Psychology*, Pearson, Boston 2004.

203 N. Chomsky, *Language and Thought*, Mayer Bell, Wakefield, Rhode Island, London 1993.

204 P. Ekman, W.V. Friesen, Constants across Cultures in the Face and Emotion [in:] D.T. Kenrick, C.L. Luce (ed.), *The Functional Mind. Readings in Evolutionary Psychology*, Pearson, Boston 2004.

205 J. Diamond, *The Third Chimpanzee. The Evolution and the Future of the Human Animal*, Harper, New York 1992, pp. 141–167.

206 E.G.G. Hofstede, *Culture's Consequences: International Differences in Work-Related Values*, Sage, Beverly Hills 1980.

and that these are a consequence of evolution[207]. Motoric differentiation, resulting directly from physiological and hormonal differences, is obvious, but the most important cognitive differences concern spatial imagination[208], mathematical and linguistic abilities[209]. On the other hand, emotional differences are related to identity in the commonly accepted 'theories of mind'[210]. The social sciences, based on the culturalist vision, used a dogma of political correctness, which consisted in levelling the differences between men and women based on biological foundations. However, empirical research conducted by evolutionary psychology allows us to see differences which may not be of fundamental significance, but can be of importance for certain aspects of social functioning. This is why management science should perhaps examine organisations in terms of the influence of relationships between the sexes, and analyse managerial and organisational processes in the context of male and female preferences.

- Evolutionary conditions of social and organisational cultures
  Culture can be understood as a system based on symbolism, being a group of beliefs, norms and models transmitted socially between individuals. The carrier of culture is a common language, while cultural transmission makes it possible to accumulate knowledge and social works. There are still evolutionarily relevant questions of whether culture is an adaption enhancing individual chances for survival, an intermediate product of the development of other evolutionary structures (such as language and communication), or a by-product, entailing certain effects harmful to the individual's survival. Today, we have no evolutionary theory of culture. There are some hypotheses, including memetics[211], which point to the analogies between biological

---

207 B.M. Frans de Waal, Sex Differences in the Formation of Coalitions among Chimpanzees, *Ethology and Sociobiology*, Vol. 5, Issue 4, 1984, pp. 239–255

208 M. Eals, I. Silverman, The Hunter-Gatherer Theory of Spatial Sex Differences: Proximate Factors Mediating the Female Advantage in Recall of Object Arrays [in:] D.T. Kenrick, C.L. Luce (ed.), *The Functional Mind. Readings in Evolutionary Psychology*, Pearson, Boston 2004.

209 Kimura, Doreen. *Sex and Cognition*. MIT press, 2000.

210 M.G. Haselton, D. M Buss, Error Management Theory: A New Perspective on Biases in Cross-Sex Mind Reading [in:] D.T. Kenrick, C.L. Luce (ed.), *The Functional Mind. Readings in Evolutionary Psychology*, Pearson, Boston 2004.

211 R. Dawkins, *The Selfish Gene*, Oxford University Press, Oxford 1976.

evolution and cultural changes[212], but so far these are only concepts in the early stages of formulation or testing. The basic research, conducted as part of neuroscience, gives us hope that we will find some basic brain mechanisms reflecting cognitive processes related to the development of the phenomenon of culture[213]. M. Tomasello believes that the human cognitive apparatus is based on cultural foundations which allow for the accumulation of works, individual identification with a community, communication and the development of abstract thinking and creativity[214]. In the social sciences, culture is regarded as the key notion. Sociology, cultural anthropology, social psychology, history and other disciplines treat culture as a root concept. Management science uses the key notion of organisational culture, which is a reflection of the understanding of culture in the humanities. The explanation of biological mechanisms of cultural transmission will probably be a groundbreaking achievement for all disciplines exploring the theory of culture. Additionally, it will undoubtedly contribute to a better understanding of the complexity of organisational culture and its related notions, such as organisational identity and image.

The evolutionary explanations of the social sciences are not just hypotheses, but theories verified by empirical research, in accordance with the basic assumptions of the neoevolutionary paradigm. The research methodology used in evolutionary psychology, socio-biology and neuroscience makes use of such traditional social science tools as surveys, comparative studies, observation and qualitative techniques, as well as techniques for studying the brain (e. g. PET), and also animal behaviour, which was previously only used by the natural sciences.

An attempt at interpreting the relationships between evolutionary human nature and its consequences in a social group's nature, leading to a description of the organisational processes, can be found in Tab. 18. This does not include all elements of the evolutionary psychology theory, as research into some aspects of human behaviour is very limited as far as it applies to management.

---

212 R. Allott, Evolution and Culture: The Missing Link [in:] J.G. Dennen, D. Smillie, D.R. Wilson, (ed.), *The Darwinian Heritage and Sociobiology*, Praeger, Westport, CT 1999, pp. 67–70.

213 B.E. Wexler, *Neurobiology, Ideology and Social Change*, A Bradford Book, The MIT Press, Cambridge 2006.

214 M.Tomasello, Michael, Ann Cale Kruger, and Hilary Horn Ratner. Cultural learning. *Behavioral and Brain Sciences* 16.03 (1993): 495–511.

4.2 Culture from the neoevolutionary perspective

According to S. Pinker, the social sciences of the second half of the 20th century were dominated by the perspective of culturalism, drawing from both the functionalist and interpretative paradigms. To put it very simply, it could be said that culturalism made the following assumptions: *tabula rasa*, cultural relativism and the empowerment of the world of symbols, values and abstraction. S. Pinker criticises the approach popularised by cultural research, which draws from Locke's idea of *tabula rasa* ('blank slate'), and assumes that no human nature originates from biological affiliation. *Tabula rasa* here means the full flexibility of a human mind, thanks to which – through socialisation – one can implement any value, norm or cultural pattern[215]. Cultural relativism, as one of the interpretations of *tabula rasa*, rejects cultural universals, i.e. elements common to all human cultures, as a consequence of human nature. The empowerment of the world of symbols, values and abstraction, characteristic of culturalism, means that these areas are characteristic only of people and that they define the essence of humanity. Language, abstract thinking and morality developed in the human world, and so are alien to the natural sciences, thus they should be studied only with the use of methods characteristic of symbolic and axiological reality.

The neoevolutionary approach to culture, although as internally diverse as the cultural one, is in clear opposition to the above-mentioned assumptions. S. Pinker points to the constant elements of human nature as being a result of our biological heritage. These concern the behavioural sphere, as well as the emotional and mental. Thanks to the cerebral 'software' gained through evolution, people learn, use languages, create, understand music, and have a moral and religious sense. But they also become addicted, fight each other and strive for power[216]. Modern anthropological and psychological research unambiguously indicates that there are indeed cultural universals. Comparative

215 Pinker, Steven. *Tabula rasa*. Edizioni Mondadori, 2010.

216 J.A. Bulbulia, The evolution of religion, [in:] R.I. M Dunbar, L. Barrett, *Evolutionary Psychology*, Oxford University Press, New York 2007; J. Carroll, Evolutionary Approaches to Literature and Drama, [in:] R.I. M Dunbar, L. Barrett, *Evolutionary Psychology*, Oxford University Press, New York 2007; I. Cross, *Music and cognitive evolution*, [in:] R.I. M Dunbar, L. Barrett, *Evolutionary Psychology*, Oxford University Press, New York 2007; S. Kirby, *The Evolution of Language*, [in:] R.I. M Dunbar, L. Barrett, *Evolutionary Psychology*, Oxford University Press, New York 2007.

Tab. 18: The nature of individuals and social groups vs. a description of organisational processes, from the perspective of the neoevolutionary paradigm. Source: Own work

Nature of an individual	Nature of a social group	Organisational process
Social nature of an individual.	Spontaneous emergence of social groups: communication, bonds, structures and relationships.	Spontaneous emergence only of organisational processes: leadership, plan, motivation.
Kin altruism	Strong family relationships, the essence of a group are coalitions between relatives and in-laws. Paternal investments.	Culturally universal influence of nepotism on organisations.
Mutual cooperation with non-kin.	Alliances and coalitions between non-kin, in order to gain common benefits.	A creation of organisations understood as purposeful social groups, striving for the fulfilment of common projects.
Natural sources of power structure and hierarchy.	Spontaneous emergence of power, structure and hierarchy, ordering a social group.	Informal, and then formal structure, as well as hierarchy and power are intuitively understood and accepted as a natural order.
Striving for dominance, fights and conflicts.	Fights for dominance and conflicts are immanent features of a social group and relationships between different groups (e. g. wars).	Striving for dominance, fights and conflicts are sources of internal organisational competition and drive rivalry between organisations.
Sexual selection.	Drive to reproduce and striving for the selection of sexual partners of the highest possible reproductive value.	Hidden significance of sexual motives in the competitive processes between individuals in organisations.
Leadership, wielding power.	Leaders or coalitions of leaders emerge naturally and strive for the consolidation of power.	Leaders are accepted, they gain or lose authority and rights, and can make decisions on behalf of the whole group.
Learning, innovation, resourcefulness, creativity.	Solving open problems in a changeable environment (also social) requires creativity, which is promoted within a group.	In organisations, entrepreneurship is a manifestation of creativity and innovativeness, and combines intellectual potential with organisational attitudes and activities.
Cognitive processes – selective memory (people, faces, narrations).	Adjustment to action and organisation in a small group, where knowing people is of a personal character.	The effects are: limited managerial differential, higher entrepreneurship of small groups and bureaucratic tendencies of large organisations.

Tab. 18: Continued

Nature of an individual	Nature of a social group	Organisational process
Planning the future.	Social decisions and survival strategies of the group take the future into consideration.	The process of informal and formal planning of variants of group activities and the supervision over their implementation.
Group and organisational communication.	Language community leads to the strengthening of relationship and the possibility of accumulating and transferring group knowledge.	Communication is the key aspect of organisation, leadership and management, from the point of view of organisational identity and the coordination of processes.
Evolutionary conditions of culture.	Spontaneous emergence of culture, based on common communication in a group.	Spontaneous emergence of organisational culture and cultural models of management.

intercultural research into grimaces and facial expressions[217], the moral sense, aesthetics and logic leaves no doubt that although culture diversifies people to a certain extent, there are a great number of physical, mental and emotional features common to all of mankind[218]. Empirical knowledge deals a final blow to radical cultural relativism, the foundation of which was the development of the postmodernist orientation in the humanities in the 20th century. The discussion covers a full list of universals; however, there is a wide range of features that appear in all human cultures. D. E. Brown collated over 500 cultural universals that have been examined by ethnographers, sociologists and psychologists[219]. These include categories of different aspects of reality, from the most general and abstract (planning, culture, language), through detailed abstract categories (economic inequality, succession, nepotism, taboo, myths), to material and symbolic artefacts (toys, tools, nouns). The neoevolutionary current also

217 P. Ekman, W.V. Friesen, *Constants across Cultures in the Face and Emotion* [in:] D.T. Kenrick, C.L. Luce (ed.), *The Functional Mind. Readings in Evolutionary Psychology*, Pearson, Boston 2004.

218 J. Panksepp, The Neuroevolutionary and Neuroaffective Psychobiology of the Prosocial Brain, [in:] R.I. M Dunbar, L. Barrett, *Evolutionary Psychology*, Oxford University Press, New York 2007.

219 D.E. Brown, *Human Universals*, McGraw-Hill, New York 1991.

rejects the empowerment of the world of symbols, values and abstraction, instead drawing mostly on analyses of animal protocultures and indicating the continuity in the mental development of species between apes and humans[220]. Extensive empirical materials show that despite the fact that certain aspects of culture are highly developed in human society, they are strongly rooted in animal protocultures. This concerns both social and cognitive skills, as well as the moral and aesthetic sense. For evolutionists, the consequence of adopting the naturalist position is the epistemological and methodological postulate of applying scientific methods taken from the natural sciences to research into the cultural sphere. D. C. Dennett, in criticism of C. Geertz's classical statement that culture is a web of meanings spun by men that cannot be examined with the use of experimental methods, as they are of an interpretative nature, states: 'The fact that we, men, spin a web of meanings is doubtless, but the webs can be analysed with the use of the scientific methods of the natural sciences[221]'. Research into cultures set in the neoevolutionary paradigm makes use of traditional observational, questionnaire and statistical methods developed by the social sciences, and also introduces experiments examining the responses of people in controlled conditions with the use of Magnetic Resonance Imaging, Positron Emission Tomography and Electroencephalography (MRI, PET, EEG). Another very important role is played by the research into the origins of cultures and civilisations carried out by palaeoanthropology. The aim of this research lies not only in cultural studies, but also in looking for generalisations, mathematical modelling and predictions, as well as in the area of cultural processes. Most evolutionist researchers are aware of the fact that this is an early stage of the development of a new approach to understanding culture, but even so, the first results are very promising. A synthetic comparison of the differences between the standard model of the social sciences, called 'culturalism' by S. Pinker, and neoevolutionism can be found in Tab. 19.

A number of evolutionists' research projects are concerned with culture, which means that there are a significant number of definitions of 'culture', referring to

220 K.N. Laland, B.G. Galef (eds.), *The Question of Animal Culture*, Mass: Harvard UP, Cambridge 2009; J. Diamond, *The Third Chimpanzee. The Evolution and the Future of the Human Animal*, Harper, New York 1992.

221 Dennett, Daniel Clement. *Breaking the spell: Religion as a natural phenomenon*. Vol. 14. Penguin, 2006.; C. **Geertz, *The Interpretation of Cultures*, Basic, New York 1973.**

Tab. 19: Standard model of the social sciences vs. neoevolutionism. Source: Own study.

Criterion	SMSC	Neoevolutionism
Nature of reality and cognition	Dualism	Monism
Features of cognition	Subjectivism and intersubjectivism	Objectivism
Epistemological assumptions	Interpretivism, social constructionism	Verificationism or falsificationism
Influence of the context of cognition and culture	Cultural or cognitive relativism	Epistemological and cultural universalism
Subject's cognition of reality	Essentialism	Evolutionary cognitivism
Research methodology	Understanding, hermeneutics, phenomenology (looking for sense)	Cause and effect explanations, experimental method.

different ways of understanding this phenomenon. Some refer to neurobiological processes[222], others to culture as understood in cognitive terms[223]. C. J. Lumsden and E. O. Wilson[224] believe that cultural transmission takes the form of a link between genes and culture (co-evolution), and that the key to explaining culture is in building a theory of information replication covering three levels: genes, mind and culture. A similar view is presented by R. Dawkins, S. Blackmore, D. C. Dennett, L. L. Cavalli-Sforza and M. W. Feldman, trying to create a mathematical theory of the 'meme' or 'culturgen'[225]. In most meanings of culture, there also appears an aspect of extra-genetic transmission of information and behaviour patterns among individuals.

222 B.E. Wexler, *Brain and Culture. Neurobiology, Ideology and Social Change*, A Bradford Book MIT Press, London Cambridge 2008, pp. 85–137.

223 Tomasello, Michael, Ann Cale Kruger, and Hilary Horn Ratner. 'Cultural learning.' *Behavioral and Brain Sciences* 16.03 (1993): 495–511. .

224 C.J. *Lumsden*, E.O. Wilson, *Genes, Mind and Culture: The Coevolutionary Process*, Harvard University Press, Cambridge *1981.*

225 R. Dawkins, *Selfish gene*, Oxford University Press, Oxford 1976; Dennett, Daniel C., and Alvin Plantinga. 'Science and religion: Are they compatible?.' (2011)., pp. 389–405, S. Blackmore, *The meme machine*, Oxford University Press, Oxford 2000.

Culture is understood by neoevolutionists in a reductionist way, as having its sources in individual behaviour and motivations which, when aggregated, form dominant values and norms in a community[226]. The most important mechanisms of cultural transmission are the learning processes, including imitation, communication, cooperation and other kinds of interaction. It is probable that in the case of humanity's ancestors, evolutionary pressure led to positive feedback between the development of social skills and the development of the brain, which translated into fast cultural development[227]. Then, possibly already as part of the development of *Homo sapiens*, culture began gaining increasing importance, allowing for the accumulation and transmission of knowledge that helped not only individuals but whole social groups to survive[228]. Innovation in both material culture (tools, clothes, weapons) and symbolic culture (language, beliefs, social institutions) began to play a key role in both our development and a growth in community size. Biological evolution was to a great extent substituted with the much faster processes of cultural evolution.

The natural origin of culture leads to a description that draws from the context of its own creation. Language is deeply rooted in the human spatial and physical understanding of the environment, and some authors even believe it is innate[229]. Most metaphors, similes and designates of abstract notions refer to physical notions[230]. For example, 'a superior is above a subordinate', 'the market grows', we keep strangers 'at a distance' or we treat them 'coolly', while our family are the 'closest' to us. We show a greater ability to understand social processes and people, as well as to tell narrating stories and histories, than to understanding

226 D.S. Wilson, *Group-level evolutionary processes*, [in:] R.I. M Dunbar, L. Barrett, *Evolutionary Psychology*, Oxford University Press, New York 2007.

227 C.J. Lumsden, E.O. Wilson, *Promethean Fire: Reflections on the Origin of Mind.*, MA: Harvard University Press, Cambridge 1983; H. Kudo, R.I.M. Dunbar, *Neocortex size and social network size in primates*, 'Animal Behaviour' October 2001, vol. 62, No. 4,, pp. 711–722; R.W. Byrne, A. Whiten, *Machiavellian Intelligence: Social Expertise and the Evolution of Intellect in Monkeys, Apes, and Humans*, Oxford University Press, New York 1988.

228 J. Tooby, L. Cosmides, Evolutionary psychology and the generation of culture, part I: Theoretical considerations, Ethology and Sociobiology, Vol. 10, Issues 1–3, January 1989, pp. 29–49.

229 S. Pinker, *Language Instinct*, Penguin 1995.

230 G. *Lakoff*, M. *Johnson, Metaphors We Live By*, University of Chicago Press, Chicago 1980.

abstractions such as the mathematical[231]. We tend to idealise our own group, to be xenophobic, sexist and to stigmatise misfits. According to D. C. Dennett and R. Dawkins, religious beliefs also have evolutionary origins[232].

Within the evolutionary framework, culture can be understood in three ways: as adaptation, an indirect product of evolution, or as its by-product[233]. Adaptations are of a hereditary character and have developed through natural selection, as they are a more efficient solution to the problem of survival or reproduction of individuals than the available alternatives. Animal protocultures evolved in this sense, providing species with hereditary mental modules, allowing them to imitate other individuals. Indirect products do not solve any adaptive or functional problems, as they just accompany other adaptations. It seems that some aspects of culture – such as art or beliefs – evolved as indirect products, accompanying the development of cultural adaptations in the form of language or technology. By-products are random variables that – in the evolutionary sense – are of no adaptive importance (such as eye colour, navel shape). Perhaps, in the case of our ancestors, this sphere includes their entire cultural variability, language structure, types of beliefs, key values and norms. As the importance of cultural evolution in human development grew, the by-products (in the evolutionary sense) – i.e. the cultural variables of different communities – began to play the key role in the selection of individuals and whole groups[234]. Possibly, for example, more aggressive, better organised or more technologically advanced communities started to gain a cultural advantage, forming the heart of the integration of whole societies.

Language and culture are elements that are uniquely characteristic of mankind, although one can find natural sources for both these phenomena. The great apes use a communication system in order to express their emotions and intentions, and to indicate external threats. However, communication and culture do not have symbolic and abstract aspects characteristic of the language and

231 P.M. Todd, G. Gigerenzer, *Mechanisms of ecological rationality: heuristics and environments that make us smart*, [in:] R.I.M. Dunbar, L. Barrett, Evolutionary Psychology, Oxford University Press, New York 2007.

232 Dennett, Daniel C., and Alvin Plantinga. 'Science and religion: Are they compatible?.' (2011).

233 D.M. Buss, *Evolutionary Psychology. The New Science of the Mind*, Pearson, Boston 2008, pp. 39–40.

234 R. McElreath, J. Henrich, *Modelling cultural evolution*, [in:] R.I. M Dunbar, L. Barrett, *Evolutionary Psychology*, Oxford University Press, New York 2007.

culture of *Homo sapiens*. Chimpanzees also show aspects of thinking and social, cooperative behaviour, as well as use of symbols[235].

The position of evolutionists on the origins of culture in animal communities is coherent and based on naturalism, i.e. an assumption that human culture is based on biological foundations that can be observed in the protoculture of apes. However, the assessment of the degree of cultural advancement of apes is highly diversified. Primatologists such as F. de Waal or J. Goodall can see the most important elements of culture in chimpanzees[236]. On the other hand, many psychologists and anthropologists believe that although we can talk of the beginnings of culture in the case of apes, many of its aspects have developed only in mankind[237].

As extensive observation has shown, apes have a kind of basic moral instinct that has its roots in the essence of the social group, and is of a functional character. Similarly to people, chimpanzees are able to show empathy and liking, altruism, mutuality, feelings of guilt and shame, as well as a sense of fair and equal sharing[238].

An important problem for evolutionary researchers looking at culture is the analysis of similarities between the models of biological and cultural evolution. Many evolutionists treat the genetic and cultural heritage as parallel, although they naturally also see significant structural differences between these two types of transmission. Most of all, genetic heritage means a limitation on the DNA pool received from the parents, while cultural heritage covers a whole group of

---

235 J. Call, *Social knowledge in primates*, [in:] R.I. M Dunbar, L. Barrett, *Evolutionary Psychology*, Oxford University Press, New York 2007, pp. 76–79.

236 Goodall, Jane. *The chimpanzees of Gombe: Patterns of behavior*. Belknap Press of Harvard University Press, 1986.; F. de Wall, A. van Roosmalen, *Reconciliation and Consolation Among Chimpanzees*, 'Behavioral Ecology and Sociobiology' 1979, No. 5, pp. 55–66.

237 J. Vauclair, *Les Animaux pendent-ils?* [in:] J.F. Dortier, *Le cerveau et la pensée*, Humaines Editions, France, 2003 p. 215. Tomasello, Michael, Ann Cale Kruger, and Hilary Horn Ratner. 'Cultural learning.' *Behavioral and brain sciences* 16.03 (1993): 495–511. .

238 F. de Waal, *Good Natured. The Origins of Right and Wrong in Humans and Other Animals*, Harvard University Press, Cambridge, London 1996, pp. 133–154 Goodall, Jane. *The chimpanzees of Gombe: Patterns of behavior*. Belknap Press of Harvard University Press, 1986.; F. de Waal, *Primates and Philosophers. How Morality Evolved*, Princeton University Press, Princeton 2006, pp. 161–182; C.M. Korsgaard, *Morality and the distinctiveness of human action* [in:] F. deWaal, S. Macedo, J. Ober (ed.), *Primates & Philosophers: How Morality Evolved*, Princeton University Press, Princeton 2006, pp. 98–119.

significant others who transmit social patterns. In many cases these are peers, teachers, authority figures and other people not related to the socialised person. Cultural transmission takes 'horizontal' forms, which means that the output is transmitted between representatives of different generations and genetic lines[239]. Additionally, the pace of cultural heritage is different, although it is usually quicker than the genetic. It is especially visible in the frequency of changes and mutations, which is very high in culture compared to genetic material. Both primary and secondary socialisation is a process of the transmission of cultural patterns, which are acquired in an active and continuous way throughout the life of an individual with developed cognitive apparatus. Genetic transmission takes place before one's birth, happens once and cannot be changed. As R. Boyd and. P. J. Richerson noted, cultural evolution is reminiscent of Lamarck's model, in that one can inherit the phenotype as well as the genotype. In other words, parents or 'cultural parents' (significant others who transmit culture), by acquiring cultural patterns can transmit, acquire and change them throughout their whole life[240]. Thus, the differences between biological and cultural heritage are significant, but the basis for both these processes remains the replication of information in the next generations.

It seems to this author that the marriage of evolutionary thinking and the theory of culture is beginning to bear fruit. On the level of the philosophy of science, it leads to a resignation from the traditional division into the social and natural sciences. The possibility of applying the theory and methods of neuroscience, cognitive science and other fields of the natural and biological sciences to cultural issues allows for the study, description, modelling and prediction of cultural changes in a more efficient way. On the other hand, it seems that the position of culture researchers stemming from science should not be orthodox. Many methods and concepts of the social sciences developed on the basis of anthropology, sociology, psychology and even philosophy can be useful for cognitive purposes. For example, traditional ethnological methods such as observation and interviews, as well as surveys and statistical methods, still play a very important role in the study of culture. Thus, culture is a kind of epistemological testing ground for combining social and natural sciences, perhaps even leading to the end of the traditional division into two cultures[241].

---

239 L.L. Cavalli-Sforza, M.W. Feldman, *Cultural Transmission and Evolution: A Quantitative Approach*, Princeton University Press 1981.

240 R. Boyd, P.J. Richerson, *Culture and the Evolutionary Process*, Chicago: University of Chicago Press 1985, pp. 8–9.

241 Snow, Charles Percy. 'Two cultures.' *Science* 130.3373 (1959): 419–419.

Many cultural phenomena appearing in psychological research are interpreted in an evolutionary context, but are not always supported by reliable studies. Brain modules developed by mankind in the Pleistocene are supposed to have equipped people with the cognitive mechanisms of cultural reproduction, such as the ability to communicate, symbolic and abstract thinking, emotions, and the ability to show empathy, and read intent[242]. However J. Fodor, the originator of the modular mind concept, does not agree with this interpretation, indicating a very high level of specialisation of cognitive mechanisms (the so-called pen-knife concept). Rather, modular minds were supposed to possess general cognitive abilities, and not the algorithms and heuristics of mankind's survival in the Pleistocene[243]. J. Gould ironically describes some of the evolutionary analyses explaining our behaviour as 'just-so stories' – an interpretation *post factum*, which is not a coherent model generating predictions that can be verified. However, this reservation is not fully legitimate, as numerous concepts of learning, imitation and culture developed in the field of evolutionary psychology have given rise to various implications about the form of examined human behaviour, which allows for verification of the hypotheses. The same cannot be said about the entire brain modules theory, except that, for example, illusions and cognitive limitations can be deduced from the species' evolution, which is confirmed by research in behavioural economics and evolutionary psychology.

4.3 Memes and culture

Memetics has its origin in the general theory of replicators proposed by R. Dawkins, which interprets culture as a process with an algorithmic character, analogous in its course to the evolution of a biological system. The basis of the replicator concept is the assumption that under appropriate conditions there are structures that are able to initiate self-replication of their organisational plan (and with limited access to resources, by an emergent selection process), and in consequence, to evolve. In a given centre, the surviving replicators should be those that enable the most efficient process of self-replication in comparison to their other versions[244]. Dawkins calls cultural replicators 'memes', from a combination of mimicry (*mimeme*) and genes (*genes*)[245]. Memetics remains a theoretical

---

242 L. Barrett, R. Dunbar, J. Lycett, *Human Evolutionary Psychology*, Palgrave Macmillan, New York 2002, pp. 295–320; D. Sperber, *Explaining Culture*, Blackwell, Oxford 1996.

243 J. Fodor, *The Modularity of Mind: An Essay on Faculty Psychology*, MIT Press, 1983.

244 R. Dawkins, *The Selfish Gene*, Oxford University Press, Oxford 1976, pp. 15–20.

245 Ibidem, p. 192.

concept, and its empirical materials are still not very rich. There is little research (for example, the studies of the mechanisms of variability in the mating songs of birds carried out by P. F. Jenkins[246]) that famous supporters of memetics can refer to. Jenkins introduced the notion of the 'song pool' as a counterpart to the gene pool, as well as 'cultural mutations', which is analogous to cultural changeability. Thus, the elaboration of the theory of replicators in biology was supposed to be biological evolution together with the perspective of the 'selfish gene', while in the social sciences, memes were supposed to be the transmitters of culture, indeed, of all information[247]. There are two main approaches to cultural information and the possibility of its transmission within a society[248]:

- The gene analogy, which assumes that the accumulation of variability in the process of evolution requires the stability of the transmitters of information coding, and that mimicry is the dominant mechanism of cultural replication[249],
- The viral analogy, which puts an emphasis on the mechanisms of horizontal information flow within a society, as opposed to genes dependant only on the vertical flow; in order to foresee the directions of a culture's evolutionary manifestations, it is necessary to apply the basic epidemiological rules[250].

At its current stage of development, memetics is a concept of a mainly qualitative and descriptive character, proven by numerous publications but very little actual research[251]. The empirical material is dominated by research into the phenomenon of the dissemination of chain letters and religious movements. Most research projects in memetics have been carried out by D. Hofstadter[252] who studied the character of the dissemination of chain letters and the factors influencing their popularity, and A. Lynch[253] who carried out major research

---

246 P.F. Jenkins, *Cultural transmission of song patterns and dialect development in a free-living bird population*, 'Animal Behaviour' 1978, No. 25, pp. 50–78.

247 R. Dawkins, *A Devil's Chaplain,* Weidenfeld & Nicholson London 2003, p. 251; M. Blute, *Memetics and evolutionary social science*, 'Journal of Memetics' 2005, No. 19, p. 6.

248 Ibidem.

249 R. Dawkins, *The Selfish Gene…* pp. 192–193.

250 R. Dawkins, *Viruses of the Mind*, Blackwell, Cambridge 1993, pp. 48–50.

251 M. Blute, *Memetics and evolutionary social science*, 'Journal of Memetics' 2005, No. 19, p. 6.

252 D. Hofstadter, *The Mind's I*, Penguin Books, London 1982.

253 A. Lynch, *Thought Contagion: How Belief Spreads Through Society*, Basic Books, London 1996.

into the mechanisms used by different religious systems and cults to increase the number of their followers.

Analysis of memetic cultural processes should begin with a definition of the replication process itself, which according to R. Aunger should fulfil four conditions:

1. Causality (the sources are a kind of a cause, giving a model to be copied).
2. Similarity (the source and its copy need to be similar in terms of chosen key aspects).
3. Information transfer (information derived from the source shapes the copy).
4. Duplication (the source and the copy have to co-exist for some time)[254].

The fulfilment of these conditions entails a number of cognitive problems, as the key issue is still finding the carrier of culture and the mechanisms of transfer and duplication. Furthermore, the question of the reason for replication remains unanswered, although this may be an error resulting from the teleological formulation of the issue, which should be avoided in the case of the natural sciences, even if it is quite common in the social sciences.

Memetics has been strongly criticised by a number of representatives of the social and biological sciences. Many serious reservations have been voiced, which at the current stage of development make memetics look like an interesting hypothesis, not a scientific theory. One needs verification which is not easy to make, taking into consideration the high level of generality of statements and the lack of a model and predictions. The 'general theory of replication' is thus only hypothetical and at the moment does not have the form of a mathematical model. So far, no one has been able to identify the transmitter of memes or even indicate the directions of their empirical research[255]. Moreover, memetics still has no precise, uniform definition. Even memes are interpreted differently by different authors[256]. In summary, the problems with the concept of memes lead to a number of as-yet unanswered questions, such as:

- Is the analogy with the Darwinian mechanism of inheritance relevant to culture?
- What is a meme? Is it a basic unit of sense? Idea? Melody? Fashion?

---

254 R. Aunger, *Memes*, in: 'The Oxford Handbook of Evolutionary Psychology', ed. R.I.M. Dunbar, L. Barrett, Oxford University Press, Oxford 2007, p. 601.

255 R. Aunger, *Darwinizing Culture: The Status of Memetics as Science*, Oxford University Press, Oxford 2001, p. 218.

256 K. Distin, *The Selfish Meme,* Cambridge University Press, 2005, p. 72.

- How to identify and study a hypothetical meme?

The lack of answers to these questions means that memetics is still a project of science, rather than science *sensu stricto*. However, it is an ambitious attempt to apply the idea of naturalism to the social sciences and humanities.

Perhaps – as the memeticians postulate – research into culture from the perspective of evolutionism will lead to the development of a broad theory of replication, describing the rules of variability in self-replicating systems, regardless of the kind of transmitter (medium). Such a theory would generalise the evolutionary theory, going beyond biological systems and perhaps, from the point of view of scientific development, would be something like the theory of relativity that generalised Newton's theory. However, it is necessary to develop both theoretical and empirical knowledge, and to cross Popper's threshold of epistemological falsifiability. Should this happen, deeper exploration of cultural processes should entail more efficient control of spontaneous, negative ideological phenomena. Thus, the tendency to replicate ideas dangerous to humanity might decrease.

4.4 The evolutionary roots of organisational culture

G. Hofstede assumed that national cultures are a part of people's mental software, which includes the basic values, while organisational cultures are mostly superficial traineeships completed in adulthood[257]. However, it seems that organisational cultures are, contrary to Hofstede's belief, very deeply rooted in the human mind and social structures, as they reflect the primitive cultures of hunter-gatherer communities, which are inscribed in the mental and genetic 'software' of *Homo sapiens*.

Organisational culture is a problematic research area in the management sciences. Its definitions are ambiguous, there is no agreement as to the paradigm, and the boundary between culture and other areas of management – as well as the assessment of the research methodology's value and the change of organisational culture – is unclear. But despite epistemological and methodological doubts, organisational culture is today a deep-rooted notion, commonly used in management.

Studies in the neoevolutionary current, located mainly within evolutionary psychology, shed new light on the interpretation of human behaviour, including organisational behaviour and organisational culture. The biological

257 G. Hofstede, *Culture's Consequences*, Sage Publications, Beverly Hills 1984.

and evolutionary basis of culture underlies the social nature of mankind. It is a kind of feedback between rivalry and cooperation. Rivalry is related to the ultimate values of the existence of biological species, which – according to neoevolutionists – are genetic reproduction and the survival of individuals. On the other hand, cooperation is an effective mechanism that enhances the chances of survival for genes and individuals.

Neoevolutionism redefines the essence and origin of culture, rejecting the innately false opposition, deeply rooted in tradition, of culture vs. nature. In fact, cultures developed based on the biology of mankind and all manifestations of human social life are derived from nature and have their origins in the behaviour of primates[258]. Communication and language were formed as a result of animal signals developing into a sophisticated system of transmitting emotions and abstract notions, which then started to evolve itself[259]. Hierarchy, power and leadership, which have contributed to the creation of the complex social structures of today's mass societies, are rooted in the fight for domination and the pecking order of social species[260]. Concern for family and relatives stems from the universal, natural instinct to reproduce one's own genetic material[261], whereas collaboration and formation of coalitions between non-kin take place in many species of apes and are the manifestations of a survival strategy based on cooperation[262]. Customs, traditions and rituals being part of each culture seem to be natural norms that regulate the functioning of social species. The studies of neoevolutionism, neoevolutionary psychology, socio-biology, neuroscience, primatology and cognitive science are able to explain more and more of the phenomena present in human social life, deriving them directly from the evolutionary mechanisms of *Homo sapiens*[263]. Therefore, it would be worth carrying out a similar analysis of organisational culture.

An analysis of evolutionary sources of human culture reveals that there is a cumulative effect of symbolic works in primitive communities, handed down from generation to generation. Over hundreds of thousands of years,

---

258 D. Sperber, *Explaining Culture*, Blackwell, Oxford 1996.

259 T.W. Deacon, *The Symbolic Species. The Co-Evolution of Language and the Brain*, W.W. Norton, New York 1997.

260 R. Boyd, P.J. Richerson, *Punishment Allows the Evolution of Cooperation in Sizable Groups*, 'Ethnology and Sociobiology' 1992, No. 13, pp. 171–195.

261 A. Hughes, *Evolution and Human Kinship*, Oxford University Press, Oxford 1988.

262 S. Bowles, H. Gintis, *Homo reciprocans*, 'Nature' 2002, No. 415, pp. 125–128.

263 J. Barkow (ed.), *Missing the Revolution. Darwinism for Social Scientists*, Oxford University Press, Oxford 2006.

hunter-gatherer groups initiated a certain organisational culture, characterised by common values, languages and communication systems, beliefs, social norms, customs, traditions and rituals, social role models and taboos, all of which were transferred between generations. This cultural system had its origin in the evolutionary biology of mankind, and provided additional, positive feedback which helped form and adopt solutions that were more functional from the perspective of the survival of individuals and communities. The cultural bond in small human communities was based on: kinship, non-kinship cooperation, and group identity, based upon the fact that one's own group was distinct from others[264]. One can draw an analogy between primitive hunter-gatherer cultures and modern organisational culture. Thus, it seems that informal organisational culture is a natural and very old system for people to adjust to life in a social group. On the one hand, it explains the spontaneous mechanism forming organisational cultures in modern companies and other organisations, and on the other, the difficulty controlling the directions of a culture's development. *Homo sapiens* identify themselves with relatively small groups, dominated by informal communication and direct contact. Identification with larger social groups, such as societies, nations or a religious community takes the form of a projection of processes transferred from a small group to a mass group. This is the source of stereotypes and the lack of functionality in the actions of large social groups[265]. Organisational culture is thus inscribed in human nature, which management should take it into consideration in the activity of all kinds of organisations.

Analyses and studies of 'soft' areas of management use the notion of functions in organisational culture. The integration function consists in uniting an organisation's members into a community (metaphorically speaking, it is the 'organisational glue'), while the perceptual function is the perception of the organisation itself and its environment in accordance with the values and norms of the culture it is part of (metaphorically speaking, these are 'organisational glasses'). The adaptive function is the socialisation of the community members in accordance with the rules of its functioning, while the function of granting identity is related to the self-identification of the community's members. Primitive communities based their unity on: kinship bonds, non-kinship cooperation,

---

264 M. Van Vugt, G. Roberts, C. Hardy, *Competitive altruism: a theory of reputation-based cooperation in groups*, [in:] R.I. M Dunbar, L. Barrett, *Evolutionary Psychology*, Oxford University Press, New York 2007.

265 F. Salter, *Ethnic nepotism as heuristic: risky transactions and public altruism*, [in:] R.I.M Dunbar, L. Barrett, *Evolutionary Psychology*, Oxford University Press, New York 2007.

leadership, communication and hostility towards other groups. Kinship was one of the strongest sources of social order, although the mechanism of sexual selection also required the development of cooperation with non-kin. The strength of kinship bonds is reflected in the nepotism and familism present in a number of modern organisational cultures. In primitive groups the hierarchy of power was based on authority, seniority and often social coalitions too, which translated into reproduction, access to goods and the possibility of sanctioning. This is reflected in culture in formal and informal organisational hierarchies with their symbolic and material attributes of power and leadership. The culture of primitive groups – similar to modern organisational culture – socialises the community members, giving them an identity and forming intentional perception. Thus, there is a clear similarity between the functions of primitive group culture and the features of organisational culture in modern companies and institutions.

Values forming the basis for the creation of culture are defined in different ways. In the case of organisational culture, some authors assume that it has certain values that are not found in other cultures, such as the national or regional[266]. Other researchers believe that the dimensions of cultural values are of a universal character, and that they can be described on the level of the culture of societies and organisations. Assuming the latter perspective, one can point to a number of different descriptions of these values' dimensions. The dimensions of cultural values used in the most important research by G. Hofstede, A. Trompenaars, C. Hampden-Turner and R. J. House are individualism – collectivism, power distance, avoiding uncertainty and masculinism – feminism[267]. From the neoevolutionary perspective one can see that these values are rooted in 'human nature'.

The formation of human identity stems from the evolutionary development of a functional community, based on the ability to recognise differences between oneself and others, as well as between fellows and strangers. This is why the attitude of an individual towards the community as a whole becomes an existential problem. The behaviour of *Homo sapiens* includes a whole range of egotistic and altruistic actions which result from two different strategies for achieving evolutionary success, measured by the reproduction and survival of individuals.

---

266 G. Hofstede, *Culture's Consequences*, Sage Publications, Beverly Hills 1984.

267 G. Hofstede, *Culture's Consequences*, Sage Publications, Beverly Hills 1984; Hampden-Turner, Charles, and Fons Trompenaars. 'The seven cultures of capitalism.' (1993).; R.J. House, P. Hanges i A. Ruiz-Quintanilla, *GLOBE. The Global Leadership and Organizational Behavior. Effectiveness: Research Program*, 1997.

Individualistic culture leads to the enhancement of selfish motivations, while collectivist cultures enhance altruism towards the members of one's own community. Thus, individualisation is based on evolution and is related to the appearance of ego and a characteristic composition of individual behavioural features[268]. In the process of the individualisation of individuals and communities, the key role is played by attributes characteristic only of mankind, such as the sense of time (temporal dimension of the ego) and abstract thinking[269].

Power is inscribed in human nature and reveals itself in different ways: pecking order, formation of hierarchy, leadership in groups, the willingness to gain control of others, creation of material and symbolic attributes of power, as well as cooperation based on social order. Power distance indicates an imaginary, symbolic space that separates those in power from their subordinates. It translates into the level of autocracy and cooperation, and the type of sanctions (e. g. physical, symbolic). Power in a human society is perceived in dualistic terms as an attribute and a relation.

The tolerance of uncertainty is part of a mental feature developed to the greatest extent in humans, i.e. awareness of the past. Animals, possibly including the great apes, can extrapolate from the past only to a limited degree. People are deeply aware of the unpredictability of the future, including their own inevitable ends. The unpredictability of the future and the risks it entails are sources of uncertainty which lead to stress. Being an emotional response to dangerous situations, stress is evolutionarily inherited from the distant ancestors of mankind. However, the abstract source of stress in the form of fear of the future is characteristic only of people. Uncertainty avoidance is a universal feature of *Homo sapiens*, while the level of the fear and stress experienced depends on the culture and individuals[270].

Attitudes towards the opposite sex, reflected in the opposition between masculinism and feminism, are connected with sexual relations and gender identity. G. Hofstede assumed a completely different understanding of this

---

268 D. Nettle, *Individual differences*, [in:] R.I. M Dunbar, L. Barrett, *Evolutionary Psychology*, Oxford University Press, New York 2007

269 M. Schaller, J.H. Park, D.T. Kenrick, *Human evolution and social cognition*, [in:] R.I. M Dunbar, L. Barrett, *Evolutionary Psychology*, Oxford University Press, New York 2007; J.J. Skowronski, C. Sedikides, *Temporal knowledge and autobiographical memory: an evolutionary perspective*, [in:] R.I. M Dunbar, L. Barrett, *Evolutionary Psychology*, Oxford University Press, New York 2007.

270 B. Winterhalder, *Risk and Decision-Making*, [in:] R.I. M Dunbar, L. Barrett, *Evolutionary Psychology*, Oxford University Press, New York 2007.

dimension and focused on the aim and quality of life[271]. Still, many other authors return to the fundamental problem of relations between the sexes, both from the biological perspective (sex) and the cultural (gender). The neoevolutionary analysis points to the most important aspects of relations between the sexes, i.e. the diversification of reproductive and life strategies, sex, the relationships with submission and threats of violence[272]. Sexual differences determine the strategies for winning partners and parental strategies; they also condition the directions of personality development and life trajectories of individuals[273].

So if the value dimensions develop on the universal grounds of human nature, where does their diversity relative to culture and individuals come from? For example, some cultures have large power distance (Mexico), others small (USA), or in the case of some, high individualism (USA), and in others the same can be said about collectivism (China)[274]. It seems that diverse histories of societies understood as communities identifying with themselves have led to a strengthening of certain values and weakening of others. This, then, is why cultures have diversified on the universal basis of human nature and its existential problems; power, attitude towards the group, attitude towards the past and relations between the sexes, as some of these have developed under conditions of group work, like the culture of rice pickers, or formed as collectivism or a cult of pioneers and individuals[275].

Anthropological research provides rich empirical materials that allow for description of elements of organisational cultures by analogy with primitive hunter-gatherer groups. Organisational ethnology developed from the methodology of field research, drawing directly from the research of cultural anthropology. The elements common to both organisational cultures and primitive groups on an advanced level of development are: social values and norms, speech and a communication system, stories and myths, beliefs, customs, traditions and

271 G. Hofstede, *Culture's Consequences*, Sage Publications, Beverly Hills 1984

272 A. Campbell, *Sex differences in Aggression*, [in:] R.I. M Dunbar, L. Barrett, *Evolutionary Psychology*, Oxford University Press, New York 2007.

273 B.S. Low, *Ecological and* Socio-Cultural Impacts on Mating Marriage Systems, [in:] R.I.M Dunbar, L. Barrett, *Evolutionary Psychology*, Oxford University Press, New York 2007; J. Belsky, Childhood Experiences and Reproductive Strategies, [w:] R.I.M Dunbar, L. Barrett, *Evolutionary Psychology*, Oxford University Press, New York 2007; S.W. Gangestad, Reproductive Strategies and Tactics, [in:] R.I.M Dunbar, L. Barrett, *Evolutionary Psychology*, Oxford University Press, New York 2007.

274 G. Hofstede, *Culture's Consequences*, Sage Publications, Beverly Hills 1984.

275 Morgan, Gareth, Fred Gregory, and Cameron Roach. 'Images of organization.' (1997).

rituals, role models (heroes, family roles), and taboos[276]. If one adopts broad, enumerative definitions of culture, these would also include art, art material products (e. g. architecture), morality, power structure and the system of ideas.

The previously described cultural values, related to solving basic existential dilemmas (attitude towards the community, power, fear of the future and relations between the sexes) result in a system of norms, i.e. dictates and prohibitions that regulate community life. Norms become rooted and consolidated, gaining functional forms over time which favour the survival of individuals and the community, though their petrifaction in the face of changes in external conditions may lead to a weakening of their functionality. In the case of organisational culture, norms stem from implemented and undeclared values, so they are functional, but in relation to the actual system of values and are not always assumed by those in charge. Social norms should not question the basic value that implicitly underlies each form of organisation, which is related to the individual pursuit of survival and genetic reproduction.

Communication systems, language and speech are developed from more primitive forms of communication and signalling used by different animals. However, language is characterised by the possibility to code and transfer theoretically unlimited amounts of complex, abstract information. The development of speech, language and communication has provided people with a sophisticated tool supporting the survival and development of mankind. The development of speech is closely related to the development of the brain, and is probably reflected in the human genome[277]. In the beginning, communication enabled the transfer of ideas and the accumulation of achievements, the development of symbolic culture, more efficient hunting, a higher level of security, and the improvement of tools. In short, it became the cornerstone of mankind. The cultures of communities create their own languages, which serve integration and communication purposes. The rhetorical figures, metaphors, and linguistic humour that people use form a cognitive framework which includes different cultural circles. The notion of the 'spirit' of a language conveys the specificity of a communication system, in which form shapes message. The development of language then contributed to the creation and dissemination of beliefs, stories,

---

276 L.G. Bolman, T.E. Deal, *Reframing Organizations. Artistry, Choice, and Leadership*, Jossey-Bass, San Francisco 2003, pp. 241–269.

277 C. Kenneally, *The First Word. The Search for the Origins of Language*, Viking Penguin, New York 2007, pp. 267–270.

myths and taboos, which form a thick tapestry of symbolic culture. The cave-dwelling people of the past were immersed in it, just as today's people are in organisational culture.

Culture also produces social role models, starting from those in charge, through subordinates, and ending with family and parental roles. Within organisational cultures one can distinguish the roles of heroes, offering models of behaviour from the point of view of leadership, with which the organisation's members identify themselves.

The cultures of primitive hunter-gatherer communities are described from the angle of the works of material culture, which on a certain level also reflect the complexity of symbolic thinking. Tools, burial methods, cave paintings and other archaeological remains allow characterisation of the level of complexity of a given local culture, but usually speak little of the actual structure of those groups. Thus, the interpretations of Cro-Magnon cultures, for example, are rather limited[278].

Reference books offer a number of typologies of organisational cultures. The most popular are the classifications by T. E. Deal and A. A. Kennedy, and by C. Handy. In a book published in 1982, *Corporate Cultures: The Rites and Rituals of Corporate Life*, Terrence Deal and A. A. Kennedy presented the typology of organisational culture based on two dimensions: feedback speed and the degree of decision risk. The combination of these two parameters gave rise to four types of organisational culture: tough-guy (rapid feedback and high risks), work-hard, play-hard (rapid feedback and low risk), bet-the-company culture (slow feed-back and high risk) and process culture (slow feedback and low risk)[279]. These four types of culture are also known as the culture of individualism, the culture of routine, the culture of gambling, and balanced culture, respectively[280]. Analysing this typology from the point of view of neoevolutionism, one can compare the cultures to the functioning of a primitive group. The tough-guy culture may have its origin in the risky teamwork of hunters; the work-hard culture is equivalent to the gathering activities of primitive communities; the bet-the-company culture

278 Stringer, Chris, and Robin McKie. *African Exodus: The Origins of Modern Humanity*. Macmillan, 1998, pp. 245–250.

279 T.E. Deal, A.A. Kennedy, *Corporate Cultures: The Rites and Rituals of Corporate Life*, Penguin Books, Harmondsworth 1982.

280 G. Jones, Enhancing Due Diligence – Examination of the Organisational Culture of A Merger and Acquisition Target, '*Journal of Business & Economics Research*' 2008, vol. 6, No. 1, p. 13.

ties in with the focus on rivalry for prestige and power within the group, while the process culture equates to subordination.

The second most popular typology of organisational cultures was presented by C. Handy[281]. It distinguishes four types of cultural orientations. Power culture is characterised by the lack of formal rules and procedures of action. Its management is of an autocratic character with power strongly centralised, and employees driven by rivalry. Role culture is distinguished by rationalism and order. Great significance is attached to the predictability of behaviour and formal rules and employees are expected to be stable and serious – employee activity and initiative are undesirable. The source of power in this organisation is in the organisational hierarchy. Task culture values the achievement of objectives. Private needs are suppressed and everyone focuses on the team and team work. Power is based on the competence of the leader. Person culture finds its basis in the belief that organisations are created in order to serve the needs of individuals. This gives individuals great freedom in their actions, and this type of culture has no mechanisms of control and hierarchy, apart from a bilateral agreement.

Using the neoevolutionary perspective allows us to link the classification by C. Handy to the culture of primitive hunter-gatherer groups. Power culture has its origin in the striving for dominance, which translated into evolutionary success in the form of reproduction and survival; role culture mostly means subordination to the hierarchy and social roles; task culture concentrates on harmonious cooperation, efficiency and community cohesion, while person culture is a relatively casual coalition of individuals cooperating together.

The culture of hunter-gatherer communities was created in primitive groups and gave rise to the mechanisms for accumulating works and transmitting values, norms and cultural models. In this sense, all other types of culture reflect the features of the primitive culture, rooted in human nature in the process of evolution[282]. It seems that organisational culture is a natural field of culture, developing spontaneously in organisations and reflecting the evolutionary past of mankind (Tab. 20).

Between organisational culture and the culture of primitive communities there are numerous analogies. However, there are also significant differences.

---

281 C.B. Handy, *Understanding Organizations*, 3rd Ed, Penguin Books, Harmondsworth 1985.

282 C. f.: R. Conniff, *The Ape in the Corner Office*, Cyan Communications Ltd., New York 2008.

Tab. 20: An analogy between the culture of hunter-gatherer communities and organisational culture. Source: Own work.

Criterion	Culture of hunter-gatherer communities	Organisational culture
Group size	From several dozen to about 150 individuals	Unlimited, but communities crystallise from several dozen to 150 individuals[a]
Type of social bond	Only direct, kin and non-kin	Direct and indirect, kin and non-kin
Type of power	Informal, hierarchical, based on authority (legitimised by cooperation)	Formal and informal, based on authority (legitimised rationally, legally or by cooperation)
Type of cooperation	Cooperation combined with rivalry	Cooperation combined with rivalry
Values	Existential dimensions: attitude towards the community, power, fear of the future and relations between sexes	Existential dimensions, dimensions characteristic of the organisation (imposed on the employees as part of secondary socialisation)
Functions of the culture	Integration, perception, identification, granting identity	Integration, perception, identification, granting identity
Culture typologies	Related to chronology and complexity of material art works	Taking into consideration diverse dimensions of culture
Language, communication and myths	Characteristic language serving information and emotive purposes	Characteristic language serving information and emotive purposes
Social roles, archetypes, heroes	Leader, subordinates, parental roles, children's roles, sexual roles, neighbour roles	Leader, subordinates, many other roles depending on the organisation
Research methodology in the culture, derived from different disciplines	Archaeology, cultural anthropology, evolutionary psychology	Organisational anthropology

[a] M. Gladwell, *The Tipping Point. How Little Things Can Make a Big Difference*, Little, Brown and Company, New York 2000, pp. 177–181.

1. Organisational culture is just one of many cultural fields, and is entangled in the correlations between the fields. The relations between national or regional culture and organisational culture are subject to a number of studies. The culture of primitive groups is a homogeneous culture, providing its members with one type of identity. Thus, modern people function within numerous cultural identities, while our distant ancestors identified themselves with one type of group (albeit one which may have included several subcultures related to, for example, kinship).
2. Organisational culture is a product of intentional, secondary social groups, while the culture of hunter-gatherer communities was created in primary groups that emerged spontaneously. Primitive groups are of an organic character; they are formed spontaneously and are subject to informal, traditional and thoroughly cultural regulations. They are dominated by direct contact, oral communication and the full involvement of their members in the life of the group. Secondary groups are of a deliberate and arbitrary character, and have formalised, business-like bonds.
3. Organisational culture can be formed by those in charge through conscious use of the tools of change, although the scope of intervention is limited. The culture of primitive communities developed spontaneously, so the results of its changes were unpredictable, and the influence of a leader was not conscious.
4. Knowledge of organisational cultures is a rich one, because it comes from copious modern research using diverse methodologies. Knowledge about the cultures of primitive communities is fragmentary and limited due to scant source materials and temporal distance. Thus, analyses taking into consideration primitive hunter-gatherer communities tend to be of a speculative character. However, it seems that in light of the development of research carried out by evolutionary psychology and other disciplines, cultural studies cannot ignore the heritage of mankind.

4.5 Neoevolutionism and other paradigms in cultural research

The dispute over culture in the discourse of the social sciences and humanities is based on the opposition between Cartesian dualism and Darwinian naturalism. Dualism, which is the belief that there is a separate sphere of 'spirit', is being increasingly undermined by naturalist explanations. Of course, there is no single, conclusive proof that the spiritual sphere, which is the subject of culture, does not exist. However, naturalist explanations are more and more effectively explaining human social behaviour without the need to refer to spiritualism. The research of neuroscience, evolutionary psychology, cognitive science, behavioural economics and socio-biology explain the mechanisms of decision-making, the evolutionary origins of social processes (interactions, communication, valuation), neuronal and biological sources of social relationships and the evolutionary basis for organisation, power distribution, leadership and institutionalization. There is more and more conclusive research within the previously-mentioned new disciplines, which allows us to analyse even the most difficult problems of the social sciences, such as awareness and culture. It is worth noting that this is only the beginning of the way ahead to empirical research into culture, as most questions remain unanswered. Today, we still do not know the transmitter of culture and the mechanisms of replications. The relationships between the individual (psychological) and collective (social) levels are also disputable. However, it seems that the proposed method of conducting research might lead to a better understanding of culture in the future.

It seems to this author that fast development of the neoevolutionary approach (neuroscience, cognitive science) is probable in the coming decades, and that this approach could become the dominant paradigm for understanding culture in the social sciences in the future. Perhaps there will be a transitory stage, when many paradigms will be used, followed by integration around a dominant paradigm. This thesis can be supported with several arguments.

At the moment, neoevolutionism is the broadest cognitive approach, integrating perspectives on the issues of culture, society, interaction, the human psyche and the interpretation of meanings. The basic assumptions of this integration are related to the concept of the 'selfishness of genes', and perhaps lead to a general replication theory. In fact, this is the first chance in the history of science to develop a single basic theory combining the natural sciences, the social sciences and the humanities. Naturally, the structure of this paradigm is, to begin with, mostly inductive, which means that increasingly advanced research is being conducted to explain and foresee the functioning of different aspects of social life. Such research has been conducted by evolutionary psychologists since the beginning of the 1980s, and so a new, neoevolutionary paradigm, which in my opinion is the most probable direction for the research into culture as a whole, should crystallise and develop in the nearest future. Today, it is only the beginning of the way ahead, and this is why the relations with other paradigms of the social sciences are important (in this work, they are presented with the use of a matrix proposed by Burrell and Morgan)[283].

---

283 Burrell, Gibson, and Gareth Morgan. *Sociological Paradigms and Organisational analysis*. Vol. 248. london: Heinemann, 1979.

Looking for a paradigm of the social sciences that would be closest to neoevolutionism, one can point to functionalism. It stems from the epistemological assumptions of neopositivism, and so its scientific criteria include cognitive objectivism, realism and empiricism, verificationism and falsificationism. It also strives for the improvement of the standards of scientific research by using methods modelled after those employed in the natural sciences. The classical, functionalist vision of social institutions and human nature assumes an adaptive function of human behaviour and has some common elements with neoevolutionism. However, functionalism does not include an assumption that the human brain, based on the link between genetics and the environment, is adapted to solving key problems of individual survival and reproduction from the ancient past, as opposed to the present. A troglodyte brain has a number of mechanisms that are non-functional from the point of view of the present time, such as the tendency to stuff oneself with the most calorific products, which although it helped primates to survive is today harmful. According to neoevolutionary assumptions, most functionalists largely overestimate the role of culture in shaping the social world, and underestimate genetic conditions. Neither is there an explanation for the significance of reproduction, which from the perspective of 'selfish genes' is the most important criterion, even more important than survival.

The neoevolutionary understanding of culture is thus quite far from functionalism and, paradoxically in the case of several aspects, closer to the interpretative-symbolic paradigm. In the neoevolutionary sense, culture is created on the micro level and includes human interactions, which lead to the emergence of collective bonds and values. In this case, there is no need to provide only functionalist explanations in relation to culture, as behaviour – stemming from the 'Pleistocene mind' – can be dysfunctional. Additionally, the need for systemic explanations is limited, because cultures are not coherent configurations of very distant values. Quite the contrary, they are variations on the universal values of people and social groups, rooted in the nature of *Homo sapiens*. And so, there are re-occurring universals in the form of the cooperative and competitive essence of the social bond, attachment to relatives, the role of speech and language, constitutive for a community, the creation of the structures of power and leadership, and the formation of similar social institutions (marriage, burial of the dead etc.). There are also cultural differences, which should be the subject of research, but the heart of the matter lies in the cultural universals.

Undoubtedly, neoevolutionism is different from the interpretative-symbolic paradigm, both on the epistemological and methodological level. Interpretivism assumes the subjectivity or inter-subjectivity of cognition, dualism and essentialism, and a characteristic methodology based on hermeneutics and phenomenology. Apart from the obvious opposition of both paradigms, one can point to slightly deeper similarities. The vision of people in interpretivism departs from the over-rationalised assumptions of *homo economicus*, which is clearly visible in functionalism. The concept of people entangled in webs of meaning of their own making is based on assumed emotional and intellectual motives, and is not internally coherent. Interpretivism also takes into consideration the influence of psychoanalysis and the discovery of the subconscious. It seems that neoevolutionism is also far from the over-rationalised image of the human mind, which is a result of the undermining of the Cartesian tradition of cognitive subjects. As part of nature, *Homo sapiens* have natural instincts, related to reproduction, survival, social life etc. However, evolutionary excess and the redundancy of the human mind lead to the creation of higher needs. Thus, the brain combines four sometimes contradictory needs and motivations on different levels of the conscious and subconscious. This is why a description of human behaviour cannot overestimate the rational sphere, omitting cognitive delusions, emotions and impulses, which are not always functional.

Neoevolutionism stands in clear opposition to the paradigm of radical structuralism. According to the assumptions of neoevolutionism, the so-called critical theory is not a theory in the scientific understanding, but an ideology. The assumptions of involving the cognitive subject in the process of change and striving for emancipation, linked with the rejection of the neopositivist epistemology, are completely antagonistic to neoevolutionism. The only element common to both paradigms seems to be a disillusioned vision of human nature and society. Radical structuralism interprets the social world in selfish categories. People strive mostly for power, ownership, control of resources and satisfaction of their own needs. Society and culture are a continuation of these tendencies. Social institutions are oppressive, use symbolic violence and produce false collective awareness, which comes down to maintaining an unjust order. The destruction of this status quo is a revolutionary action, requiring involvement of disadvantaged social groups. Similarly to radical structuralism, neoevolutionism points rather to the selfish motives of individuals. Genetic 'programming' leads to the tendency to idealise oneself, rationalise one's own negative actions, and nepotism. Even 'altruism' from the neoevolutionary perspective is not selfless. By saving kin, we save our genes, but by cooperating with strangers, we improve our chances of survival and reproduction. In consolation, it can only be added that neither neoevolutionism nor the critical theory goes completely towards full, selfish determinism. Genetic 'programming' is never full and is only a tendency, not a behavioural automatism. Thus, overcoming biological pressure is possible, and this is proven everyday by, for example, people adopting children. Furthermore, the creation of both these paradigms is proof of the emancipation of people from the biological and political mechanisms.

There is a huge gap between radical humanism, sometimes identified with postmodernism, and neoevolutionism. Postmodernism is subjectivist and relativist, and at the same time, sceptical of science. In contrast, neoevolutionism has an objectivist orientation, strives for generalisation and universalism in cognition, and places a large measure of trust in the institution of science.

The opposition between a standard model of the social sciences and neoevolutionism seems not to be fully true. In reality, neoevolutionism, although it proposes a radical change of the cognitive perspective in the social sciences, maintains more complex relationships with other paradigms of the social sciences. In the sense of the philosophy of science, it draws mostly on neopositivism, although its vision of the human mind is far from the rationalism and empiricism of the Vienna Circle. Of four paradigms of the social sciences, neoevolutionism seems to be the closest to functionalism. Although most assumptions of neoevolutionism are contrary to the interpretative-symbolic paradigm, there are certain common threads, related to the vision of *homo sociologicus*, such as limited rationality, the barriers of interpretation and cognitive delusions. Neoevolutionism stands in clear opposition to subjectivist paradigms, thoroughly rejecting radical structuralism, radical humanism and, naturally, postmodern approaches based on extreme epistemological relativism.

Applied to the understanding of culture, the concept of neoevolutionism has creative consequences. However, it is a controversial approach, often criticised by representatives of the social sciences and humanities. The most important accusations concern determinism, the issue of free will and consciousness, and scientism. According to critics, neoevolutionism is too determinist, as it explains human behaviour in categories of 'selfish genes', without leaving space for free will, and thus treats people as genetic and cultural 'puppets'. However, neoevolutionary explanations concern probability and the tendency to certain activities, not certainty and full determination. For example, neoevolutionary analyses show that nepotism, directly proportional to kinship, is a universal tendency in all cultures. Still, this does not mean that everyone behaves in the same way, or even that everyone acts nepotistically. Consciousness remains a difficult

Tab. 21: Neoevolutionism and the paradigms of culture in the social sciences. Source: Own work.

	Epistemology	Methodology	Pragmatics
Neoevolutionism	Objectivism Rationalism	Methods of brain studies (MRI, EEG, POS), social experiments	Neuro-marketing, research into social transmission of information and culture
	Homo Sociologicus	Quantitative, standardised, methods	
	Economicus Culture seen from the perspective of cerebral processes (a significant role of subconscious processes)	Researcher-outsider, uninvolved, non-evaluative	
Functionalism	Objectivism	Quantitative, standardised methods	Research into the influence of cultural dimensions on management
	Logical empiricism Homo Economicus Culture seen from the perspective of social functions	Researcher-outsider, uninvolved, non-evaluative	Optimisation of organisational culture
Interpretivism	Intersubjectivism	Understanding, qualitative, non-standardised methods	Improvement of organisation by cultural studies, individual and non-generalising
	Hermeneutics Homo Sociologicus Culture seen from the perspective of meanings	Researcher-insider, involved, evaluative	
Critical current	Objectivism Neo-Marxism	Methods involved in the change of an unjust reality	The criticism of practices and theories of organisation and management
	Homo Sociologicus Culture seen from the perspective of fighting for power and ideology	Researcher-insider, evaluative	Making organisations more fair by cultural studies and action research
Postmodernism	Subjectivism Postmodernism Homo Sociologicus Culture as meta-narration	Glossing, essay-writing, deconstruction	The criticism of practices and theories of organisation and management

issue, and is still in the initial stages of research[284]. Nevertheless, there are already some promising studies in neuroscience, which shed light on this phenomenon from the evolutionary and cognitivist perspectives, showing how the complexity of neuronal network gives rise to reasoning[285]. Neoevolutionism is scientistic, because it is an attempt to apply the methods of the natural sciences to the social sciences and humanities. However, I believe that at the current stage of research, this does not eliminate epistemological and methodological pluralism. Different paradigms offer different visions of culture and methods of studying them, and lead to different changes, which can be treated in complementary or metaphorical terms as images of organisations from different perspectives.

284 J.M. Bering, T.K. Shackelford, The Causal Role of Consciousness: A Conceptual Addendum to Human Evolutionary Psychology, *Review of General Psychology*, Vol. 8(4), Dec 2004, pp. 227–248.

285 A. Revonsuo, *Inner Presence: Consciousness as a Biological Phenomenon*, Cambridge, MA, US: MIT Press. (2006). xxv 473.

5 The interpretative understanding of culture in management

5.1 A description of the interpretative-symbolic paradigm

Culture is a constituent notion of the interpretative-symbolic current, also known as symbolic interactionism. It was developed within the humanities in the middle of the 20th century, in such disciplines as sociology, cultural anthropology and linguistics, thanks to researchers from the American school of F. Boas. The inspirations for the development of this concept were, among others, hermeneutics, research into the 'linguistic breakthrough' (the so-called Sapir-Whorf hypothesis) and the concepts of the 'family of words' of L. Wittgenstein. The paradigm of symbolic interactionism also has historical significance as an attempt at synthesising opposing approaches with the functionalist paradigm, which dominated in the first half of the 20th century and is commonly believed to have been originated by G.H. Mead, whose collected lectures were published by his students in the book *Mind, Self, and Society*. In the USA, the interpretative approach quickly divided into different scientific schools, of which the leading roles were played by cultural anthropology (C. Geertz), ethnomethodology (Garfinkel and Cicourel), the dramaturgic approach (E. Goffman) and the grounded theory (A. Strauss). Symbolic interactionism, which is often referred to interchangeably with the term 'interpretative-symbolic', also became a very important current[286]. In Europe, the interpretative approach had its most significant representatives in Germany and France. In the 1960s, A. Shutz created the philosophical and methodological basis for interpretative sociology, using the thought of phenomenologists and hermeneutists, mainly E. Husserl, M. Heidegger and H.G. Gadamer[287]. In France, the interpretative approach became rooted in the research methodology of the social sciences, and is still used by representatives of different theoretical schools. For example, P. Bourdieu, one of the most important modern sociologists, located close to neo-Marxism, used the interpretative and qualitative methodology extensively in his research, similarly to other French sociologists and anthropologists

286 H. Blumer, *Symbolic Interactionism*, Englewood Cliffs, N.J., 1969.
287 A. Schutze, *Phenomenology of the Social World*, Heinemann, London 1972.

concerned with culture (such as A. Tourraine, M. Wieviorka and M. Crozier). As the first alternative paradigm to the dominant functionalist approach, the interpretative-symbolic approach became the basis for the development of more radical cognitive approaches, including the critical current and postmodernism in different social sciences.

Over the last few decades, management science has seen a development of concepts that can be located in the interpretative current[288]. Based on similar assumptions, these concepts draw from the humanities. Symbolic interactionism, considered to be the source of the interpretative perspective, emerged from within sociology and cultural anthropology, and its influences can be found in philosophy, linguistics, and the historical and political sciences[289]. The transfer of the achievements of the extensive and heterogeneous interpretative paradigm to management is also becoming increasingly visible, which is why it is worth attempting to identify the basic assumptions, adapted to management science[290].

Interpretative research into organisational culture offers a number of diverse cognitive and pragmatic concepts, drawing inspirations from interpretivism, interactionism, the dramatic approach, ethnomethodology, cultural anthropology and other currents of the social sciences and humanities[291]. Most researchers treat many of these approaches as stemming from the interpretative-symbolic paradigm. However, there are also authors who point to significant differences between these concepts[292]. Before undertaking a more detailed analysis, it is worth examining the differences between these currents within the paradigm of symbolic interactionism (Tab. 22).

Historically, interpretivism is the oldest current of the symbolic interactionism paradigm, and was created thanks to G.H. Mead and his students from the University of Chicago[293]. Culture was understood from the perspective of

---

288 M.J. Hatch, *Organization Theory: Modern, Symbolic-Interpretive and Postmodern Perspectives* . Oxford: Oxford University Press,1997

289 H. Blumer, *Symbolic Interactionism*, Englewood Cliffs, N.J., 1969.

290 In this article, the notions: approach, current, perspective and interpretative orientation are used interchangeably.

291 H. Garfinkel, Studies in Ethnomethodology. Englewood Cliffs, NJ: Prentice-Hall, 1967.

292 M.J. Gallant, S. Kleinman, Symbolic interactionism vs. ethnomethodology, Symbolic Interaction, 1983, 6: 1–18.

293 G.H. Mead, *Mind, Self, and Society*, Ed. by Charles W. Morris. University of Chicago Press 1934.

social relationships and roles, reflected in the concepts of self, social games and the other. The interpretivist current focused on the sociological analyses of the creative process and the crystallisation of the social self, using interviews and observations.

Symbolic interactionism is a term coined by H. Blumer in 1937. Blumer proposed a new humanist current, which opposed neopositivism, referring to the works of G. H. Mead. He believed in studying culture by getting at the subjective meanings and senses, which are constructed by social actors in the process of their interactions. Blumer's most important contribution to the development of the cultural discourse in science is the formulation of a coherent cognitive approach within the social sciences, as an alternative to the dominant neopositivist-functionalist paradigm[294]. Symbolic interactionism has developed into an extensive research current, the subjects of which include, among others, social activities (including organisational behaviour).

The originator of the dramatic approach was E. Goffman, who developed a unique concept of social roles, based on symbolic interactionism and the theatre metaphor[295]. Goffman's works about stigmatisation and social exclusion are still used in interpretative and critical analyses of organisational culture[296]. The drama current marks a kind of return to the dramatic perspective, developing today, and the narrative approach. The drama current is applied to improve the organisation and its employees through role-playing, the aim of which is to reduce stress or release emotions[297]. On the other hand, the narrative and textual approach developed its own concept of conducting organisational research, which shall be discussed below.

Ethnomethodology was created in the 1960s by H. Garfinkel[298]. The assumptions of this concept are based on the need to discover the rules by which

---

294 H. Blumer, *Symbolic Interactionism: Perspective and Method.* New Jersey: Prentice-Hall 1969.

295 E. Goffman, *The Presentation of Self in Everyday Life*, University of Edinburgh Social Sciences Research Centre, 1959

296 E. Goffman, Stigma: Notes on the Management of Spoiled Identity. Prentice-Hall, 1963, pp. 151–152; A.P. Brief, *Still Servants of Power*, 'Journal of Management Inquiry', 9/4, 2000.

297 I.L. Mangham, M.A. Overington, *Dramatism and the Theatrical Metaphor*, in: 'Beyond Method. Strategies for Social Research', ed. G. Morgan, Sage, Beverly Hills, London, New Delhi 1983, pp. 219–233.

298 H. Garfinkel, Ethnomethodology's Program, New York: Rowman and Littlefield 2002.

Tab. 22: The currents of symbolic interactionism in management. Source: Own work.

Symbolic interactionism currents	**The main research issues**	**The dominant research methodology**	**The most important researchers**
Interpretivism	Self and identity of managers and other organisational actors	In-depth interviews, participant observation, covert and overt	G.H. Mead, the Chicago School
Symbolic interactionism	Social games, communication and negotiations in management	Subjectivist analyses of meanings and interpretations, self-analysis, in-depth interviews	H. Blumer, K. Weick, G. Morgan
Dramatic approach	Social roles of managers, image management, oppressiveness of the organisation	Observations, self-analysis, frame analysis	E. Goffman, I.L. Mangham, M.A. Overington
Ethnomethodology	Research into the process of work and creation, consolidation of organisational rules and practices	Conversational analyses (e.g. of sequentiality), breaching experiment	H. Garfinkel, A. Cicourel, H. Sacks, D. Maynard, S. Clayman
Organisational anthropology	Understanding organisational culture and identity, and the processes of wielding power	Field observations (overt and covert), shadowing, in-depth, biographical interviews	C. Geertz, M.J. Hatch, K. Weick, G. Morgan, G. Burrell
Narrative and textual approach	Interpretation of narratives and texts in the process of their creation	Conversational analyses, narrative research, storytelling, metaphorical analysis Analyses of text through metaphors, archetypes, organisational paradoxes	B. Czarniawska, J. Denning, A. Daphne, L. Giles, Ch. Huang, M. Kets de Vries, S. Clegg, M. Kostera
Organisational cognitivism	Giving meaning to the organisational reality	Metaphorical analysis of text analyses, conversational analyses	C. Eden, P. Cossette, A.E. Tenbrunsel, A. Jelinek, J.A. Litterer and C. Ouelet

Tab. 22: Continued

Symbolic interactionism currents	**The main research issues**	**The dominant research methodology**	**The most important researchers**
Grounded theory	Looking for the meaning of culture as created by social groups	Methodology of the grounded theory, observations, interviews, literary analyses	A. Strauss, B.G. Glaser, J. Corbin, K. Konecki

people, through their behaviour, give meaning to reality. The key role in ethnomethodology is played by conversational analyses based on the interpretative assumption that language plays a constituent role in the social world[299]. Another characteristic method was supposed to be the breaching experiment, consisting in provocative behaviour that was supposed to breach social conventions and allow for discovery of ways of maintaining order by social actors. In the organisational sphere, the processes of communication and work are the subjects of ethnomethodological[300].

Organisational anthropology became the first current located within the interpretative-symbolic paradigm to allow for a return to the issue of the definition and typology of culture in management. Anthropology drew an interest in culture from cultural anthropology and its interpretation after the anti-functionalist breakthrough. At first, in the 19th century and at the beginning of the 20th century, anthropology (ethnology, ethnography) was based on neopositivist-functionalist, and then structuralist assumptions. However, in the second half of the 20th century, there was a turnaround in the discourse of cultural anthropology, which moved towards the social constructivism approach. Then, the key role was played by the moderate approaches of cultural relativism, such as the interpretative-symbolic paradigm, and with time, some more radical approaches such as post-structuralism and postmodernism. The

299 A. Cicourel, *Language and Social Interaction: Philosophical and Empirical Issues*, 'Sociological Inquiry', 1980, vol. 50, no. ¾, 1980; H. Sacks, E.A. Schegloff, 'Two Preferences in the Organization of Reference to Persons in Conversation and Their Interaction' in: G. Psathas (ed.) Everyday Language: Studies in Ethnomethodology, Irvington Press, New York, NY, 1979, pp. 15–21.

300 H. Garfinkel, ed., *Ethnomethodological Studies of Work*, 1986, pp. 160–193.

works of C. Geertz, J. Clifford and G. Marcuse were all of key significance to the development of the constructivist version of cultural anthropology[301]. Organisational anthropology was born out of this non-fundamentalist version of the social sciences in the 1970s. It is broadly and increasingly often applied in the research into organisational culture and identity, as well as in the analyses of incremental strategies, organisational image, processes of management and human resources management[302]. Organisational researchers, using the anthropological approach, include K. Weick, G. Morgan, M.J. Hatch and G. Burrell. The methodology of organisational anthropology is rich, but its core still includes field research: overt and covert observations (participant and non-participant), shadowing, biographical research, in-depth case studies etc.

Organisational anthropology is more and more often the basis for documentary texts, forming a kind of organisational literature. Organisational stories and role-playing scenarios are used as tools for the purpose of organisational diagnosis[303]. In this sense, anthropology is also a source of the narrative and textual approach, which interprets the theoretical discourse and practice of management from the perspective of narratives and texts. The methodology is based on qualitative text analysis and conversational analysis, making use of

301 C. Geertz, *After the Fact: Two Countries, Four Decades, One Anthropologist*. Cambridge, MA: Harvard University Press 1995; A. Gupta, J. Ferguson, *Beyond 'Culture': Space, Identity, and the Politics of Difference*, Cultural Anthropology, 1992, 7: 6–23.

302 L. Smircich, Concepts of Culture and Organizational Analysis, *Administrative Science Quarterly*: 28(3), 1983, pp. 160–172.; M. Rosen, *Coming to the Terms with the field: Understanding and doing organisational ethnography*, 'Journal of Management Studies', no. 28, 1991, pp. 1–24; M.J. Hatch, *Irony and the Social Construction of Contradiction in the Humor of a Management Team*, 'Organization Studies', 1997, pp. 275–288; L. *Smircich*, G. *Morgan*, *Leadership: The Management of Meaning*, ' Journal of Applied Behavioural Studies', 18: 257–273, 1982; M.A. Hogg, D. J Terry, *Social identity and self-categorization processes in organizational contexts*, 'Academy of Management Review', 25, 2000, pp. 121–140.

303 J.S. Brown, S. Denning, K. Groh, L. Prusak, *Storytelling in Organizations. Why Storytelling is Transforming 21st Century Organizations and Management*, Elsevier Butterwoth-Heinemann, Oxford, 2005; M. Rosen, *Coming to the Terms with the field: Understanding and doing organisational ethnography*, '*Journal of Management Studies*', no. 28, 1991, pp. 1–24; M.J. Hatch, *Irony and the Social Construction of Contradiction in the Humor of a Management Team*, 'Organization Studies', 1997, pp. 275–288.

the methodological experiences of the interpretative-symbolic discourse and the hermeneutic tradition[304]. The group of theoreticians and practitioners, concerned with narrative research, and especially storytelling, grows rapidly. Today, the most important representatives of this current are believed to be M. E. Boyce, J. Denning, A. Daphne, L. Giles, and C. Huang[305].

The different kinds of textual tools in the interpretative-symbolic current include metaphors, archetypes and paradoxes. Metaphor has its roots in poetry and comes from the Greek word for transfer (*meta* – change, *phora* – move), and is one of numerous rhetorical figures. As R. Jacobson said, metaphors and metonymy are elementary language operations, present in all utterances[306]. A metaphor is the departure from the literal, original meaning of a word towards a figurative meaning[307]. Metaphors serve communication and didactic purposes, making it easier to understand organisational culture[308]. The metaphors have the function of generalisation and regulation, as they describe new phenomena, referring to linguistic structures rooted and familiar in culture. If we assume that national language is secondary to colloquial language, metaphorical references have to be an inseparable element of each discourse.

The concept of archetypes comes from Carl Gustav Jung[309], who assumed that humanity has a collective unconsciousness, having an effect on our entire perception and interpretation of reality[310]. The archetypes rooted in the collective unconsciousness are universal, existential challenges and social roles, which are

---

304 B. Czarniawska-Joerges, *Narratives of Individual and Organisational Identities*, in: 'Organisational Identity. A Reader', ed. M.J. Hatch, M. Schultz, Oxford University Press, Oxford – New York 2004, pp. 407–435; A. De Fina, A. Georgakopoulou, Analysing Narratives as Practices, *Qualitative Research*, vol. 8(3) 379–387, 2008; B. Czarniawska, P. Gagliardi (ed.), *Narratives We Organize By*. Amsterdam/ Philadelphia: John Benjamin's Publishing Company 2003; B. Flyvberg, *Case study*, in: N.K. Denzin, Y.S. Lincoln. eds. *The Sage Handbook of Qualitative Research*, 4th Edition. Thousand Oaks, CA: Sage 2011, Chapter 17, pp. 301–316.

305 M.E. Boyce, *Organizational story and storytelling: a critical review*, Journal of Organizational Change Management, 1996, Vol. 9 Iss: 5, pp. 5 – 26

306 R. Jacobson, *Essais de linguistique générale*, Paris 1969, p. 244.

307 M. Black, More about Metaphor, in: *Metaphor and Thought*, ed. A. Ortony, Cambridge 1979.

308 T.D. Taber, Using Metaphor to Teach Organization Theory, *Journal of Management Education*, 2007, 31(4): 541–554.

309 C.G. Jung, *The Archetypes and the Collective Unconscious*, Princeton, NJ: Bollingen, 1968.

310 E.F. Edinger, Ego and Archetype, Shambhala Publications 1992.

reflected in culture. Archetypes are used in management mostly in relation to the creation of organisational strategy, management of culture, identity and marketing, as well as human resources management and marketing[311].

M. Kostera describes the possibility of applying archetypes in the world of organisation and management, pointing to the possibility of setting the concept of archetypes in the theory of culture in an epistemological way[312]. The notion 'archetype' is also used in a meaning close to the Weberian 'ideal model'[313] and in the Jungian understanding as reflecting structures and systems, enhanced by one interpretative pattern[314]. Analysis by M. Kostera of a number of Jungian archetypes related to transformation (birth, death, rebirth), personality (the shadow, the anima and animus, the self), family (mother, father), stories (the hero, the maiden, the wise old man) and animals (the lion, the dog, the cat), describes a number of possibilities for applying them to management science[315]. They also form a basis for reflection on the key management problems, such as identity, power, leadership, change and so on. Perceived from the perspective of archetypes, these issues are interpreted in a broad cultural context, and it is not necessary to artificially divide isolated scientific disciplines into discourses. It is research based on intuition and ethical and aesthetic sensitivity, not only on rational studies. However, not all archetypes seem to be equally useful cognitively and pragmatically.

Another unconventional method of managing culture is with the use of paradox. A paradox (from Greek *parádoxos* – unexpected, unbelievable) means thinking about the apparently obvious truth of its elements but – because of an error or vagueness of expression – leading to clearly opposing conclusions. V.W. Quine and many other authors analysed the reasons and types of paradoxes, noting that in most cases they are related to logical and linguistic issues, such as self-reference, juxtaposition and vicious circles[316]. In the case of management

---

311 D. Miller, P.H. Friesen, Archetypes of Strategy Formulation, *Management Science*, 24: 921–933, 1978.; R. Greenwood, C.R. Hinings, Understanding Strategic Change: the Contribution of Archetypes, *Academy of Management Journal*', vol. 36, no. 5, 1993.

312 M. Kostera, *Organizations and Archetypes*, Edward Elgar Publishing, 2012

313 D.P. Rutenberg, *Organizational Archetype of a Multi-national Company*, 'Management Science', no. 16 (6), 1970, pp. 337–348.

314 M. Kostera, *Organizations and Archetypes*, Edward Elgar Publishing, 2012

315 M. Kostera, *Organizations and Archetypes*, Edward Elgar Publishing, 2012

316 W. Van Orman Quine, 'The Ways of Paradox', The Ways of Paradox and Other Essays, Random House, 1996, p. 5; P. Hughes, G. Brecht, *Vicious Circles and Infinity - A Panoply of Paradoxes*. Garden City, New York: Doubleday 1975.

science, paradoxes are used in the cognitive and pragmatic sphere[317]. They often take the form of oxymorons – figures of speech combining contradictory terms[318]. A pioneer in terms of using the concept of paradoxes in management is M. Kets de Vries[319]. Whereas in management, the concept of paradoxes is used by, for example, S. Clegg, J. Fletcher and K. Olwyler. Problems that are seen as paradoxes, or studied with the use of paradoxes, concern organisational culture and identity[320].

Today, we can see the spread of such non-orthodox concepts in management as metaphors, archetypes and paradoxes, as well as lesser-known textual and literary methods (e.g. allegories, parallels, catharsis). Comparing these ideas, we can point to certain similarities: humanist origins; a striving for the revealing of deep structures and patterns rooted in the human cognitive apparatus; applications (mostly related to the theory of organisation, organisational culture and strategy); human resources management, strategic management and leadership.

Organisational cognitivism is a new proposal for understanding organisational culture. It is located within the interpretative-symbolic paradigm, which can be slightly misleading, as it is associated with cognitive science and neuroscience. Its main assumption is in reaching collective meanings, subjectively created and consolidated, by analysing the metaphors used to perceive reality[321]. The research

---

317 A. Zohar, *Paradoxical Dimensions of Organization*. Working Paper, Toronto: Schulich School of Business, 1995.

318 K.E. Weick, F. Westley, Organizational Learning: Affirming an Oxymoron. in: S.R. Clegg, C. Hardy, W.R. Nord (Eds.), *Handbook of Organization Studies* (pp. 440–458). Sage 1996.

319 M. Kets de Vries, *Organizational Paradoxes*. London: Tavistock, 1980.

320 P.J. Streatfield, *The Paradox of Control in Organizations*. London: Routledge, 2001; Ch. Handy, *The age of paradox;* Harvard Business Review Press, 1995;

321 C. Eden, J. Spender (ed.), *Managerial and Organisational Cognition. Theory, Methods and Research*, Sage, London 1998; P. Cossette, *L'organisation. Une perspective cognitiviste*, Les Presses de l'Universite Laval, Canada 2004; A.E. Tenbrunsel, T.E. Galvin, M.A. Neale, M.H. Bazerman, *Cognitions in Organisations*, in: 'Handbook of Organisations Studies', ed. S.R. Glegg, C. Hardy, W.N. Nord, Sage, London 1996. A. Jelinek, J.A. Litterer, Toward a Cognitive Theory of Organisation, in: *Advances in Managerial Cognition and Organisational Information Processing*, ed. C. Stubbart, J.R. Meindl, J.F. Porac, JAI Press, Greenwich 1994 ; C. Ouellet, P. Cossette, *Les travaux des chercheurs utilisant le concept de cognition en sciences de l'administration: une etude exploratoire*, 'Actes de la 8 Conference Internationale,de Management Strategique', Paris 1999.

into organisational culture, with reference to the phenomenological inspiration, is still at the initial stage. It uses the philosophy of E. Husserl, M. Merleau-Ponty, and R. Ingarden to analyse the values and the process of work[322].

I would like to finish the analysis of cultural research currents with a description of the 'grounded theory', which is an example of a concept set within the interpretative-symbolic paradigm, but that draws inspiration from the functional paradigm[323]. The grounded theory is a methodological approach and a scientific school developed by A. Strauss and B.G. Glaser in the 1960s[324]. Use of the word 'theory' is here a bit misleading, as in fact we are dealing a with methodology and research methods supported by epistemology. They postulate a consolidation of the theorising process in the primary, inductive process of acquiring knowledge about the studied social reality. This concept is an attempt at bringing together the paradigm of symbolic interactionism and the neopositivist-functionalist-systemic paradigm, while breaking with the assumptions of epistemological relativism[325]. Perhaps this is connected with the biography of the grounded theory's creator – A. Strauss – who was a student of H. Blumer, the creator of symbolic interactionism, and P. Lazersfeld, the father of the empirical method in modern sociology. The grounded theory is located on the borderline between paradigms, both from the epistemological and methodological perspectives. The assumptions it draws from symbolic interactionism include:

- Lack of the researcher's pre- of a researcher (*tabula rasa*), who instead develops a cognitive network only during the research process,
- Looking for local meanings, constructed in the processes of interaction by social actors,
- Assuming a moderate version of social constructivism as the epistemological basis,
- Qualitative, open research methodology, based on the inductive approach,
- Methodological pluralism, allowing for the combination of research methods and techniques, even when they are drawn from different paradigms.

---

322 W. Küpers, *Embodied Symbolic Consumption - Phenomenological Perspectives of Interpretative Consumer Research*, [in:] R. Elliot, S. Beckmann, *Perspectives on Interpretative Consumer Research*, CBS, Kopenhagen, 2000.

323 A.E. Clarke, Situational Analyses: Grounded Theory Mapping After the Postmodern Turn, *Symbolic Interaction*, 2003, 26: 553–576.

324 B.G. Glaser; A.L. Strauss, The Discovery of Grounded Theory. *Strategies for Qualitative Research*, 1967.

325 A. Clarke, *Situational Analysis: Grounded Theory after the Postmodern Turn*, Thousand Oaks, CA: Sage Publications 2005.

On the other hand, it draws the following assumptions from the neopositivist-functionalist-systemic paradigm:

- Striving for the creation of a theory that allows for generalisation of research results and explanations,
- A process of quasi-verification, consisting in proposing hypotheses at the advanced stages of research and testing them,
- A tendency to give cause-and-effect or systemic explanations for social interactions.

The methodology of the grounded theory is of a qualitative character and assumes a consistent, quite strict, multi-stage process of gathering data[326]. The key subjects of interest are social interactions, understood as a process, which are analysed with the use of the incident technique[327]. The methodology of research is supposed to be grounded, which means that all generalisations and hypotheses are created only after the first stages of research, which usually takes the form of field work or data collection with the use of all available techniques[328]. By definition, research is supposed to begin inductively, which means that it does not propose theories and hypotheses, and that only during the process of enriching knowledge can one begin thinking deductively and formulating working theories and hypotheses. Thus, the grounded theory is qualitative, open to different data collection techniques, but on the other hand, it postulates generalisations and testing of hypotheses at a more advanced stage of research. It also departs from the correspondent concept of truth, assumed to be the traditional aim of empirical research, and moves towards pragmatic cognitive categories of the theories so developed, such as cognitive usefulness, relevance and operationality[329]. The grounded theory is used in research into organisational culture and identity, as well as many other problems of management, such as human resources management, leadership and marketing[330]. It is quite a popular methodology of

326 B.G. Glaser, *Doing Grounded Theory - Issues and Discussions*, Sociology Press 1998.

327 B.G. Glaser; A.L. Strauss, *The Discovery of Grounded Theory. Strategies for Qualitative Research*, 1967.

328 A.L. Strauss, J. Corbin, *Basics of Qualitative Research. Grounded Theory Procedures and Techniques*, Newbury Park, CA: Sage 1990.

329 B.G. Glaser, *The Grounded Theory Perspective I: Conceptualization Contrasted with Description*, Sociology Press 2001.
Anselm L. Strauss; Juliet Corbin: 'Grounded Theory in Practice' (1997)

330 C. Goulding, Grounded Theory, Ethnography and Phenomenology: A Comparative Analysis of Three Qualitative Strategies for Marketing Research, *European Journal*

qualitative research, especially in the USA, but one could also point to a number of interesting research projects all over the world[331].

The brief description of the currents located within the interpretative-symbolic paradigm presented here includes both historical approaches, such as interpretivism, currents related mostly to the sociological analysis of societies and organisations (interactionism, dramatic current, ethnomethodology), currents developed and used within modern management, such as organisational anthropology, and marginal or new approaches, such as cognitivism and organisational phenomenology. As we can see, the interpretative-symbolic paradigm is internally diverse, although there are some common cognitive assumptions about different currents that integrate this cognitive approach:

1. People are perceived as social actors, entangled in interactions and the process of their interpretation (interactionism).
2. People create their own identities in an active way, in a social group (social identity).
3. People and a group create and transform social senses and meanings through interactions (symbolisation).
4. Culture equates to local networks of meanings, created by people in social and linguistic games (webs of meaning).
5. Getting to know the social reality is subjective or intersubjective, so by definition is limited and one-sided (intersubjectivism).
6. One can get to know social reality and culture only by penetrating the local meanings created by people (interpretation).

Apart from the similarities with the sphere of epistemological assumptions, the research and pragmatic methods used are also very close to each other. The above description of the different currents located within the interpretative-symbolic paradigm indicates that they use very similar research methods, which are

---

of Marketing, 2005, Vol. 39 Iss: 3/4, pp. 294 – 308; S.R. Komives, J.E. Owen, S.D. Longerbeam, Developing a Leadership Identity: A Grounded Theory, *Journal of College Student Development*, 46, 593–611; K.D. Locke, *Grounded Theory in Management Research*, London Sage 2001; P.Y. Martin, B.A. Turner, Grounded Theory and Organizational Research, *The Journal of Applied Behavioral Science*, April 1986 22: 141–157.

331 C. Goulding, *Grounded Theory: A Practical Guide for Management*, Business and Market Researchers. London: Sage 2002; K. Konecki, The Methodology of Grounded Theory in the Research of the Situation of Work, *The Polish Sociological Bulletin*, 2: 59–74, 1989.

based on similar assumptions. In-depth interviews are a very popular method, assuming reaching to the real meanings used by social actors. Furthermore, observations are often used to capture the sense of behaviour. Unlike in the neopositivist-functionalist approach, assuming a subjective, participant or even emotionally involved position is recommended. Another valuable source of data is auto-analysis, as subjectivism is an inherent feature of this paradigm, while other methods include conversational analyses, text analyses and other in-depth research methods.

5.2 Concepts of symbolic interactionism in management

Attempts to reconstruct the assumptions of the interpretative-symbolic paradigm in management reveal several aspects, including social constructivism, organisation understood as a social agreement, the cognitive role of language in management and the entanglement of cognitive activity in practice. These epistemological assumptions are fulfilled in research programmes based on the qualitative, 'soft' methodology, drawing inspirations mostly from the humanities.

1 Social constructivism

The epistemological starting point is the perspective of a reflective cognitive subject, entangled in relationships with other people. Social constructivism is an assumption that reality is created socially. K. Weick, referring to the organisation process, just like P. Berger and T. Luckmann in the sphere of social processes, believed that reality is created by social actors[332]. According to the assumptions of realism, relationships between people, group communication, the wielding of power, leadership and management are neither entities nor relationships existing objectively. Rather, they are intersubjective, which means they are created by collective and individual processes of negotiating meanings. Their ontological status is different from the status of material objects. However, no one can ignore the fact that the organisational world is also based on material foundations, which can offer certain meanings, even if they are not solely meanings. Material aspects of the organisation's functioning have the ontological status of objective – and not only intersubjective – entities. This concerns, for example, machines, devices, resources and material products. However, one can propose the thesis

332 P.L. Berger, T. Luckmann, *The Social Construction of Reality: A Treatise in the Sociology of Knowledge*, Doubleday, Garden City 1966; K.E. Weick, *The Social Psychology of Organizing*, Addison-Wesley, Reading Mass. 1979.

that in the organisational world there is feedback between objectively existing reality, subject to the process of interpretation, and the granting of meanings. Social conventions are formed around the material reality, influencing that reality. Thus, the ontology of the intersubjective world of social groups and organisations emerges, harmonising with the objectively existing objects.

The interpretative approach is characterised by a moderate social constructivism, unlike the radical postmodernist options[333]. According to the constructivist epistemology, people are the creators of the world. In the process of interpretation, they give meaning to their environment, structuring it into cognisable entities that can be shaped. The interpretative approach emphasises the feedback between discovery of the world and creation of the world by people in the cognitive process. Naturally, reality is not only a social or linguistic construct, but cultural elements do help to create the organisational world and aid in perception of it. In this sense, the subject is not only a discoverer but also a creator.

Social constructivism causes researchers focusing on the interpretative-symbolic perspective to perceive organisations mostly from the perspective of social processes related to the granting and understanding of meanings. Popular examples of constructivism in management include the concepts of organisational culture (inc. L. Smircich, M.J. Hatch), organisational subcultures (J. Van Maanen, R.S. Barley), meanings management (G. Morgan, L. Smircich) and the dominant strategic logics[334].

2 The organisational process understood as building a social agreement

According to interpretative researchers, organisational order does not exist objectively, but is constantly maintained, reconstructed and modified by individuals and groups functioning within and around an organisation. Organisational and managerial processes are created by groups as a result of institutionalization, empowerment and internalisation processes, and are of a conventional character

333 Cf.: D.M. Boje, R.P. Gephart Jr, T.J. Thatchenkery, *Postmodern Management and Organization Theory*, Thousand Oaks: Sage Publications, 1996.

334 L. Smircich, *Organizations as Shared Meaning*, in: 'Organization Symbolism', JAI Press, Greenwich 1983, pp. 55–65; E.H. Schein, *Organization Psychology*, Englewood Cliffs, Prentice-Hall 1965, p. 60; J. Van Maanen, R.S. Barley, *Occupational Communities: Culture and Control in Organizations*, in: 'Research in Organizational Behaviour', ed. B.M. Staw, L.L. Cummings, JAI Press, Greenwich 1984, pp. 287–366.

as they form a group consensus[335]. Economic interests have as much impact as political, social and psychological factors. Organisational order is a process of dynamic establishment of social structures, which are subject to temporary conventions.

Naturally, the process of the negotiation of meaning is not only of a rational character. Participants in an organisation's life accept the conventional reality as something pre-existing and obvious, but unconsciously still play the negotiating social game. Organisational hierarchy, charismatic leadership, authority, informal groups, subcultures, and even strategies are conventions which temporarily serve as the social consensus and are maintained in a given organisation by the interaction's participants themselves. The strength, stability and rationalism of these agreements differ. Organisations exist thanks to strong social conventions, which are reflected in law. It can be said that the organisation's continuity is maintained by involvement in a social game and the subconscious belief that these fragile conventions are stable.

3 The cognitive role of language

After the 'linguistic breakthrough', many currents of the social sciences began to assume that language is the cognitive basis for understanding the world[336]. Language is far from the idealised image of formalised language, and close to its cultural understanding. The Wittgensteinian term 'family of words', transferred into management, is related to the fluidity of meanings given to different notions in the organisational world. Organisation and the process of management are by definition ambiguous. Related notions, which build the whole sphere of organisation and management, such as power, leadership, management, organisational structure, strategy and organisational culture, do not have one single designatum and are defined and combined in a number of different ways.

The interpretative current emphasises the changeability of social meanings, which is closely related to constructivist assumptions. Ways of thinking and speaking form a characteristic discourse in a number of management currents, which cannot be unified. Thus, the social nature and linguistic character of cognition themselves give rise to the multiplicity and ambiguity of management that, similarly to other social sciences, cannot aspire to the creation of general

335 P.L. Berger, T. Luckmann, *The Social Construction of Reality: A Treatise in the Sociology of Knowledge*, Doubleday, Garden City 1966.

336 Compare: Whorf, B.L., Lee, P., Levinson, S.C., & Carroll, J.B. (2012). *Language, thought, and reality: Selected writings of Benjamin Lee Whorf.* MIT press., pp. 329–361.

syntheses and universal theories. Attempts at the creation of a single discourse in management are, by definition, utopian and bring to mind the Lyotardian 'meta-narrations', characteristic of radical epistemological fundamentalism[337]. The interpretative approach is different from the postmodern in the assumption that the processes of cognition and changing reality are carried out by self-replicating language games, and not only glossing. Language creates multiple interpretations which shape the network of meanings in a fluid way. The acts of cognition and thinking about organisational processes and management can be found in the hermeneutic circle. Forsaking the idealised concept of language as a medium offering a perfect reflection of reality, and assuming the constructivist and pragmatic approaches (language shapes the reality described), has significant epistemological consequences. The limits of the cognition of organisation, structure and the reasons for their existence are determined by language[338]. The discourse in management science imposes intersubjective mental constructs on us, in the form of organisation, enterprises, environment, strategies, structures, cultures.

4 Entanglement in praxis

In making interpretations, a researcher of organisations loses their position as an objective, non-interfering observer and becomes a subject actively involved in the changes of the reality being studied – changed by the fact of the studies, as such. The link between the researcher and the studied reality should be described as inseparable entanglement in the reality being studied and changed. In his Hawthorne experiment, E. Mayo noted that organisation researchers wield significant influence over their subjects. This is why management science and other social sciences should reject the distinction between the subject and the cognition subject.

Popular explanations are primary in management, or at least equally important as or harmonising with scientific explanations[339]. The emphasis on categories of everyday life is clear (the everyday epistemology[340]). Management specialists

---

337 Lyotard, Jean-Francois. 'Excerpts from The postmodern condition: A report on knowledge.' *A postmodern reader* (1993): 71–90., p. 111.

338 L. Wittgenstein, *Tractatus logico-philosophicus*, PWN, Warszawa, 2002, thesis 5. 6, p. 64.

339 A. Schutze, *Phenomenology of the Social World*, Heinemann, London 1972.

340 J. Surowiecki, *The Wisdom of Crowds: Why the Many Are Smarter Than the Few and How Collective Wisdom Shapes Business, Economies, Societies, and Nations.*

use the hermeneutic language of theory or the colloquial language of practice. There is an obvious problem with the disproportion between these discourses, but – as management specialists – we have to assess both the theoreticians' concepts, sophisticated in terms of terminology, and the ideas of management gurus, stemming from practice and strongly rooted in the colloquial discourse[341].

The concepts which point to the entanglement of the organisational process in praxis, the result of which is the lack of the possibility of creating an objective subject-object cognition process, can be found within change management, human resources management, strategic management, organisational learning and organisational culture. M. Crozier describes the processes of changes, based on the involvement of the interfering researcher, with the use of colloquial categories (using examples such as the SNCF and Air France)[342]. Involved social researchers become participants in the dynamic change process developed and implemented by a group.

5 Management as a symbolic activity

A person in an organisation is a searcher for meaning, oriented towards values and involved in the research situation. The process of management, understood as a symbolic activity, can be described as a correlation between organisational activities and perception, communication and the interpretation of organisational activity (Figure 26). The cognitive act is entangled in language and is culturally relative, and so it is a symbolic activity. Organisation and management are to the same degree based on the manipulation of objects and meanings. The symbols of organisational status, function, position and rights are a manifestation of power. Organisational culture forms a symbolic system. Strategic, cognitive and structural processes in organisations are also based on semantic systems, which results in the management's entanglement in the linguistic and semantic context.

This aspect of management as a symbolic activity is emphasised by research into organisational culture. M.J. Hatch proposes a description of culture as a dynamic process of creating artefacts, symbols, assumptions and values with use

New York: Doubleday, 2004; M. Suk-Young Chwe, *Rational Ritual. Culture, Coordination and Common Knowledge*, Princeton University Press, Princeton and Oxford 2001, pp. 79–82.

341 J. Micklethwait, A. Wooldridge, *The Witch Doctors: Making Sense of the Management Gurus, Three Rivers Press, 1998*

342 M. Crozier, *L'entreprise à l'écoute*, Seuil 1994.

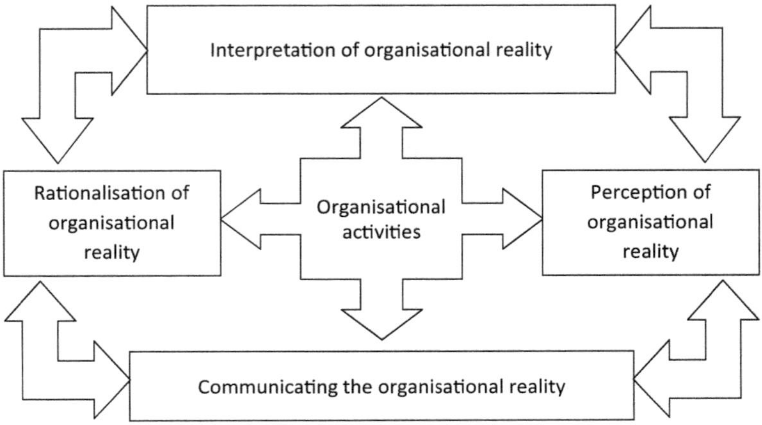

Fig. 8: Organisational culture in the interpretative understanding. Source: Own work.

of interpretation and symbolisation[343]. Problems stemming from the analyses of symbolic culture, such as construction of the identity of organisations and individuals[344] and the anthropology of everyday life, words and language, are increasingly often reflected in management[345].

6 Qualitative methodology of the IS paradigm

Management science is more often using methods drawn from the interpretative-symbolic current of the social sciences. Thus, there is a transfer of research methods from sociology, cultural anthropology, linguistics and social psychology to management science. The most important methods include the management methods of humanist psychology, organisational anthropology, ethnomethodology, intervention sociology, the previously-discussed grounded theory, in-depth case analysis, participatory action research, discourse analysis and metaphorical methods. All listed methods and techniques focus on qualitative and field research. Organisations and their participants are studied in the process of action, with the use of colloquial categories. The emphasis is put on

343 M.J. Hatch, *The Dynamics of Organizational Culture*, Academy of Management Review, no. 18, 1993.

344 M.J. Hatch, M. Schultz (ed.), *Organizational Identity*, Oxford University Press, 2004.

345 S. Linsted (ed.), *Text/Work. Representing Organization and Organizing Representation*, Routledge, London-New York, 2003.

the understanding of a situation by the researcher. And so the cognitive method merges with the method of making changes and improvement. The axiological element becomes indispensable, and an important role is plated by language and the cultural context.

The interpretative methodology is criticised for a number of reasons: (1) it is very heterogeneous and its results are often difficult to compare, (2) it is not suitable for studying mass processes and phenomena, (3) by definition, it is not objective, (4) it gives rise to problems concerning the reliability of the results, (5) the involvement of a researcher can lead to ethical doubts[346].

The methodology of the interpretative-symbolic current is based on the epistemological reflection and has developed a number of interesting research tools. The methodological approaches which gain more and more significance in management science include mostly the methods of organisational anthropology (organisational ethnology), psychoanalysis, ethnomethodology, intervention sociology, the grounded theory, extended case studies and participatory research.

The interpretative current covers certain epistemological assumptions, which have been reflected in a number of concepts and methods in management. Apart from the previously mentioned interpretative concepts of organisational culture, strategy and structuralisation, one can also point to the localisation and transfer of meanings[347], organisational learning[348], life history methodology[349], the creation of cognitive maps[350] and the dramatic perspective[351]. The interpretative approach describes organisational reality which is entangled in the hermeneutic circle. The movement of thoughts is what leads to understanding, anticipating the sense of the whole from the perspective of its elements, and constructing the sense of individual elements within the

---

346 E. Babbie, The Practice of Social Research, Wadsworth Publishing; 13th edition, 2012

347 S. Sampson, Money without Culture, Culture without Money: Eastern Europe`s Nouveux Riches, in: *World View. Political Behaviour and Economy in the Post-communist Transition*, Co-Editor Birgit Muller, vol. 3, no. 1, 1994, p. 10.

348 D.A. Schön, Organizational Learning, in: *Beyond Method. Strategies for Social Research*, ed. G. Morgan, Sage, Beverly Hills, London, New Delhi 1983, pp. 115–128.

349 G.R. Jones, Life History Methodology, in: *Beyond Method. Strategies for Social Research*, ed. G. Morgan, Sage, Beverly Hills, London, New Delhi 1983, pp. 147–159.

350 M.G. Bougon, Uncovering Cognitive Maps. The Self-Q Technique, in: *Beyond Method. Strategies for Social Research*, red. G. Morgan, Sage, Beverly Hills, London, New Delhi 1983, pp. 173–188.

351 I.L. Mangham, M.A. Overington, Dramatism and the Theatrical Metaphor, *in*: *Beyond Method. Strategies for Social Research*, ed. G. Morgan, Sage, Beverly Hills, London, New Delhi 1983, pp. 219–233.

unity of the whole. The application of the interpretative project to management science leads to a functional view of the organisational process, which can be considered from the point of view of the creation and interpretation of strategy, organisational structure and the development of organisational culture.

5.3 Interpretative vision of culture in management

The interpretative-symbolic paradigm is often used in the research into organisational cultures. A vast majority of works and scientific research, being an alternative to functionalism, are based on interpretative assumptions. Relatively little research into organisational culture is based on the paradigm of radical structuralism (CMS) or postmodernism (POST). The interpretative approach spread in organisational research in the 1980s and the 1990s, as a result of an increase in the popularity of qualitative research methods and a gradual absorption of the works of other social sciences and humanities, including mostly sociology and cultural anthropology.

Looking for the most important features distinguishing the interpretative-symbolic paradigm in relation to organisational culture, one can use the comparison with the functionalist paradigm (Tab. 23).

Interpretative theories focus on the description of correlations in complex social and organisational structures, departing from the neopositivist cause and effect pattern. The key to the creation of a scientific theory is to understand, to capture the meaning from the perspective of an involved observer or an organisation member[352]. Theories are not supposed to be created in the spirit of objectivism and axiological neutrality, but should highlight the intersubjective differentiation of senses and interpretations of different organisational actors. Many theories in management science on organisational culture, human resources management, managerial processes and change management are based on the assumptions of the interpretative approach. The methodology of the interpretative approach is related to the project of idiographic science, which can be identified with the emic approach. The idiographic way of practicing science means focusing on unique descriptions and analysing individual cases as characteristic. Unlike nomothetic science, idiographic science does not strive for generalisations[353]. K. Pike proposed a diversification of human linguistic

352 L. Sulkowski, Interpretative Approach in Management Sciences, *Argumenta Oeconomica*, no. 2, 2009.

353 H. Thomae, The Nomothetic-Idiographic Issue: Some Roots and Recent Trends, *International Journal of Group Tensions*, 1999, 28(1), 187–215.

Tab. 23: Interpretative-symbolic paradigm vs. functionalist paradigm of culture in management. Source: Own work.

Criterion	Interpretative-symbolic paradigm	Neopositivist-functionalist-systemic paradigm
Epistemological orientation	Emic, intersubjective perspective, idiographic science	Etic, quasi-objectivist perspective, nomothetic science
Essence of culture	Network of meanings and interpretations, integrating a social group	Values, norms and believes of a systemic character, commonly accepted in the organisation
Significance of culture in management	Key, the foundation of cognitive and social processes	Significant, one of the variables shaping organisational behaviour
Categories of the cognition of culture	Root metaphor	Internal or external variable
The aims of cultural research in management	Understanding, description, synthesis, stimulation of changes	Generalisation, verification, analysis, forecasting and programming changes
The researcher's attitude towards culture	Participant of the studied phenomena and processes (insider), involved	Objective, external point of view (outsider)
The researcher's attitude towards cultural values	Consciousness entangled in values and culture (axiological position)	Striving for objective cognition, which is free from valuation
The relationships between social and organisational cultures	Mutual permeation, correlations	Values from social culture spread to organisational culture
Culture description	'Thick'[a], vivid, axiological	Quasi-objective, comparable with others
Subcultures	Inherent elements of culture; culture undergoes constant fragmentation and tension	Undesirable elements of culture; culture should be heterogeneous
Relationships between culture elements	Correlations, repetitive and individual	Cause and effect, repetitive
Organisational identity	A derivative of culture, cognitively and pragmatically useful	A useless notion, unnecessary multiplication of notions
Currents of cultural research in management	Interpretive, dramatic, critical, psychodynamic, cognitivist	Comparable cultural studies, functionalist research into organisational culture, neoevolutionism

(*continued on next page*)

Tab. 23: Continued

Criterion	Interpretative-symbolic paradigm	Neopositivist-functionalist-systemic paradigm
Preferred methodology	Descriptive and explanatory or understanding (hermeneutic)	Explanatory – providing predictions based on abstract systems of notions
Preferred methods	Non-standard, qualitative, non-structured, field, anthropological methods	Standard, quantitative, structured, representative, mostly survey methods
Representatives	L. Smircich, G. Morgan, M.J. Hatch, K. Weick, M. Schultz, D.A. Goia, K. Corley, R.P. McDermott, J. Church	G. Hofstede, F. Trompenaars, Triandis, C. Hampden-Turner, E. Schein, R. House, T. Deal, A. Kennedy, T. Peters, Waterman, C. Handy

[a] C. Geertz, '*Thick Description: Toward an Interpretive Theory of Culture*'. In The Interpretation of Cultures: Selected Essays. New York: Basic Books, 1973.

behaviour, taking into consideration the possibility of applying this dichotomy to research into all social activities[354]. Both terms come from fundamental linguistic terms – phonemic and phonetic. This methodological division has gained significance in cultural anthropology and ethnology, but is also vividly reflected in the cultural research of other disciplines, from psychology, sociology and linguistics, to archaeology, medicine and psychiatry. In the case of management science, it is not completely unknown, although it appears only occasionally[355]. The emic vs. etic approach has been used in comparative cultural analyses by such researchers as M. Harris, W. Goodenough, J. Berry, and E. Hall[356]. The dichotomy between emic and etic has become the basis for the development of

354 K. Pike, L. Kenneth, *Language in Relation to a Unified Theory of the Structure of Human Behavior*, 2nd ed. The Hague, Mouton 1967.

355 T. Headland, K. Pike, M. Harris, *Emics and Etics, The Insider/Outsider Debate,* Sage Publications, 1990.

356 M. Harris, *Cultural Anthropology*, 2nd ed. New York: Harper & Row,1987; T.E. Hall, Adumbration as a Feature of Intercultural Communication, In the Ethnography of Communication, 1964; J.J. Gumperz, D. Hymes, *The Ethnography of Communication*, American Anthropologist (special publication) 66(6), Part 2. eds. Pp. 154–163; J.W. Berry, On Cross-Cultural Comparability, *International Journal of Psychology* 1969, 4:119–128; H.W. Goodenough, *Description and Comparison in Cultural Anthropology*, Aldine, Chicago, 1970.

a qualitative, involved and participatory methodology of cultural research, proposed by C. Geertz and called 'thick versus thin description'.

Trying to describe the distinction between emic and etic in cultural research, one can point to two different cognitive perspectives. The epistemological foundation for the emic approach is the interpretative-symbolic paradigm, hermeneutics and phenomenology. The emic approach means looking for the perspective of a culture participant, who understands their culture and is able to treat it analytically (an insider). Participation allows for construction of research categories, set in social reality, which are particular, and not universal. Colloquial, contextual concepts, set in a given culture are primarily for research, and form the discourse subject. The regular research method is the in-depth cultural study, often using interviews, participatory observation and other qualitative and anthropological methods. Examples of the development of methodologies located within the emic approach include C. Geertz's thick description, and the grounded theory of A. Strauss and A. Tourraine's intervention sociology[357]. The etic orientation is set in the neopositivist paradigm, together with its postulates of striving for objectivity and axiological neutrality. In consequence, researchers are external, uninvolved observers who try to distance themselves from the social reality being studied (outsiders). Social realities exist objectively and should be reflected in the research process based on the scientific method. Characteristic features of the etic approach include striving for generalisations, objectivism and looking for a more universal reference framework, drawn from outside culture. Research methods cover a full spectrum of survey and statistical methods, as well as other qualitative and standardised methods used in empirical sociology, psychometrics, evolutionary anthropology, management science and other disciplines. It is worth noting that the creators of the emic\etic concept accepted the fact that both culture participants (insiders) and researchers from outside culture (outsiders) can assume one of the two perspectives by choosing the orientation and the research method[358]. Many researchers believe that being an external observer itself determines the choice of the etic perspective in cultural research.

Research into organisational culture draws inspirations from other scientific disciplines, which take culture as their subject of interest. Thus, the elementary

357 C. Geertz, Thick Description: Toward an Interpretive Theory of Culture. In *The Interpretation of Cultures: Selected Essays*. New York: Basic Books, 1973.; B. Glaser, A. Strauss, *Discovery of Grounded Theory: Strategies for Qualitative Research*, Aldine, Chicago 1967; A. Touraine, *La voix et le regard*, Seulil, Paris 1978.

358 T. Headland, K. Pike, M. Harris, *Emics and Etics, The Insider/Outsider Debate,* Sage Publications, 1990.

methodological differentiation between the emic and etic perspectives is reflected mostly in the cultural research within management[359].

Culture in management, as seen from the interpretative-symbolic perspective, includes mostly those issues concerning:

- Symbolic and interpretative aspects of management,
- Social game and interactions between organisational actors,
- Organisations seen as constructions of the social reality,
- Managerial discourse, the emergence of meanings.

The most important representatives of this orientation, conducting cultural research in management, include L. Smircich, G. Morgan, M.J. Hatch, M. Shultz, and B. Czarniawska[360].

In the research into organisational cultures, the perspective of symbolic interactionism is multi-current and methodologically diverse, although generally it can be identified with the qualitative methodology[361]. It covers organisational anthropology and ethnology, dramatic methods, as well as psychodynamic and cognitive approaches. The field involves understanding and research into culture using a wide range of interpretative and critical methods, from participatory observation, through metaphorical and narrative methods, to action research. The interpretative-symbolic methodology (emic) is criticised for the radicalism of the assumptions of cultural relativism, which negate searching for cultural universals. Many researchers are sceptical about the lack of standardisation and representativeness of the research, believing its qualitative methods are not rigorous enough. Cultural studies are criticised by many researchers as individual descriptions, which depart from the scientific discourse because of the lack of generalisations.

---

359 D.R. Deniso, What Is the Difference between Organizational Culture and Organizational Climate? A Native's Point of View on a Decade of Paradigm Wars, *The Academy of Management Review*, Vol. 21, No. 3, Jul., 1996, pp. 619–654.

360 L. Smircich, Studying Organisations as Cultures, in: *Beyond Method: Strategies for Social Research*, ed. G. Morgan, Beverly Hills-London-New Delhi 1983; G. Morgan, Paradigms, Metaphors and Puzzle Solving in Organization Theory, *Administrative Science Quarterly*, 25, 1980; M. Schultz, M.J. Hatch, Living with Multiple Paradigms: The Case of Interplay in Organizational Culture Studies, *Academy of Management Review*, no. 4, 1996..

361 N.K. Denzin, Y.S. Lincoln: *The sage handbook of qualitative research*, Third Edition, Sage Publications, London 2005.

To sum up, the cultural discourse of management, practiced on the basis of symbolic interactionism – and despite its internal diversity – has a number of common features, including:

1. Emic epistemology and methodology.
2. Idiographic vision of science.
3. Criticism of the instrument al approach to culture, characteristic of functionalism.
4. Cultural relativism.
5. Social constructivism.
6. Culture as a root metaphor in an organisation.
7. Management understood as a symbolic activity.
8. Social and processual understanding of management.
9. Meanings and identity management.
10. Defragmentation of organisational culture and a significant role of subcultures.
11. Entanglement in praxis.
12. Everyday epistemology.
13. Discourse locality.
14. Anthropological and ethnological methodology of research.

Qualitative cognitive and pragmatic methodology.

5.4 Organisation identity and organisational culture

The controversial notion of organisational culture and the development of the interpretative-symbolic paradigm in management have led to an increase in interest in the concept of organisational identity. In the subject literature, organisational identity is treated in two ways. Some authors believe it is located in the cultural current and is a cognitively valuable notion that can be used together with organisational culture. On the other hand, other researchers have indicated that organisational identity could become the core of the cultural discourse, and even substitute the vague notion of organisational culture, so it is perhaps worth attempting to assess the possibilities for application of the concept of organisational identity in the cultural current in management[362].

---

362 M.J. Hatch, M. Schultz, Living with Multiple Paradigms. The Case of Paradigm Interplay in Organizational Culture Studies, *Academy of Management Review*, 1996. M.J. Hatch, M. Schultz, "A cultural perspective on corporate branding." *Brand culture* (2006): 15-31.

Both collective and individual identity belong to the most important concepts in social sciences and humanities. The concept of 'identity' itself is deeply rooted in the interpretative-symbolic paradigm, commonly used by the creators of idea, such as G.H. Mead and H. Blumer[363]. The originators of symbolic interactionism described identity as the 'concept of the self'[364] – a symbolic interpretation of individuals referring to who they believe they are and who they would like to be[365], as well as all subject constructs, referring to oneself, and not just a simple sum of the elements, but their synthesis[366]. 'Identity' is a significant notion for the social sciences, but it is ambiguous and forms a 'family of words'[367]. When considering the extensive literature and research of the concept of identity, the classics: G.H. Mead, H. Tajfel and J. Turner[368], and E. Goffman have to be mentioned[369]. The interactionist understanding of identity was originally derived from sociology, but with time, spread to field such as social psychology, cultural anthropology and management science. It occupies a level characteristic of their research issues in each of these sciences. For example, psychology is more concerned with individual identity, sociology, while anthropology - with collective identities, and management science - with organisational identity.

The postmodern and critical approaches to the issue of identity were elaborated with post-structuralism, thanks to M. Foucault, J.-F. Lyotard, J. Derrida[370]. The most significant aspects of the postmodern view on identity are related to defragmentation, deconstruction, internal contradiction and paradox. On the other hand, the critical understanding, closely related to postmodernism, focuses on the understanding of identity as a kind of 'prison' for 'ego' that disciplines

363 G.H. Mead, *Mind Self and Society from the Standpoint of a Social Behaviorist*, Chicago: University of Chicago, 1934.

364 A. Brittan, *The Privatized World*, Routledge and Kegan Paul, London 1977, p. 102.

365 H.R. Tomé,, F. Bariaud, *La structure de l'identité à l'adolescence*, in: 'Identités collectives et changements sociaux', red. P. Tap, Privat, Toulouse 1980, p. 61..

366 H. Bausinger, Senseless Identity, in: *Identity: Personal and Socio-Cultural. A Symposium*, 'Acta Universitatis Upsaliensis', Uppsala, 1983, p. 337,.

367 F. François, *Identité et hétérogénite de l'espase discursif*, in: 'Identités collectives et changements sociaux', ed. P. Tap, Privat, Toulouse 1980, p. 345,.

368 H. Tajfel, J. Turner, An Integrative Theory of Intergroup Conflict, in: *The Social Psychology of Intergroup Relations*, ed. W.G. Austin, S. Worchel, Oxford University Press, Oxford 1979.

369 E. Goffman, *The Presentation of Self in Everyday Life*, University of Edinburgh Social Sciences Research Centre, 1959

370 M. Foucault, *Power Knowledge Selected Interviews & Other Writings*, Random House, New York 2000.

and sanctions ways of expression. In the critical sense, identity, although disintegrated, can be an object of different forms of manipulation, hiding the striving for dominance and wielding of power[371].

In management science, the concept of 'organisational identity' is quite new, emerging only in the 1980s and starting to spread at the end of the 20th century. This may also be the reason also why interpretative, postmodern and critical approaches to organisational identity grew at the same time.

Studies of identity, carried out within social psychology and sociology, concern the creation and development of the 'social self' by individuals. But should they be conducted at the level of a collective actor, i.e. the organisation?

There are many scholars who prefer to transfer the notion of identity to the level of community, including organisations. R. Jenkins uses the concept of collectively shared identities[372]. M.J. Hatch and M. Schultz draw on G.H. Mead's concept, and also say that organisations have identities ('subjective self' and 'objective self')[373]. J. Dutton and J. Dukerich describe the process of the reflection of organisational identity in the organisation's image[374]. Thus, it is clear that the idea of identity is becoming rooted in the theory of management science.

Organisational identity is the response from organisation members to questions such as 'Who are we as an organisation?', and 'Who we would like to be?' If we believe that an organisation is something more than a collection of individual actions, it seems logical to look for social manifestations of organisation, such as culture, management, strategy and structure. Describing identity as a 'symbolic, collective interpretation of people who create an organisation, with reference to what organisation is and what it would like to be' seems clear. However, in order for the notion to be fruitful, it identity must be distinguished from culture, and image from organisational mission and vision.

Under stable circumstances, organisational identity remains the subject of a collective agreement that is often implied. The issue becomes explicit only when tensions and changes arise, when the questions of key values re-occur and contradictory visions of the organisation's development clash. S. Albert

---

371 B. Czarniawska, H. Höpfl (ed.), *Casting the Other: the Production and Maintenance of Inequalities in Work Organizations*, Routledge, London 2002.

372 R. Jenkins, *Social Identity*, Routledge, London 1996.

373 M.J. Hatch, M. Schultz, The Dynamics of Organisational Identity, in: *Organisational Identity. A Reader*, ed. M.J. Hatch, M. Schultz, Oxford University Press, Oxford – New York 2004, p. 380.

374 J. Dutton, J. Dukerich, Keeping Eye on the Mirror: Image and Identity in Organisational Adaptation, *Academy of Management Journal*, 1991, no. 34, pp. 517–554.

and D.A. Whetten claimed that the effects of studies are the result of a collective agreement on values, organisational culture, action philosophy, orientation, market position, the domain of the activity, mission, vision and organisational membership as manifestations of organisational identity[375]. Thus, organisational identity should meet three key criteria: firstly, the criterion of determining key organisational features. Organisational identity should reflect its essence and the basic existential issues around which the consensus between organisational members was developed. Secondly, the criterion of differentiation: organisational identity exists when the members of the organisation feel distinct from others. They identify themselves with the organisation, define their boundaries, the criteria for membership and exclusion. And thirdly, the criterion of temporal continuity: an organisation is integrated by legal and managerial conventions, which are kept thanks to the conviction of the organisation's members and other people from its environment that there is continuity to the organisation's existence, despite changes[376]. These three criteria, proposed by S. Albert and D.A. Whetten, can be supplemented with a fourth: organisational identity, which is a supra-individual and social phenomenon. The distinguishing sense of existence, maintained by the organisation's members in time (esprit du corps) is a manifestation of the functioning of a social group, and not only of selected individuals (such as owners, managers or other interested parties).

Can it be possible to analyse the social aspects of organisation without the notion of 'identity'? B.E. Ashforth and F. Mael propose that the process of gaining social identity is a necessary condition for undertaking any group action. The 'psychological group' is defined in the categories of membership. Identifying oneself with a group is at the same time the most important mechanism of belonging. When discussing the manifestations of the emergence of social identity, one can mention a group's sense of difference, its striving for its continuation, and group prestige[377]. The concept of identity is closely related to identification, that is identifying oneself with a group. However, as with most studies of organisational culture and leadership, identifying oneself with an organisation used to be taken as internalisation of its values and involvement. The two phenomena are different as identification with a group means identifying oneself

375 S. Albert, D.A. Whetten, Organizational Identity, in: '*Organisational Identity. A Reader*', ed. M.J. Hatch, M. Schultz, Oxford University Press, Oxford – New York 2004, p. 90.

376 Ibid., pp. 90–91.

377 B.E. Ashforth, F. Mael, Social Identification Theory and the Organisation, in: *Organisational Identity. A Reader*, ed. M.J. Hatch, M. Schultz, Oxford University Press, Oxford – New York 2004, pp. 134–142.

with it, while internalisation is the acceptance and assimilation of values shared by the group. Identification with an organisation does not necessarily lead to the internalisation of the organisation's values, while identification with the whole organisation does not condition identification with the members of this organisation. Being involved refers to making a relatively large effort while working for the organisation, the source of which can be, but does not need to be, identification with a group. Distinguishing these three notions makes it possible to view identification as a source of organisational identity, and to internalisation as a mechanism of its consolidation and spreading to trainees. Organisational identity is developed in the processes of communication and negotiation of meanings, which implies that it is strongly rooted on the level of groups and teams, although according to many authors its presence at the level of the whole organisation gives rise to theoretical problems[378]. Therefore, it appears that the topic of identity should not be missed in the analyses of the organisation's functioning. The final question is whether there exists any purpose in the creation of the theory 'organisational identity', understood as a whole, and the study of the processes of the creation, maintenance and changes of group identity.

The issue of the differentiation between organisational identity and culture is problematic, as descriptions of organisational culture are so broad that they usually cover organisational identity as well, at least to a some extent. This is especially true of the definitions of organisational culture developed within the interpretative-symbolic paradigm (Tab. 24).

Comparing the descriptions of organisational culture to the criteria for defining organisational identity, one can see similarities, but also a number of differences. All quoted definitions concern temporal continuity and social constitution of organisational culture, which is also a description of organisational identity. Additionally, more recent definitions fulfil the first criterion, describing culture, similarly to identity, as key values ('essence'). The difference is the lack of a criterion that would distinguish organisations based on a unique configuration of values, which is a feature of identity. Despite the fact that the definitions of organisational culture and identity are similar, it seems that it would be useful to distinguish these two notions. Strategor distinguished culture from identity, locating culture on the level of the symbolic space (ideas, values, norms, beliefs, myths), and identity on the level of the individual interpretation of this

378 Ibid., p. 150.

Tab. 24: Definitions of organisational culture and the criteria for defining organisational identity. Source: Own work.

Author	**Organisational culture definitions**	**Comparison to organisational identity**
R. and J. Likert	The dominant pattern of values, myths, beliefs, assumptions, norms, their manifestations in language, symbols, artefacts, technology, aims and practices of management, feelings, attitudes, activities and interactions[a].	Criteria met: the 'essence' of the organisation and temporal continuity.
E. Schein	A model of shared, fundamental assumptions, developed by a given group by solving problems of adaptation to the environment and internal integration. This model can be regarded as binding. It is instilled in new members as the correct way of solving problems[b].	Criteria met: the 'essence' of the organisation, temporal continuity and social constitution.
G. Hofstede	'Mind programming' of the organisation's members, which means a collection of organisational values, norms and rules implemented by the group[c].	Criteria met: differentiation, temporal continuity.
C. Siehl and J. Martin	Organisational culture can be seen as the glue which binds the organisation by sharing patterns of meanings. Culture is concentrated around the values, beliefs and expectations shared by the organisation's members[d].	Criteria met: the 'essence' of the organisation, temporal continuity and social constitution.
P.M. Blau	A kind of set of the unwritten rules of the social game in an organisation, which allow the participants of its social life to understand the organisation and identify with it[e].	Criteria met: differentiation, social constitution.
A. Pettigrew	Culture is a system of publically and commonly accepted meanings by a given group at a given time. This system of notions, forms, categories and images allows people to interpret their own situation[f].	Criteria met: the 'essence' of the organisation, temporal continuity and social constitution.
J. van Maanen	Culture refers to knowledge which is transmitted to group members in order to share it; knowledge of this type is used to inform, set, shape and bear responsibility for routine and non-routine activities of the members of a given culture. Culture is expressed (or constituted) only by activities or words of its own members, and has to be interpreted by organisation employees. Culture as such is not visible, it can only be seen by its manifestations[g].	Criteria met: the 'essence' of the organisation, differentiation, temporal continuity and social constitution.

Tab. 24: Continued

Author	Organisational culture definitions	Comparison to organisational identity
L. Smircich	Webs of meanings woven by people in the process of organising[h].	Criterion met: social constitution.
G. Morgan	Organisational culture usually refers to a development pattern which is reflected by social systems of knowledge, ideology, values, laws and everyday rituals[i].	Criterion met: social constitution.
D. Denison	Culture refers to deep structures of organisations, which are rooted in the values, beliefs and assumptions of the organisation's members. Meaning is constituted by socialisation with different groups gathered in the workplace. Interaction reconstructs the symbolic world which gives cultures large stability and an uncertain character and fragility, rooted in the dependence of the system on different activities[j].	Criteria met: the 'essence' of the organisation, temporal continuity and social constitution.
R. Deshapande, R. Parasurman	Unwritten, often subconsciously perceived rules that fill the gap between unwritten and actual events in an organisation[k].	Criterion met: social constitution.

[a] R. Likert, J. Likert, *New Ways of Managing Conflict*, New York: McGraw-Hill, 1976.

[b] E. Schein, *Organisational Culture and Leadership*, Jossey-Bass, San Francisco 1982, p. 12.

[c] G. Hofstede, *Culture and organizations--Software of the mind.* McGraw-Hill, 1997.

[d] C. Siehl, J. Martin, *The role of symbolic management: How can managers effectively transmit organizational culture?*, in: J. Hunt, D. Hosking, C. Schriesheim, R. Stewart (eds). *Leaders and Managers: International Perspectives on Managerial Behaviour and Leadership*, Elmsford, NY: Pergamon., 1984., pp. 227–39.

[e] P. M. Blau, R. Scott, *Formal organizations: A comparative approach*, Stanford University Press, 2003, p. 298.

[f] A. M. Pettigrew, *On studying organizational cultures*, Administrative Science Quarterly, Vol. 24, No. 4, Qualitative Methodology, 1979, pp. 570–581.

[g] J. van Maanen, *Tales of the Field: On Writing Ethnography*, Series: (CGWEP) Chicago Guides to Writing, Editing, and Publishing, 1988.

[h] L. Smircich, *Studying Organisations as Cultures*, in: G. Morgan, *Beyond Method: Strategies for Social Research*, Beverly Hills-London-New Delhi 1983; C. Geertz, *The Interpretation of Cultures*, Basic Books New York 1973, p. 39

[i] G. Morgan, *Images of Organization*, Thousand Oaks, CA: Sage Publications, 1997.

[j] D. Denison, *What is the difference between organizational culture and organizational climate? A native's point of view on a decade of paradigm wars*, Academy of Management Review, 21(3), 1996, pp. 1–36.

[k] R. Deshapande, R. Parasurman, *Linking Corporate Culture to Strategic Planning*, in: 'Organizacja i Kierowanie', 1987, no. 6.

space – the external image (imagination, passion, inhibitions)[379]. This definition applies to the psycho-social understanding of identity.

Deliberations on relatively permanent and key values distinguishing organisations refer not only to the notion of organisational identity, but also mission, vision, corporate culture and image. It is necessary to distinguish these notions and find common points.

Organisational mission and vision are notions drawn from strategic management, and are defined in different ways. L.W. Rue and P.G. Holland believe that mission determines the essence and meanings of the organisation's existence by formulating its most general aims and fields of activity[380]. According to J. Brilman, vision is a short formula, detailing the main organisational vocation and aims[381]. The organisational mission should be based on organisational culture and identity, although it has to include only those values that are considered worthy of spreading, in order to create a positive organisational image. Vision is usually created by the managers, but does not need to be spread and serves as a projection of the organisation's development, based on its chosen aims and values. Thus, both these terms are close in meaning, being realised, forward-looking and expressed aims and key values. Mission and vision are purposefully created, realised and usually spread with the aim to be fulfilled in the future. Thus, mission is different from organisational identity, although it often plays an important role in its formulation[382]. One can see the relationship between the mission of an organisation and its identity and culture. Organisational culture and identity are based on key values, and are created thanks to the correlations between spontaneous and intentional collective activities.

M.J. Hatch and M. Schultz clearly distinguish between the culture, identity and image of an organisation, pointing to the correlations between these elements. Organisational culture is neither fully culture-conditioned, nor fully dependent on the organisation's image, as it is formed by the correlations between these two spheres (Fig. 9)[383].

---

379 *Strategor: politique générale de l'entreprise: stratégie, structure, décision, identité.* Dunod, 2005., p. 503.

380 L.W. Rue, P.G. Holland, *Strategic Management. Concepts and Experiences*, McGraw-Hill, New York 1989, pp. 7–8.

381 Brilman, Jean, and Jacques Hérard. *Les meilleures pratiques de management: dans le nouveau contexte économique mondial.* Editions Eyrolles, 2006., p. 79.

382 L. Leuthesser, C. Kohli, Corporate Identity: The Role of Mission Statements, *Business Horizons*, May-June 1997, p. 59.

383 M.J. Hatch, M.S. Schultz, Scaling the Tower of Babel: Relational Differences Between Identity, Image and Culture in Organizations, in: *The Expressive Organisation: Linking*

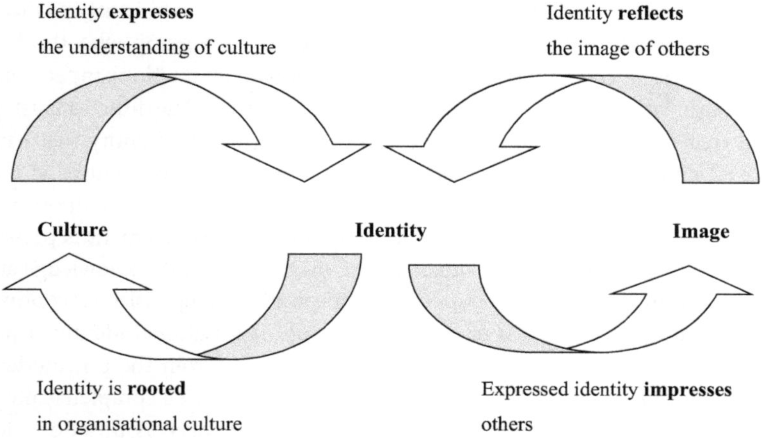

Fig. 9: The dynamics of an organisational identity. Source: M.J. Hatch, M. Schultz, *The Dynamics of Organisational Identity*, in: 'Organisational Identity. A Reader', ed. M.J. Hatch, M. Schultz, Oxford University Press, Oxford – New York 2004, p. 379.

The correlations between organisational culture, identity and image are reflected in four interpretative processes, which take place between these spheres. The first is the mirroring of the organisation's images, created by others within its identity. Mirroring links the organisational image (the way it is seen by others – the environment) with its identity. The second is the process of the reflection of identity in the organisational culture. Identity leaves its mark on the shape of the organisation's values, norms and cultural patterns, and so it has to be set in culture. This leads to the expression of organisational culture in identity. Organisational culture is known and spread by the expressions of identity, based on culture. On the other hand, identity impresses others through image, and the whole model forms feedback[384]. It seems that it would be useful to add mission and vision, which are a kind of idealised image of an organisation and its future, although in most cases these are created for internal purposes only. Thus, apart from the organisational image, mission and vision are also used to manage expressions and should be located on the proposed diagram next to image.

Identity, Reputation and the Corporate Brand, Oxford University Press, Oxford 2000, pp. 24–25.

384 M.J. Hatch, M. Schultz, The Dynamics of Organisational Identity, in: *Organisational Identity. A Reader*, ed. M.J. Hatch, M. Schultz, Oxford University Press, Oxford – New York 2004, p. 379.

Most researchers believe that the concept of organisational identity is rooted in the interpretative-symbolic paradigm. There are also many who think that although it is a concept stemming from symbolic interactionism, it can be interpreted within other cognitive perspectives as well. The functionalist paradigm treats organisational identity as an objective, material entity that can be managed and measured[385]. The interpretative approach treats identity as a network of meanings and social communication, being a subject of temporary and partial agreement of the organisational group. Identity management is pointless, but it is possible to manage the organisation, making use of the knowledge about changes within its identity. Postmodernist inspirations emphasise discontinuity, ambiguity and the vagueness of the categories of organisational identity, leading to fundamental cognitive and pragmatic limitations[386]. From the postmodernist perspective, organisational identity management seems to be a completely utopian project[387]. A summary of the key differences between the ways organisational identity is understood within different cognitive approaches can be found in Tab. 25.

The assumption of such a way of thinking and distinguishing organisational identity allows us to use the concept of 'identity' in management science. But is applying the concept of organisational identity together with the already rooted notion of organisational culture promising in cognitive terms? It is worth considering the applications of the concept of organisational identity. Organisational identity is a manifestation of an organisation's community's attempts at broadening its influence, and at the same is a reflection of the internal game of interests. This is why it is unstable, changeable and expressed in different ways, depending on the context. This is reflected in the concept of multiplicity and flexibility of organisational identity[388]. M.G. Pratt and A. Rafaeli propose a multi-layer concept of organisational identity, the manifestation of which is the research into organisational symbols and artefacts, such as clothes and dress[389].

---

385 B.M. van Riel Cees, J.M.T. Balmer, Corporate Identity: The Concept, Its Measurement and Management, *European Journal of Ma*rketing, 1997, Vol. 31 Iss: 5/6, pp. 340 – 355

386 R.G. Dunn, *Identity of Postmodernity Crises*, University of Minnesota Press, Minneapolis 1998, pp. 51–80.

387 M. Parker, *Utopia and the Organizational Imagination: Outopia*, 'Utopia and Organization', ed. M. Parker, Blackwell Publishing, Oxford 2002.

388 M.J. Hatch, M. Schultz (ed.), *Organisational Identity. A Reader*, Oxford University Press, Oxford – New York 2004, pp. 4–5.

389 M.G. Pratt, A. Rafaeli, Organizational Dress as a Symbol of Multilayered Social Identities, in: *Organisational Identity. A Reader*, ed. M.J. Hatch, M. Schultz, Oxford University Press, Oxford – New York 2004, pp. 275–312.

Tab. 25: Three perspectives on organisational identity. Source: Based on D.A. Whetten, P.C. Godfrey (ed.), *Identity in Organisations. Building Theory through Conversations*, Sage, London 1998, pp. 42–43.

	Functionalist perspective	**Interpretative perspective**	**Postmodern perspective**
Key problem	How does OI influence the activities of organisations and people?	How do we socially create the sense of who we are ('we')?	1. Problematisation, breaking the continuity, defragmentation of the sense of identity.
Identity definition	1. Institutionalised belief in who we are. 2. Objective dimensions – aims, organisational rules, core activity.	Constantly socially renegotiated collection of meanings of who we are as an organisation.	Temporary and fragmented reflection on who we believe we are as an organisation.
Basic assumptions	1. OI is a social fact. 2. OI is objective, observable and can be manipulated.	1. People need to agree on stable meanings. 2. OI is constructed socially. 3. Social groups strive for OI by agreeing on common meanings.	1. Vagueness of meanings. 2. OI is a random and temporary collection of meanings. 3. OI takes the form of a paradox. 4. Multiplicity and diversity.
The aims of research into OI	1. To discover 2. To describe 3. To measure 4. To use (manage)	To reveal the senses and structures of the creation of meanings, negotiated between the organisation members.	1. To provoke 2. To encourage reflection 3. To give voice to 'the silent'
Data	1. Observing the activities that influence OI 2. Analysing statements 3. Demographic studies 4. Psychometric data	1. Data significant to the organisation members - symbols 2. Data significant to researchers: - symbols - interpretation patterns	1. Language and discourse 2. Cracks, discontinuity 3. Lacks, absence
Consequences	1. The key significance of OI – key values and beliefs are instilled	1. The key significance of OI – group agrees on key meanings	1. The key significance of OI – constantly changing

(*continued on next page*)

Tab. 25: Continued

	Functionalist perspective	Interpretative perspective	Postmodern perspective
	2. The permanence of OI – it is difficult to change	2. The permanence of OI – social context determines the permanence	2. The permanence of OI – constantly deconstructed and reconstructed
	3. Distinction through OI – accepted and manageable	3. Distinction through OI – introduction of categories of similarities and differences	3. Distinction through OI – respect for 'others', fragmentation
Metaphors	1. Subject 2. Assets, resources	1. Brain: hologram 2. Improvisation in a scene	Collage – a combination of unexpected elements

(OI – *organisational identity*)

D.A. Gioia, M. Schultz and K. Corley describe the 'adaptive instability' of the ways organisational identity is defined, which on the one hand provides for maintenance of the continuity of the sense of belonging to the organisation, but on the other, to preparation for changes in its environment[390]. Identity work can be found in all organisational interactions, in the form of the routine maintenance of existing patterns of action, as well as their interpretation and radical changes[391]. The research conducted by N. Monin and B. Czarniawska-Joerges explores the concept of the narrative creation of organisational identity[392]. Another promising idea is the analysis of the relationships between the creation

390 D.A. Gioia, M. Schultz and K. Corley, Organisational Identity, Image and Adaptive Instability, in: *Organisational Identity. A Reader*, ed. M.J. Hatch, M. Schultz, Oxford University Press, Oxford – New York 2004, pp. 349–376.

391 R.P. McDermott, J. Church, Making Sense and Feeling Good: The Ethnography of Communication and Identity Work, in: *Communication and Identity*, ed. L. Thayer, 'Communication', vol. 2, no. 2.

392 N. Monin, *Management Theory. A Critical and reflective Reading*, Routledge, London, New York 2004, pp. 167, 190–191; B. Czarniawska-Joerges, Narratives of Individual and Organisational Identities, in: *Organisational Identity. A Reader*, ed. M.J. Hatch, M. Schultz, Oxford University Press, Oxford – New York 2004, pp. 407–435.

of power, organisational control and identity[393], as well as between communication and identity[394].

Another very interesting area of research is the search for dysfunctions in the process of an organisation's identity's development. M.J. Hatch and M. Schultz mention two basic options: organisational narcissism and organisational hyper-adaptation. Following A.D. Brown, these authors define organisational narcissism as the organisation's lack of will or ability to respond to its own image, existing in the environment[395]. This is related to a lack of interest in the opinions of interested external parties and a focus on maintaining its own self-esteem, fantasising about its own grandeur and having a disturbed perception and interpretation of information from the environment. M.J. Hatch and M. Schulz diagnose narcissism as a sign of distorted organisational identity, characterised by the fact it is dominated by references to organisational culture. In the case of the relationships between culture, identity and image, the last of the elements loses its significance. The mechanism of organisational narcissism includes the focus on the creation of a strong culture, reflecting identity in culture, expressing culture through identity and neglecting image. Narcissism is dangerous to organisations. The authors use the example of Royal Dutch Shell, which ignored the outcry of ecologists against their disposal of an old oil rig in the North Sea. Shell's engineering culture and identity led to a narcissistic feedback, which completely rejected the information about the deteriorating image of the company. Only after a series of crises did the company begin to reflect, opening itself to interested parties and rejecting its narcissism. The opposite of narcissism is organisational hyper-adaptation, which means a close link between the organisation's identity and image. Organisations which focus on external image, the opinions of interested parties and market research results can lose the sense of their existence. The necessity to constantly adapt to external changes makes a company lose contact with its cultural heritage. According to M.J. Hatch and M. Schultz, dangers entailed by hyper-adaptation include the loss of continuity, outer-direction and the weakening of the organisational culture. Examples of hyper-adaptive

393 M. Alvesson, H. Willmott, Identity Regulations as Organisational Control Producing the Appropriate Individual, in: *Organisational Identity. A Reader*, ed. M.J. Hatch, M. Schultz, Oxford University Press, Oxford – New York 2004, pp. 436–465.

394 G. Cheney, L.T. Christensen, Organisational Identity: Linkages Between Internal and External Communication, in: *Organisational Identity. A Reader*, ed. M.J. Hatch, M. Schultz, Oxford University Press, Oxford – New York 2004, pp. 510–557.

395 A.D. Brown, Narcissism, Identity and Legitimacy, *Academy of Management Review*, no. 22, 1997, pp. 643–686.

activities include the attempt to replace 'classic' Coca-Cola with New Coke and the temporary breaking with the cultural heritage of such companies as Gucci and Yves Saint Laurent[396]. However, opinions about the 'loss of organisational culture' differ. M. Alvesson suggests that substituting organisational culture with a rapidly changing image, dependent on the customers' perception, is a standard element of modern organisations' flexibility and is not a significantly dysfunctional feature[397]. Regardless of opinion though, research into the relationships between organisational culture, identity and image seems to be an interesting, as yet inexhaustible area.

Some authors use notions close to 'organisational identity', such as 'organisational character'[398]. However, it seems that this work has not been successful. The notion of identity, despite its ambiguity, is rooted in the discourse of the interpretative social sciences and thus can be transferred to management. There is much research and numerous analyses of organisations, drawing from the current of organisational anthropology and organisational sociology. This is why, at the current stage, multiplying the notions that are supposed to synthetically describe the essence of an organisation seems useless, unless we assume that it is a kind of metaphor, the basic aim of which is the stimulation of thinking, and not explanation or understanding.

In summary, it can be said that organisational identity is a new concept in management, and is developing fast. Researchers function mostly within alternative paradigms to the neopositivist-functionalist approach, which dominates in management science. Most concepts are based on symbolic interactionism, but there are also postmodern and critical references to organisational identity. Some especially promising applications concern organisational culture, leadership and maintenance of an organisation's image.

396 Ibid., pp. 398–399.

397 M. Alvesson, Organisation: From Substance to Image, *Organization Studies*, no. 11, pp. 373–394.

398 V. Srinivasan, Organisational character: the key to transforming organisations of the future, *Human Resources Development and Management*, vol. 3, no. 1, 2003.

6 The radical vision of culture in management

6.1 Critical management studies

Critical Management Studies are a relatively new perspective, which crystallised only at the beginning of the 1990s. The pioneer works undertaking the issue of ideological demystifications, based on the structure of dominance in management, had already appeared by the 1970s[399], but over the last two decades Critical Management Studies has taken the form of an institutionalised discourse thanks to a number of publications, research papers, conferences, journals and associations (such as the CMS section of the American Academy of Management)[400].

Reconstruction of the most important assumptions of the critical current allows us to find several common assumptions, forming an internally diverse paradigm of Critical Management Studies. Most of all, it treats management science as a persuasive discourse stemming from capitalist assumptions aimed at maintenance of the existing status quo, based on dominance and exploitation. Critical Management Studies aspire to reveal the truth, in order to question the seemingly objective and natural status of various subjects, including organisational order, managerial power, institutions, managerial practices and identity[401]. This 'denaturalisation' of the managerism discourse leads to a description of oppressive activities and institutions based on dominance, which are often harmful to people and society and hidden within the apparent rationality of management science. The postulate of exposing the interests of different social groups who wield power by controlling the scientific discourse is supposed to result in criticism and a change of existing, unjust social orders. In consequence, the development of the critical current is supposed to develop the awareness, grant the possibility of expression and fulfil the interests of the disadvantaged groups, who are subject to power, such as ethnic and social minorities, and women[402]. Their emancipation is supposed to be accompanied by the mechanisms of symbolic violence, the demystification of the managerism ideology and the departure from

399 H. Braverman, *Labor and Monopoly Capital: The Degradation of Work in the Twentieth Century*, New York: Monthly Review Press 1974.

400 M. Alvesson, H. Willmott (eds), *Critical Management Studies*, London: Sage 1992.

401 M. Alvesson, H. Willmott (eds), *Studying Management Critically*, London: Sage 2003.

402 C. Grey, H.C. Willmott, *Critical Management Studies: A Reader*, Oxford University Press 2005.

irresponsible and instrumental managerial practices. The tools developed by the critical current include deconstruction and denaturalisation of the managerial discourse, critical and reflective analyses of the language of power-wielding, and methods of enhancing the autonomy and self-control of the disadvantaged groups (such as empowerment)[403].

In the case of organisational culture, the critical perspective can be considered in two ways. The first is the broadly understood criticism of organisational culture theory, which has functioned within the social sciences and management since the 1970s. Interpretivists critical of the functionalist approach, which in their opinion is an instrumentalist approach to culture, include L. Smircich, M.J. Hatch, G. Morgan[404]. On the other hand, functionalists are also sceptical of the achievements of alternative paradigms, pointing to their locality, lack of generalisations and methodological weaknesses. Postmodernism is especially criticised, although it is consistently described as an attempt to view culture in management in an anti-theoretical, non-systemic and non-methodological way, which forsakes cognitive ambitions and turns to literature (essay-writing, glossing)[405]. There is also criticism of the representatives of other scientific disciplines, such as cultural anthropology, sociology, cultural science, and even psychology and linguistics[406]. As to the second current, it is a narrowly understood criticism of organisational culture and culture in management – a radical structuralism paradigm (Critical Management Studies)[407]. The critical current is distinguished by radicalism in questioning cognitive, pragmatic and ideological values of the previous output of research into culture within management science. It is a rapidly developing current, becoming more and more significant and making use of most sceptical threads, raised even before the institutionalisation of Critical Management Studies as part of the broadly construed criticism of the cultural management current. It is worth considering the main aspects of the

---

403 M. Parker, *Against Management: Organisation in the Age of Managerialism*. Oxford: Polity 2002.

404 M.J. Hatch, M. Schultz, Living with Multiple Paradigms: The Case of Paradigm Interplay in Organizational Culture Studies, *Academy of Management Review*, 1996, Vol. 21. No. 2, pp. 529–557; G. Morgan, (ed.), *Beyond Method: Strategies for Social Research*, Beverly Hills, California: Sage 1983.

405 G.A. Olson, *Justifying Belief: Stanley Fish and the Work of Rhetoric*, State University of New York Press, 2002, 90 State Street, Suite 700, Albany, NY, 12207.

406 Smircich, Linda. 'Concepts of culture and organizational analysis.' *Administrative science quarterly* (1983): 339–358.

407 M. Alvesson, H. Willmott, *Critical Management Studies*, Sage, London 1992.

criticism because of 1) its institutional crystallization, 2) its increasing significance and 3) the clear, radical position of the representatives of this current.

6.2 The critical understanding of organisational culture

Organisational culture has been controversial since the notion first appeared. Thus, the critical reflection is not present only within the critical current of management (Critical Management Studies). However, representatives of the critical current have proposed the most radical and reflective approach, which synthesises a number of currents that have appeared in previous criticism[408].

The analysis presented below uses issues undertaken by the representatives of Critical Management Studies and researchers of other currents. The most important problems of organisational culture, raised as part of the critical current, mostly concern:

- Culture as a tool of dominance and oppression,
- Organisational culture as hypostasis and ideology,
- Organisational culture as a pseudo-scientific current and fashion,
- Culture as a mental prison.

CMS raises numerous threads of criticism of the cultural current in management science. These include critical aspects and proposals for theoretical and methodological solutions. The criticism of the output of the cultural current in management is presented with the use of concepts drawn both from CMS and earlier sceptical orientations within the social sciences, such as neo-Marxism, post-structuralism, the Frankfurt School, as well as radical feminism[409].

The aims of CMS can be presented metaphorically, referring to a medical sphere as a process of 'healing' modern organisations, according to the pattern 'diagnosis, shock therapy, convalescence'. Diagnosis is here supposed to identify the 'dark side' of organisational culture, which is the instrumental and repressive treatment of individuals in order to fulfil the interests of the groups who wield power. The shock therapy consists in the dissemination of criticism leading to a revolutionary, or at least evolutionary change, destroying the unjust order and eliminating, or at least reconstructing, the exploitative organisational culture. Convalescence is the implementation of a new cultural project, which assumes

408 M. Rowlinson, S. Procter, *Organizational Culture and Business History*, Organization Studies May 1999 vol. 20 no. 3 369–396.

409 C. Grey, H.C. Willmott, *Critical Management Studies: A Reader*, Oxford University Press, 2005.

the subjectivity of people in the organisation, and justice, thus guaranteeing the emancipation of the disadvantaged groups.

The metaphorical aims of CMS in relation to organisational culture can be presented as *catharsis*. The recuperative shock leads to a transgression and a radical transformation of identity.

The critical aims of CMS include:

- Diagnosis of the oppressiveness of organisational culture,
- Recognising and exposing the ideological function and the creation of false awareness within cultural processes in modern organisations[410],
- Exposing the mechanisms of 'symbolic violence' in cultures and organisations[411],
- Describing the instrumental and manipulative methods, as well as the methods of social engineering of 'culturalism' in organisations[412],
- Presenting the cultural visions of the controlling mechanisms, which move organisations towards the ideal type of 'total institutions',
- Discovery of neo-colonial concepts and practices of international corporations that are hidden under a façade of intercultural management and globalisation processes,
- Exposing the mechanisms of 'mind control', the creation of 'one-dimensional people', controlled by the consumerist culture[413],
- Analysing the entire output of management as a projection of culture which legitimises power and maintains the status quo[414],

---

410 M. Alvesson, S. Deetz, *Critical Theory and Postmodernism Approaches to the Study of Organization*, pp. 191–217 in S. Clegg, C. Hardy, and W. Nord (eds.) *Handbook of Organization Studies*. Thousand Oaks: Sage, 1996; H. Willmott, Breaking the Paradigm Mentality. *Organization Studies*, 1993, Nr 14/5, pp. 681–719.

411 J. Brewis, J. Gavin, *Culture: Broadening the Critical Repertoire* [in:] Alvesson M., Bridgman T., Willmott H. (ed.). *The Oxford Handbook of Critical Management Studies*. Oxford: Oxford University Press 2009.

412 H. Willmott, Strength Is Ignorance; Slavery Is Freedom: Managing Culture in Modern Organizations, Journal of Management *Studies*, 1993, no. 30/4, pp. 515–552.

413 S.A. Deetz, *Democracy in an Age of Corporate Colonization*, State University of New York Press, 1992.

414 D. Lyon, *Theorizing Surveillance: The Panopticon and Beyond - Reference, Information and Interdisciplinary Subjects Series,* Willan Publishing 2006.

- Criticism of the culture of managerial, business and economic education around the world[415].

Criticism is the basis of the CMS current, but its aims go deeper, as they are supposed to lead to radical change. This can be presented as a list of the pragmatic-methodological aims of the cultural current of CMS:

- Creating organisational cultures based on real democracy in organisations,
- Cleansing organisational culture of all signs of violence by the rejection of 'false awareness' or 'enlightened false awareness' ('organisational cynicism'[416]), reflection, managing sensemaking), humanisation and moral and ethical sensitivity[417],
- Improving the social position of disadvantaged groups using emancipatory methods, including empowerment, parity, political correctness[418],
- Implementing emancipation culture on the level of relationships between organisations, within organisations and between employees[419],
- Rejecting the functionalist paradigm and the instrumental mind in cultural interpretations[420],
- Developing qualitative, interpretative and involved methods of research into organisational cultures,
- Creating a reflective and critical organisational culture that would direct the development of organisations, society and people towards the increase in humanisation[421].

---

415 A. Contu, *Critical Management Education* w: Alvesson M., Bridgman T., Willmott H. (ed.). *The Oxford Handbook of Critical Management Studies.* Oxford: Oxford University Press 2009.

416 P. Sloterdijk, *Critique of Cynical Reason*; Minneapolis, University of Minnesota Press, 1988

417 H. Willmott, Breaking the Paradigm Mentality. *Organization Studies*', 1993, no. 14/5, pp. 681–719.

418 M. Alvesson, H. Willmott, *Making Sense of Management.* A Critical Introduction. London: Sage, 1996.

419 T. Potterfield, *The Business of Employee Empowerment: Democracy and Ideology in the Workplace*, Quorum Books, 1999.

420 M. Alvesson, *Understanding Organizational Culture*, London: Sage, 2002.

421 H. Willmott, *Strength Is Ignorance; Slavery Is Freedom: Managing Culture in Modern Organizations*, *Journal of Management Studies*, 1993, No. 30/4, pp. 515–552.

1. The oppressiveness of organisational culture.
   According to the representatives of CMS, organisational culture is not axiologically neutral and reflects the structure of power. It is oppressive, because it fulfils the interests of some groups at the expense of others. It disfavours people who are subject to power, and sanctions an unjust order. Critical researchers generally agree with interpretivists, assuming that organisational culture can be understood as a root metaphor, which refers to what an organisation is, and not what it owns. As a consequence of this perspective, cultural problems become fundamental to the organisation's functioning in all its dimensions[422]. Thus, the oppressiveness of culture translates directly into the repressiveness of organisations.
2. Ideology and 'false awareness' in the cultural processes of modern organisations.
   By promoting indoctrination and manipulation, culture is a mechanism for wielding power, which is of a systemic character. Owners, managers and employees do not have to realise the injustice and repressiveness of culture in modern organisations. Oppressive culture is assimilated, considered natural, obvious, and so impossible to be changed. Culture becomes an ideology and builds 'false awareness', which rationalises – for the purpose of those in power and those subject to it – the unjust order as the only possible option, the alternative to which can only be chaos and destruction[423].
3. 'Symbolic violence' in organisations.
   Modern organisational, managerial and consumerist culture has become the most important tool for control and wielding power. This tool is very effective and dangerous, because it is concealed and often works implicitly and in a systemic way, rather than personally. It is not the bare-faced violence of physical repression, but subtle mechanisms of control and social self-control, which – following P. Bourdieu – can be called 'symbolic violence'[424]. Language, systems of values and norms, organisational structures and communication networks are all hierarchical and control minds in the interest of the owners of the financial, political, relational and cultural capital. 'Symbolic violence' through culture, which – according to the root metaphor – is an organisation, has spread to all aspects

---

422 D. Knights, H.C. Willmott, Organizational Culture as Management Strategy: A Critique and Illustration from the Financial Services Industry, *International Studies of Management & Organization*, Vol. XVII. No. 3, 1987, pp. 40–63.

423 N. Monin, *Management Theory. A Critical and reflective Reading*, Routledge, London, New York 2004 p. 191.

424 P. Bourdieu, *Espace social et pouvoir symbolique*, in: *Choses dites*, Minuit, Paris 1987.

of organising[425]. Using the Foucauldian metaphor, culture becomes a Panopticon which controls organisations and instils systems of self-control in their members[426].

4. Instrumental methods of 'culturism' in organisations.
According to H. Willimott's description, corporations practice 'organisational culturism', which is manifested by the striving for the creation of a monoculture, oriented only towards the fulfilment of the aims and interests of owners and managers[427]. This means regular implementation of practices which integrate organisations, and the promotion of conformism in striving for a strong, homogenous organisational culture[428]. 'Organisational culturalism' is a reflection of the functionalist understanding of culture as a variable subject that can be controlled, and at the same time serve as a tool of control. According to the representatives of CMS, functionalists have propagated a concept of organisational culture that can be easily manipulated, which gives those wielding power another tool of oppression. Such instrumental concepts of culture are indicated by, for example, researchers from the CMS currents who criticise the use of methods of instrumentalisation, manipulation and social engineering in the management of culture, human resources and meanings, and point to their basis in the maintenance of the status quo. However, they also draw attention to the increase in the sophistication of controlling and power methods stemming from the fulfilment of the interests of those wielding power. Employee autonomy – which gives meaning to an organisation's work, non-financial motivations, loyalty-building and organisational loyalty – can be used as a tool for increasing profits. This means that autonomy, loyalty and identification are not autotelic, as they are only a means of increasing effectiveness and profitability. Thus, this is only 'apparent empowerment', developed by such concepts as 'Y theory', the school of human relations, corporate social responsibility, self-direction etc., which are in fact of a manipulative character[429].

---

425 Smircich, Linda. 'Concepts of culture and organizational analysis.' *Administrative science quarterly* (1983): 339–358.

426 D. Lyon, *Theorizing Surveillance: The Panopticon and Beyond - Reference, Information and Interdisciplinary Subjects Series*, Willan Publishing 2006.

427 H. Willmott, *Strength Is Ignorance; Slavery Is Freedom: Managing Culture in Modern Organizations, Journal of Management Studies*, 1993b, Nr 30/4, pp. 515–552.

428 M. Alvesson, *Understanding Organizational Culture*, London: Sage, 2002, p. 35.

429 Compare: H. Willmott, Strength Is Ignorance; Slavery Is Freedom: Managing Culture in Modern Organizations, *Journal of Management Studies*, 1993b., Nr 30/4, pp. 515–552.

5. Organisation and organisational culture as a 'total institution'.
   In creating the concept of total institutions, E. Goffman described organisations that are relatively isolated and develop their own, highly effective mechanisms of supervision, which lead to elimination of their members' individuality[430]. As a result of planned and spontaneous development of controlling systems in institutions such as hospitals, penal institutions and monasteries, truly Kafkaesque, bureaucratic and de-subjectivised systems are created, the priority of which are only organisational aims, at the expense of their members'. Visions of such dehumanised management, reminiscent of a total institution or even totalitarian systems, together with their dreams about single, coherent and real culture and ideology are sometimes presented as threats to modern organisations. They concern whole organisations, which create sophisticated systems of bureaucratic supervision, and more and more often use modern technologies of surveillance and permanent control[431]. The systems of self-control and self-censorship, which are of a cultural character, contribute to the homogenisation of their culture and the building of a strong organisational identity, but at the same time lead to the suppression of non-conformism, individuality and perhaps even creativity[432]. The reflection of the dehumanised organisation, reminiscent of a total institution, can be seen in the individual areas of organisation, such as the system of managing human resources[433]. According to CMS representatives, the personal function, oriented towards the maximisation of the exploitation of people, and so exploitation and indoctrination, is the reason for the expansion of the sub-discipline and practice of human resources management[434]. The mechanisms of total institutions, manifestations of which can be found in modern organisations,

430 Goffman, Erving. On the Characteristics of Total Institutions. *Symposium On Preventive and Social Psychiatry*, 1961.

431 D. Lyon, *Surveillance as Social Sorting: Privacy, Risk, and Digital Discrimination*, Routledge, 2003; *Organization for Economic Cooperation and Development* OECD Publishing, 2004.

432 J. Brewis, J. Gavin, *Culture: Broadening the Critical Repertoire*, in: M. Alvesson, T. Bridgman, H. Willmott (ed.), *The Oxford Handbook of Critical Management Studies*, Oxford: Oxford University Press 2009, pp. 234–235; Cf. İ. Erdoğan, *Recommendations on Media and Ethics*, Proceedings 'International Symposium on Media and Ethics' November 3–4, 2006, http://www.siyasaliletisim.org/pdf/medyaveetikkongrebildirileri.pdf, p. 207.

433 A.P. Brief, Still Servants of Power, *Journal of Management Inquiry*, 9/4, 2000.

434 P. Boxall, J. Purcell, P. Wright, *The Oxford Handbook of Human Resource Management*, Oxford 2007.

can also be found on the level of organisational subcultures. In a famous experiment, P. Zimbardo divided students into groups of 'prisoners' and 'guards', showing how the fragmentation of culture and the creation of subcultures catalyses violence in organisations, which can take symbolic and physical forms[435]. Other bases for total institutions are the human psyche and the authority mechanisms set in culture. In a different experiment, and probably the most famous in social psychology, S. Milgram showed how the pressure of authority can lead to creation of social structures using violence[436]. For most people, all kinds of authority pressure are able to force them to use violence against others.

6. 'Neo-colonialism' of intercultural management and globalisation.
   CMS representatives cite the criticism of neo-imperialism, which has been present in the discourse of management and other social sciences and humanities for several decades. N. Chomsky publishes and conducts social campaigns in order to build awareness of the necessity to change the neo-imperial orientation of American culture and the process of 'colonisation', which uses globalisation mechanisms[437]. According to Chomsky, international corporations, worldwide financial institutions and the governments of the richest countries create an exploitative order and maintain the status quo in their own interest[438]. This is reflected in the freedom of the capital flow and the hegemony of the financial and banking sector in economy, which is politically protected. In order to fulfil their economic interests, governments of many countries are ready to take military action. Culture plays an important role in this neo-imperial system, as it rationalises, conceals and glorifies the activities of corporations and managers. According to many researchers, managerial culture and intercultural management are only a cover for neo-imperialism and exploitation, while on the other hand, are also the instrumentally-understood tools and techniques of obtaining high effectiveness of work in an international environment. Thus, the theory of management in the context

---

435 P.G. Zimbardo, C. Maslach, C. Haney, *Reflections on the Stanford Prison Experiment: Genesis, transformations, consequences*, in: T. Blass, *Obedience to authority: Current Perspectives on the Milgram paradigm*, Mahwah, N.J.: Erlbaum, 2000, (pp. 193–237).

436 S. Milgram, *Obedience to authority*. New York: Harper & Row, 1974.

437 N. Chomsky, *Making the Future: The Unipolar Imperial Moment*, City Lights Publishers 2010.

438 N. Chomsky, *Powers and Prospects: Reflections on Human Nature and the Social Order*, Boston: South End Press, 2006.

of globalisation is developed mostly as a rationalisation of interests of people wielding power. Intellectuals, researchers, the academic environment and the consulting sector, enthusing over globalisation processes, can have their own interests in glorifying this current, but they also play the role of Lenin's 'useful idiots', brainwashed by the idea of worldwide unity.

7. Colonisation of the minds of one-dimensional people, controlled by consumerist culture.
   Consumerist culture channels human nature in accordance with the interests of those wielding power. It is not a coincidence, but a systemic feature, that culture often becomes a tool of exercising power. The projection of modern power, dispersed among corporations, managers and owners on the one hand, and governments, politicians and media on the other, is the postmodernist culture of modern consumerism. The Janus-faced nature of power is reflected in a seemingly individualist culture, while in fact – as S. Deetz said – we live in a world of everyday life colonised by concerns, using the mechanisms of cultural social and media communication to shape our consumerist needs[439]. N. Klein describes the practice of inflating consumer needs in an artificial way, with the use of sophisticated tools of psychomanipulation and social engineering in marketing. People become slaves to brands which – thanks to effective advertising, PR and branding – become their basic source of identification, satisfaction and self-esteem[440]. Thus, paradoxically, although people's standard of living is incomparably higher than several decades ago, and despite the fact that technological development has improved living comfort by a whole order of magnitude, social structure and the human condition remain unchanged. The world is divided into the privileged, who wield power, and the subordinate, who are subject to power and are disadvantaged. In order to maintain the social order and effective exploitation, the systemic mechanism in the form of culture, mass media and education 'programmes' people's minds, emphasising the natural and inevitable character of the existing order. Thus, culture implicitly creates a 'model', standardised, postmodernist consumer, who is limited to the role of a 'one-dimensional' and 'outer-directed' person through their freedom of market choice[441]. In the context of granting identity through identification with brands and the confusing

439 S.A. Deetz, *Democracy in an age of corporate colonization*, State University of New York Press, 1992.

440 N. Klein, *No Logo*, Fourth Estate, 2010.

441 H. Marcuse, 'Introduction to the Second Edition', *One-dimensional Man: studies in ideology of advanced industrial society*, London: Routledge 1991.

excess of alternative information, consumers' choices are still in line with the interests of the dominant groups.

8. The output of management science as a projection of culture that legitimises power.
   The threads of power have been inseparably linked with the concept of culture in management science. According to the representatives of CMS, this is a result of the instrumental character of the scientific discipline itself and its practices, created mostly in order to exploit people in a more effective way. This is reflected in most concepts created within management. Human resources management, using the dehumanised language of 'resources', 'human capital', 'personnel' and 'staff', indoctrinates in a spirit of power legitimisation. Marketing culture creates illusions of choice, channelling disadvantaged groups along narrow, consumerist pathways[442]. Accounting and financial management are thoroughly de-subjectivised and treat people as money transfers[443]. Strategic management rationalises profits and the development of organisations at the expense of people.
9. Critical Management Education.
   Critical Management Education, a current of CMS, develops, on the one hand, the criticism of the dehumanised management education, based on the instrumental mind, and on the other, proposes a breakthrough in the form of in-depth reflection and the development of methods, treating people in organisations in a subjective way. CMS criticises the ideology of managerial culture, expressed in business education, which is a kind of secondary socialisation, based on instrumental rationality. The education system maintains power relations, closely linking theory with practice. Graduates of business, economic and MBA schools are educated in the spirit of business ethics, and not general human ethics, and so they focus on the effectiveness of action, cost-effectiveness, and loyalty towards owners and managers[444]. The managerial ethos is a rationalisation of the lack of moral scruples. After such education, employees are treated as a 'resource', a means leading to the achievement of economic and market

442 D. Brownlie, M. Saren, R. Wensley, R. Whittington (eds.), *Rethinking Marketing: Towards Critical Marketing Accounting*, London: Sage 1999.

443 T. Tinker, *Paper Prophets: A social critique of accounting*, New York, 1985, Praegar.

444 See A. Contu, Critical Management Education, in: M. Alvesson, T. Bridgman, *The Oxford Handbook of Critical Management Studies*, Oxford 2009; Czarniawska B., Gagliardi P. (ed.). *Management Education and Humanities*, Cheltenham, Northampton: Edward Elgar, 2006.

goals. Management education is thus based on indoctrination and transfer of technocratic knowledge, used for the instrumentalisation of people in organisations[445]. Another purpose of the education and socialisation of employees is reproduction, which means transferring power to chosen ones. Using P. Bourdieu's nomenclature, management education creates a *habitus* supporting the reproduction of power structures, which is a manifestation of symbolic violence[446]. Thus, it can be said that ideology, as well as managerial ethos and profession (*habitus*) are 'inherited' or instilled in the process of education. According to the research conducted by P. Bourdieu and J.C. Passeron, the system of higher education schools awards students who have cultural capital, i.e. those from the ruling classes. The earlier research of B. Bernstein gave similar results[447]. The education system effectively eliminates nonconformists who do not want to accept the managerial ethos and culture.

10. Gurus within power structures.
Managerial culture is based on socially-created authorities, which reflect power structures. Some of the most popular and influential representatives of management occupy the positions of gurus, instead of reflective and critical researchers. Thus, gurus are 'heroes' and the most important popularisers of oppressive culture and managerial ideology. Gurus, who 'produce' the most popular guides, as well as simple and 'practical' concepts of management, focus on a clear, contagious idea, combined with effective marketing. Gurus are read because their concepts 'seduce' their readers, which means that they require no deep reflection, are simple to understand and remember, include a 'shocking' novelty, and are presented in simple, non-academic language. In spite of their appearances, gurus are not rebels out to destroy the existing power structures. Quite the contrary – they maintain them. They play the role of 'cultural industry' in management, which is a mechanism described by the Frankfurt School. They generate media interest in the concepts and structures of management, sanctioning the obviousness and natural state

---

445 L. Perriton, M. Reynolds, *Critical Management Education: From Pedagogy of Possibility to Pedagogy of Refusal?*, Management Learning 2004, 35, 1: 61–77.

446 P. Bourdieu, *Raisons pratiques.* Sur la théorie de l'action, Seuil, 1994; P. Bourdieu, J. -C. Passeron, *A Reproduction. Eléments pour une théorie du système d'enseignement*, Les Éditions de Minuit Collection Sens Commun, Paris 1970.

447 B. Berenstein, *Towards a Theory Of Educational Transmissions*, 1975; B. Berenstein, *Selection and Control*, 1974.

of this order. They occupy minds with 'memes' of contagious concepts and, at the same time, put aside reflection on issues which are fundamental to organisations, such as power and justice. Consciously or not, gurus try to 'program' the minds of managers, in accordance with the interests of those wielding power[448]. The gurus' 'cultural industry' is supported by mass advertising campaigns, PR and scientific marketing, which leads to the creation of 'idols' for managers. Gurus are treated in management in a special way, as their publications are of a popular character and do not fulfil the requirements of a scientific discipline, and so are rarely subject to reliable criticism from the academic environment[449]. It is also worth emphasising that – as the relationships with practice and the consulting sector are an inherent element of management understood as a scientific discipline – in the case of practitioners and managers, writing as such is a value. However, some management gurus from the past, such as P. Drucker, P. Kotler and I. Ansoff, have created some valuable scientific works, some of which became the basis for whole sub-disciplines of management.

6.3 Emancipation aims of cultural criticism

Criticism is the basis of the CMS current, although its aims go deeper, as it is supposed to lead to change. Thus, diagnosis leads to therapy, which entails humanist methods of management. This can be presented as a list of the aims of the cultural current of CMS:

- Creating organisational cultures based on real democracy in organisations.
- Cleansing organisational culture of all signs of violence by rejecting 'false awareness' or 'enlightened false awareness' ('organisational cynicism'), reflection, managing sensemaking, humanisation and moral and ethical sensitivity,
- Improvement of the social position of disadvantaged groups using emancipatory methods, including empowerment, parity, political correctness.
- Implementing emancipation culture on the level of relationships between organisations, within organisations and between employees.

448 J. Micklethwait, A. Wooldridge, the World Tomorrow: The Essentials of Globalization, Times Books (New York), 2000, p. 9

449 Chiapello, Eve, and Norman Fairclough. 'Understanding the New Management Ideology: A Transdisciplinary Contribution from Critical Discourse Analysis and New Sociology of Capitalism.' *Discourse & society* 13.2 (2002): 185–208.

- Rejecting the functionalist paradigm (neopositivist-functionalist-systemic) and the instrumental mind in cultural interpretations.
- Developing qualitative, interpretative and involved methods of research into organisational cultures.
- Transforming the profession-centrism and technocracy of the academic environment and management practitioners into methodological pluralism.
- Creating a reflective and critical organisational culture that would direct the development of organisations, society and people towards the increase in humanisation.
- Developing humanist management projects by the radicalisation of methods.

1 Democratisation of organisations

A critical view of organisational cultures leads to the conclusion that through 'symbolic violence', they are the key mechanism of maintaining and reproducing inequality. According to H. Willmott, the discourse of organisational culture in management as such is based on the instrumental approach to employees. T. Peters and R. Waterman, and their continuators[450], are often ideologists of 'corporate culturism', which seemingly promotes employee autonomy and democratic management, but in practice is a method of manipulation, the aim of which is to indoctrinate employees, involve them in the work of the organisation and obtain their obedience[451]. According to CMS representatives, a change for the better should entail a significant increase in democracy within organisations, aimed at the real, and not just instrumental, autonomy of their employees. The first thing to be implemented should be a method of radically increasing the participation of employees and subordinates in key organisational decisions. Thus, the concepts of employee participation, internal organisational democracy and self-directed teams present in the management literature even before the institutionalisation of CMS are radicalised, as they are not supposed to be the means leading to higher effectiveness.

450 T.J. Peters, R.H. Waterman, Jr., In Search of Excellence: Lessons From America's Best-Run Companies, New York, NY: Harper & Row 1982; R. Koch, I. Godden, *Managing without Management: A Post-Management Manifesto for Business Simplicity*, London: Nicholas Brealey 1996.

451 H. Willmott, Renewing Strength: Corporate Culture Revisited, *Management*, Vol. 6, No. 3, 2003, 73–87.

2 Rejection of violence through reflection of the culture

The culture of 'symbolic violence' (mobbing, bullying, harassment and sometimes even physical violence) should be 'healed' by the deepening of the reflection and adoption of a critical view based on the humanist orientation and moral sensitivity. After rejecting the cost-effectiveness of activities as the core of management science, it is necessary to find a new organisational order, one of the most important assumptions of which will be the increase in equality. One of the most important methods that can be applied here is the management of meanings, which on the one hand leads to a determination of the dominant discourses, while on the other makes it possible to promote the alternatives[452].

3 Methods which emancipate marginalised groups in organisations

A common element in both CMS and Marxism is radical criticism of the existing social and organisational order. Representatives of the critical current propose changes that are designed to lead to a change in position of the disadvantaged groups. The striving for a radical change of the disadvantaged groups' position is also an element which links CMS with the feminist current[453]. One of the most important methods leading to the emancipation of the disadvantaged groups is supposed to be empowerment, which empowers oppressed groups and makes them more aware. It is difficult to translate the term 'empowerment' into Polish because the sense of 'delegation of power and responsibilities' in management is set in the functionalist paradigm, while 'authorisation' and 'transfer of power' are too narrow and do not include the aspect of a change of awareness. Thus, I propose using the English term, as it means support leading to the transfer of full responsibility and power, in consequence of which representatives of the marginalised group become aware and empowered. In practice, empowerment is used in projects of the critical current, and is more and more often appearing in works oriented towards other paradigms[454].

---

452 M. Alvesson, H. Willmott, *Making Sense of Management: A Critical Introduction*, SAGE, 1996.

453 T. Potterfield, *The Business of Employee Empowerment: Democracy and Ideology in the Workplace*, Quorum Books, 1999.

454 L. Sulkowski, *Application des techniques d'empowerment dans les projects d'emamcipation dirige vers les groupes defavorise*, « L'Europe et le developpement regional. Politiques communautaires, entrepreneuriat et mobilisation de la societe civile » ed. C. Martin, PGV/AESIC ISLA, Lisboa 2007.

Parity means requiring the participation of disadvantaged groups in the structures of organisational management, based on legal norms or an organisation's normative regulations. In the case of management, the most frequent solution is having a minimum number of female employees or employees from disadvantaged groups as members of the organisation's management. This solution is being increasingly often applied in Scandinavian countries and in the USA. Even so, it is a very controversial practise, as in fact it discriminates against individuals from non-marginalised groups (e.g. men).

Critical researchers, using the concepts of the 'linguistic breakthrough', postmodernism and textualism, are oriented towards social constructivism, and so they can see that language is the fundamental tool for the creation of reality. This is culturalism, which makes language the most important tool for shaping the world of organisation and human communities. The change of reality is impossible without the change of language, which means that the need for radical reconstruction is a result of being anchored in culture and language. The method of changing the existing order is 'political correctness', literally translated into Polish as *poprawność polityczna*, which is a striving to cleanse the language, mostly in the public discourse, of pejorative expressions that could discriminate or negatively stigmatise certain social groups, and especially minorities and disadvantaged groups. 'Political correctness' became popular in the USA but is, again, very controversial, as some argue that it limits the freedom of speech[455]. In the case of management, when we deal with the public discourse, the norms of political correctness become more and more popular, although the notion itself is rarely used. For most CMS representatives, political correctness is a positive tendency, although it is strongly resisted by the power structures and should be radicalised. There are also many critics who point to negative aspects, citing limits on expression, communication freedom, or even destruction of the cultural programme of organising things[456].

4 Popularisation of emancipation culture

Culture, and so organisational culture as well, can be seen as a method of emancipation[457]. However, this means an important change in the dominant

455 D. Ravitch, *The Language Police: How Pressure Groups Restrict What Students Learn*, Knopf, 2003

456 H.S. Schwartz, *Society against Itself: Political Correctness and Organizational Self-Destruction*, London: Karnac Books, 2010

457 M. Alvesson, H. Willmott, On the Idea of Emancipation in Management and Organization Studies. *Academy of Management Review*, 1992, 17(3), 432–464.

epistemological, methodological and praxeological perspective in management science. In the cognitive sphere, this is related to the rejection of the researcher's axiological neutrality and a move to the position of social constructivism, which entails methodological consequences. Whereas in the praxeological sense, this includes the management of core values in the cultural project, towards which organisational culture shall be oriented. These values include human subjectivity, equality and tolerance for diversity. CMS researchers assume, although it may be a utopian thought, that it is possible to reorient from the currently dominant culture of cost-effectiveness and effectiveness, and – as a subtext – power, towards humanisation. The transformation, or cultural transgression, is supposed to take place on numerous levels, including different cultural circles (social culture, mass culture, organisational cultures) and human relationships. Thus, cultural transgression would require us to deal with changes concerning macroculture (whole society, mass culture), mezzoculture (organisational culture) and microcultures (microemancipation in human relationships).

5 Anti-functionalism

The epistemology of organisational culture is one of the key problems of CMS. In the case of CMS, the acceptance of the central role of culture in the process of organising leads to the criticism of the mainstream, which is the neopositivist paradigm and the functionalism of cultural processes and their management[458]. The most radical current of criticism postulates the rejection of the entire management science project, while the moderate version is a kind of 'repair', related to the rejection of the instrumental mind and the primacy of cost-effectiveness in human activities[459].

---

458 H. Höpfl, The Making of the Corporate Acolyte: Some Thoughts on Charismatic Leadership and the Reality of Organizational Commitment, *Journal of Management Studies*, 1992, No. 29/1, pp. 23–33; G. Kunda, *Engineering Culture. Control and Commitment in a High-Tech Corporation,* Philadelphia: Temple University Press 1992; H. Willmott, Strength Is Ignorance; Slavery Is Freedom: Managing Culture in Modern Organizations. *Journal of Management Studies*, 1993, No. 30/4, pp. 515–552; H.C. Willmott, What has been happening in organization theory and does it matter?, *Personnel Review*, 1995, No. 24 (9), pp. 33–53; A. Chan. *Toward a Genealogy of Organizational Culture. The Perspectives of Foucault*, Amsterdam-Philadelphia: John Benjamins publishing Company, 2001; M. Alvesson, *Understanding Organizational Culture*. London: Sage, 2002.

459 M. Parker, *Against Management: Organization in the Age of Managerialism*, Wiley-Blackwell, 2002.

CMS representatives are very critical about the output of research into culture within the social sciences. The research of the main current concerning organisational culture, conducted in the 1970s and the first half of the 1980s, is regarded as 'corporate culturalism', which is a striving for the instrumentalisation of culture as a tool of effective management. Apart from the problem of the effectiveness of organisational culture management, which is a reservation voiced by many authors, the key question is the ethically doubtful character of the project[460].

CMS representatives are much closer to the cognitive assumptions of symbolic interactionism and postmodernism than the functionalist current. Alternative paradigms criticise resource-based, determinist and instrumentalist approach to organisational culture, rooted in the neopositivist-functionalist-systemic paradigm. Similarly to other alternative paradigms, CMS accepts the vision of culture as an area of conflict, fragmentation and the creation of subcultures. The view of the fluidity of individual and collective identities is similar. Organisational culture is perceived as being indeterminist, while the possibility of managing or steering culture is assessed sceptically[461].

However, there are significant differences between critical, interpretative and postmodern understandings of organisational culture. Most of all, the critical current, unlike postmodernism and interpretivism, is based on ontological realism with a moderate version of social constructivism[462]. Thus, according to CMS representatives, reality, including social reality, exists objectively or at least intersubjectively. CMS representatives believe that culture is linked with inequality and power, and that it is possible to change this situation. Therefore, they propose to develop the project of emancipation culture, which should be characterised by egalitarianism, inclusiveness and orientation towards humanist values, instead of the economic.

6 Methodology of the critical research into culture

Because of the ambiguity and multidimensionality of culture, CMS representatives have accepted the methodological pluralism approach. However, there is a quite clear preference for qualitative methods, stemming from such humanist currents as hermeneutics, phenomenology and those used by researchers

460 H. Willmott, *Renewing Strength: Corporate Culture Revisited*, Vol. 6, No. 3, 2003, pp. 77–81.

461 M. Alvesson, *Understanding Organizational Culture*, London: Sage 2002.

462 J. Duberley, P. Johnson, *Understanding Management Research: An Introduction to Epistemology*. London: SAGE Publications Inc 2003b.

identified with the Frankfurt School, radical feminism, interpretivism and postmodernism[463].

The most important characteristic of CMS methodology, and especially of cultural research, is the postulate of a researcher involved in the change of the social reality. This is a rejection of axiological neutrality and requires the research process to become a process of changing culture. Thus, the division between critical and pragmatic aims of CMS presented here is, from the point of view of this perspective, artificial, as all aims have to be, by definition, both critical and pragmatic. Cognition should lead to the emancipation change.

The methodological pragmatism allows for the possibility of using a number of methods, as long as they are subordinated to the emancipation aim[464]. The methodological pluralism allows CMS representatives to use the arsenal of methods developed within different paradigms. Most often, they use interpretative methods, such as cultural studies, comparative analyses, discourse analyses, organisational anthropology methods, in-depth interviews, participant observation, dramatic and narrative methods. Several methodological concepts, appearing in CMS, were drawn from postmodernism, and they include deconstruction, denaturalisation, textual and metaphorical methods. Critical researchers could also use methods stemming from the functionalist paradigm, such as statistical analyses and standard survey methods, although in this case there is a limitation in the form of the postulate of axiological neutrality underlying the research methodology. Furthermore, it seems that the sociological methods include a number of tools that are useful from the point of view of critical culture researchers, such as A. Touraine's intervention sociology, the grounded theory of A. Strauss and the methods of phenomenological sociology. In the case of cultural methods used in management, the subject of criticism is the 'corporate culturism' and the orientation towards instrumental rationality. In the case of deductive methods, CMS focus on philosophical, sociological and anthropological analyses.

7 Critical methodological pluralism

As N. Harding noted, creators and promoters of management have built an extensive system of social legitimisation of power, including business schools, the market of business publishing houses, an academic environment and a lobby

463 M. Alvesson, S. Deetz, *Doing Critical Management Research*, London: Sage 2000.

464 J. Duberley, P. Johnson, *Understanding Management Research: An Introduction to Epistemology*. London: SAGE Publications Inc. 2003, p. 133.

concentrated around management. With the use of this machinery of symbolic violence, the social discourse is filled with seemingly indisputable assumptions and concepts, maintaining the reproduction and legitimising power, such as 'management protects the world against chaos and offers an objective truth about reality' and 'it is an art, allowing for the wielding of power over other people'[465].

Under the influence of CMS criticism, the attitude of organisational researchers and advisors should also undergo a radical change. At the moment, they are focused on building their own position through profession-centrism. As a result, they mostly legitimise unjust orders, lending the managerial ideology the authority of science. Moreover, referring to the authority of science and the relationships with those in power, they derive unjustified – in the opinion of CMS researchers –benefits.

8 Critical organisational culture

Reflective and critical culture means that the project of the transgression of organisational culture towards emancipation is permanent. It requires criticism not only at the stage of the diagnosis of the status quo, but also during the process of implementing changes. It is a kind of promise that culture and its values will not only be celebrated and maintained, but will undergo constant reflection and critical examination from the point of view of the fulfilment of the aims of emancipation[466]. Concern for the autonomy of people and the humanisation of organisations should be permanently present in the management science project, which would allow gradual implementation of emancipation's aims. In order for this project to be successful, it is necessary to shape the awareness of an organisation's members and researchers, and to develop appropriate sensitivity and reflection. CMS have ambitions to fulfil this task.

9 Development of humanist management projects through the radicalisation of methods

A chance for the development of the critical current that would humanise management, are certain threads already present in the theoretical discourse and in practice, such as corporate social responsibility, subjectivity in managerial processes (self-directed teams, substitute management), social and partner

465 N. Harding, *The Social Construction of Management*, Routledge, London 2003, p. 14.

466 Cf. L. Smircich, *Concepts of Culture and Organizational Analysis* transl. J. Gonciarz, in: A. Marcinkowski, J.B. Sobczak (ed.). *Wybrane zagadnienia socjologii organizacji*, Część II: Perspektywa kulturowa w badaniach organizacji. Kraków: UJ, 1989, p. 59.

marketing, social ownership forms, heterarchies, network structures and cooperation. All these concepts go towards greater autonomy, freedom of decisions and equality of employees and consumers. However, as H. Willimott noted, in the case of organisational culture, such striving for an increase in employee autonomy is paradoxically oppressive[467]. It is a kind of innovativeness, the aim of which is to better control people's minds and hearts through culture and values. In this sense, this approach is oppressive and manipulative. It seems that most managerial concepts do not fulfil the emancipation criterion because, by definition, they strive for higher effectiveness, and not for the greater autonomy of people. The critical view of the theory of corporate social responsibility of business suggests that it is often a smokescreen or the creation of an image in order to derive greater benefits. A smokescreen is supposed to conceal the negative aspects of the organisation, often presenting an image that is drastically different from reality. A classic example is Royal Dutch Shell, which changed its image as a great polluter by focusing on ecology and alternative energy sources[468]. From the point of view of CMS researchers, substitute management and other forms of delegating responsibilities to employees are not empowerment, because their aim is to control employees in a more effective and sophisticated way (including self-control and self-censorship), and, naturally, to achieve higher effectiveness. The partner, and even social marketing, can be interpreted in a similar way. It seemingly promotes partner relationships between enterprises and customers, but on the other hand, it is a form of sophisticated manipulation. By gathering and processing detailed information about consumers and maintaining permanent communication, companies create personal obligations and exploit them for their own benefit. Thus, it seems that consumers are even more controlled, kept under surveillance, and manipulated. This is because, as a result of individualisation and personalisation, they are no longer anonymous and have become easy targets for social engineering[469]. The assumption of branding, which means building loyalty towards a brand through the identification process, is even more important in partner marketing than the classical marketing[470]. The key is psychomanipulation, which leads to consumers' pathological attachment

---

467 H. Willmott, *Renewing Strength: Corporate Culture Revisited*, Management, Vol. 6, No. 3, 2003, pp. 77–81.

468 Cf. https://www.shell.com/home/content/environment_society.html/.

469 S. Lace, *The glass consumer: life in a surveillance society*, National Consumer Council, Policy Press, 2005

470 J. Hart, *Loyal Subjects?: Consumer Surveillance in the Personal Information Economy*, Library and Archives Canada, 2009.

to objects, which generate somebody's profit, instead of people. According to some representatives of management, network structures, heterarchy and cooperation are supposed to create organisations without power. However, viewing them from the perspective of the CMS interpretative framework, one can see an increase in sophistication, and not a decrease of the organisational power's oppressiveness. Flexible forms of employment shift the entire risk and responsibility entailed by business activity onto the employees, reducing operational costs. By outsourcing and offshoring, cooperative market structures give entrepreneurs and managers the possibility to exploit employees in countries of the lowest labour cost, without causing unnecessary worry about the social effects in their home countries. At the same time, corporations are absolved of the responsibility for working conditions in their overseas co-operators. According to CMS representatives, loose internal structures of organisations are also oppressive, although in a subtler way. Another consequence of the pressure to reduce costs is the implementation of restructuring activities, which are usually harmful to employees. Euphemistic expressions for restructuring include business process reengineering, job sharing, downsizing, consolidation strategies, lean management and divestment, and all conceal the practices of reducing employment and extorting workaholism in order to increase effectiveness.

CMS representatives believe that in order for management theory and practice to receive a humanist dimension, it is necessary to include emancipation in the organisational culture as a core value. Without this, all theories and methods of management will be instrumental.

The issues of culture in management have been a space for the creation and development of management currents which run alternatively to the dominant. It is similar in the case of CMS, which treats cultural issues as being of key significance from the epistemological, methodological and pragmatic perspectives.

One value of CMS is its use of the culture of neo-Marxism, the Frankfurt School and feminism in research, previously applied in the political sciences and sociology. Another of CMS' assets is its stimulation of the awareness of researchers, managers and employees, in order to increase their ethical sensitivity and the social responsibility of management science. This entails a proposal to develop new, involved methods and techniques of cultural research, such as empowerment, parity, action research and discursive tools.

6.4 Limitations of the critical current in management

The critical current of management is quite controversial, because its underlying assumptions are of an ideological character. Management, described as a discourse of persuasion, maintaining oppressive social structures, is perceived one-sidedly and ideologically. At the same time, Critical Management Studies have scientific ambitions, referring to the neo-Marxist objectivism. Marxism postulated the scientific nature of its own discourse, but it never managed to reach beyond ideology.

The critical current in management science should be re-assessed, and not only by its supporters. I would like to propose a critical analysis of the CMS current, located on two levels. The first is a general criticism of the whole CMS current in epistemological, methodological and praxeological areas. The other level of analysis is quite detailed and involves applying the critical current to different sub-disciplines and problems of management science.

Starting with the general criticism of CMS, one can point to several key problems of a general nature:

1. A dubious philosophical basis in the form of neo-Marxism and postmodernism.
2. Erroneous understanding of the human nature, leading to a utopia.
3. Lack of epistemological and institutional maturity.
4. Methodological superficiality.
5. Pragmatic weakness.
6. Discourse insularity.

1. The critical current is derived from neo-Marxism and is linked with postmodernism. This is why it is a reflection of the key cognitive problems of both these philosophies. CMS use a modified perspective of the Marxist class struggle. The key notions of this current are power, dominance, control, dominant and subordinate classes, and false awareness[471]. It also includes categories borrowed from other neo-Marxists, such as symbolic violence[472] and neo-imperialism[473]. The Marxist vision compromised itself in economy, politics and society in the previous century, but persists in the concepts of the critical current in management, sociology and cultural anthropology. The criticism of Marxism in economic sciences has rich tradition, mostly in terms of the confrontation with the neoclassical[474] and the Keynesian[475] schools. As a result of the fall of real socialism and the

471 J. Larrain, *Marxism and Ideology*, London, Macmillan, 1983.

472 P. Bourrdieu, *Language & Symbolic Power*, Harvard University Press, 1991.

473 N. Chomsky, *The Corporate Takeover of U.S. Democracy* - chomsky. info, access on January 24th, 2010; M. Hardt, A. Negri, *Empire*, Harvard University Press, Cambridge, London 2001.

474 F. Hayek, *The Road to Serfdom*, Chicago, 1994.

475 J.K. Galbraith, *The Affluent Society*, New York, 1958.

bankruptcy of the communist idea in many countries, Marxism, which for over a hundred years was a significant economic school, became a completely marginal orientation in economy. Just like neo-Marxism, postmodernism is problematic, especially when understood as the epistemological basis for the development of the social sciences. Mats Alvesson clearly emphasises the difference between postmodernism and CMS but many researchers, and indeed many ideas, remain common to both these currents. Examples include M. Foucault, J. F. Lyotard, Z. Bauman, and in the case of our own science, G. Burrell, M. Schultz, M.J. Hatch, B. Czarniawska, M. Kostera. Both currents' common problems include scepticism about the development of science and progress, the key role of power in organisations, postulates of an increase in moral sensitivity and the preference for discursive methods. The scepticism about social progress links neo-Marxism with postmodernism, and is present in CMS as well. Researchers functioning within this paradigm, focus on inequalities, injustice, discrimination and violence, and often do not want to see the evident organisational and social progress, which improves the conditions of people's functioning. Organising enabled technical, political and social progress, covering the whole mankind. CMS researchers do not want to accept the fact that although economic differences between countries and social groups are deepening, this is to a large extent a result of the rapid increase in the wealth of the people and countries already present in the high income segments, and not because of a regression in the case of groups having the lowest income. An analysis similar to conducted for social and economic progress can be carried out in relation to scientific scepticism. Lack of faith in the scientific progress, being one of the most important threads of postmodernism and a significant thread in the case of CMS, is largely irrational, because scientific progress, including in the social sciences, is a fact. Naturally, the social sciences develop much slower than the natural sciences, but the progress is clearly visible. Science is entangled in society and is not axiologically neutral, although it undoubtedly contributes to the development of people and human communities. Other root concepts of CMS, such as a fight for dominance, false awareness, symbolic violence, can also be criticised as exaggerated and excessively ideological. Thus, postmodernism, together with its extreme cultural and epistemological relativism, is not a good basis for the development of science, unless as a source of inspirations and metaphors.

2. The evolution of neo-Marxism towards Critical Management Studies is an attempt to transfer the concept of class struggle to the organisational level. It seems that it is a failed attempt because of its assumptions concerning human nature. The vision of CMS is striving for cleansing the human nature of tendencies that were imprinted in the minds of people and their preceding species

over millions of years of evolutions. *Homo sapiens* are neither a tabula rasa, nor cultural clay, which can be freely shaped by society[476]. Striving for the wielding of power is natural, and although it is socially corrected, its character is not fully culture-relative. The consequences of wielding power include social and organisational inequalities, closely tied to prestige and hierarchy. Another manifestation of human nature is our cooperative-competitive orientation, which can be easily identified in the organisational world. In addition, the source of leadership, organisational culture[477], communication process, sex differences are fully natural. Culture and the process of socialisation shape our nature, but they cannot fully negate it. From this point of view, the CMS project is utopian because it strives for a radical reconstruction of organisations and management, following ethical postulates, which is against human nature.

3. CMS is at an initial stage of development and, in a way, attracts mostly the enthusiasts of this approach. It lacks the maturity of a paradigm that has been through a number of stages of development and shocks. Undoubtedly, a critical view of CMS is needed, both from its own perspective and from the perspective of other paradigms. Moreover, it would be advisable to popularise this concept, so that it is present in the managerial discourse in a number of countries.

4. CMS also face a number of methodological problems. CMS researchers mostly use the tool kit of qualitative and involved methods, indicating that they are characteristic of the critical current. However, as the experience of numerous projects shows, using methods such as empowerment or action research in management does not necessarily mean the acceptance of the critical paradigm. Empowerment, the striving for equality and enhancement of the position of disadvantaged groups are all examples of methodological postulates adopted by the European Union as criteria for the assessment of projects. Methodological pluralism assumes that, from the point of view of research reliability, a research triangulation is needed which could combine qualitative and quantitative methods, as well as those both neutral and involved. Another problem is the lower methodological rigor and higher freedom of the interpretation of the involved studies. Some of them can be regarded as too interfering, or almost manipulative. For example, A. Tourrain's intervention sociology can be accused of provoking the social movement and organisations to change[478].

---

476 S. Pinker, *The Blank Slate*. New York: Penguin. 2002

477 L. Sulkowski, The Problems of Epistemology of Corporate Culture, *Journal of Intercultural Management*, Volume 1, Number 1, April 2009.

478 A. Touraine, *La voix et le regard*, Seulil, Paris 1978.

5. CMS also has a limited pragmatic effectiveness because there are few significant research projects carried out within the critical paradigm of management. The concepts of an improving organisational change, taking into consideration higher ethical sensitivity, are carried out within other paradigms of management science, not only within CMS. For example, business ethics is an important, developing current combining philosophical and business threads. Another example is corporate social responsibility, the aim of which is to sensitise organisations to social needs. Similarly, on the level of organisational behaviour in management science, there is an increasing significance to the humanist current, which emphasises the significance of subjectivity, self-fulfilment and creativity of people in organisations. Thus, undertaking projects that make organisations more ethical and friendly does not have to entail adoption of the CMS paradigm. Additionally, criticism of the management concept is made within different paradigms, and one does not have to be a CMS representative to criticise managerial theory and practice. However, as CMS representatives point out, not every attempt at a critical view of management science's results falls within the critical current[479]. The prerequisite for making criticism from the perspective of the CMS paradigm is the use of intellectual tools in this mental formation, such as the striving for the emancipation of the disadvantaged groups and adopting the assumptions of the discourse denaturalization in management science.

The critical view of CMS has to be diverse, depending on the problems undertaken and its sub-disciplines. It seems that the critical and postmodernist currents are useful from the point of view of marketing analyses, as they point to the manipulative aspects of this sub-discipline. On the other hand, CMS researchers do not accept the fact that marketing also witnesses the development of humanising concepts, which emphasise subjectivity and ethics, such as relationship marketing, relationship marketing and social marketing[480]. It is difficult to distinguish the elements of postmodernism and CMS in management. Another creative solution is the application of the critical current to human resources management, although the image of the sub-discipline itself is distorted by CMS. And the criticism of strategic management from the CMS perspective is less successful. Pointing to the rationalisations of the top management, which are supposed to conceal the unethical practices is interesting, but was already known in the previous management concepts, proposed by, among others, Karl

479 J. Duberley, P. Johnson, *Understanding Management Research: An Introduction to Epistemology*. London: SAGE 2003b.

480 See: N. Lee, Ph. Kotler, *Social marketing*, Free Press, 1989.

Weick[481]. There are some interesting applications for CMS in organisational culture, as they point to the possibly oppressive and ideological influence of norms and values. Other threads, creatively developed by CMS, include ideology, management oppressiveness, issues of organisational power, communication and business ethics[482]. The deliberations of some representatives of the critical current, concerning management accounting, quality management and logistics, are rather exotic and poorly grounded in theory. Generally, the applications for CMS are diverse, depending on the research issue and sub-discipline, and the subject literature offers us examples of innovative and appropriate applications of the critical current, as well as of some less successful attempts.

481 K. Weick, Substitutes for Corporate Strategy, in: *The Competitive Challenge*, Ballinger, Cambridge 1987.

482 K. Blanchard, N.V. Peale, *The Power of Ethical Management*, William Morrow; 1988.

7 The cultural changeability of organisations

7.1 Cultural conditions of organisational changes

The concept of change differs depending on the management paradigm assumed, and naturally, there is no agreement among researchers about which classification to use. Some opt for linking change management with the schools or currents of organisational thought, which would be the image of enrichment of the theory and methods of the last century. Other researchers look for paradigms, characteristic mostly of change management, one example of which is the dichotomy between evolutionary (continuous) and revolutionary (radical) changes[483]. There are also attempts at an integrated approach to change management, which would include different cognitive perspectives[484]. Another interpretation, used in this book, points to the relationships between change management and the social sciences paradigms, which here means looking for the widest possible point of reference.

Regardless of the assumed paradigm of the social sciences, one can point to different types of organisational changes, depending on the assumed criterion. Naturally, the basic distinction is the division into evolutionary and revolutionary changes, which is part of the dichotomy between superficial and in-depth changes. Thus, changes can be located in a continuum from full control to full spontaneity. Compared to other aspects of management, cultural changes are more often located in the spontaneous sphere, although the assessment of the control level depends on the paradigm. Functionalists more often move towards controlled changes, while representatives of the alternative paradigms prefer spontaneous changes of culture. A gentler version of this dichotomy is the dualism of planned and controlled changes vs. coordinated and ad hoc (improvised) changes[485]. This, in turn, is part of the juxtaposition of changes controlled by a leader with changes that take place beyond their control[486]. Organisational

483 L.E. Greiner, *Evolution and Revolution as Organizations Grow*, Harvard Business Review, 1998 May-Jun;76(3):55–60, 62–6, 68, 1972.

484 D. Meyerson, J. Martin, *Cultural Change:* An Integration of Three Different Views, *Journal of Management Studies*, 1987, 24: 623–647; Y. Allaire, M.E. Firsirotu, *Theories of Organizational Culture*, Organization Studies July 1984 vol. 5 no. 3 193–226.

485 W.J. OrlikowskI, J.D. Hofman, An *improvisational model for change management: the case of groupware technologies*, *Sloan Management Review*, 1997.

486 M. Fullan, *Leading in a Culture of Change*, San Francisco, California: Jossey-Bass 2001.

changes are usually based on one of the two cores of crystallisation, as they are either strategically or culturally oriented[487]. Strategic changes are based on a planned transformation, inscribed in the aims, mission and concept of the competitive advantage[488]. On the other hand, cultural changes are oriented towards the transformation of mentality, and only then towards strategic and structural changes[489].

The functionalist understanding of change is based on increases in effectiveness or cost-effectiveness of an organisation's functioning. Thus, a positive change results in progress and improvement of the organisation and its members, thanks to which their actions are more effective. Negative change is regression, so a decrease either in effectiveness or in cost-effectiveness of the organisation's activities. Functionalists strive for full control over the process of changes, understood as a transformation of the organisational system and its subsystems, leading to a better use of resources and the adjustment to the environment. The most important objects of changes are the organisations themselves, but changes also include organisation's subsystems (such as strategy, structure, culture) and employees. Because of the necessity to maintain the organisation's integrity in the process of change, the preference for evolutionary and continuous change dominates. Thus, most methods of making changes are aimed at the process of improving the organisation, and not reconstructing it radically, examples of which include TQM, organisational development, and lean management. However, instrumental functionalism also includes methods that – at least on the level of assumptions – postulate in-depth changes, such as reengineering. The functionalist paradigm draws from neopositivism, which translates into the postulate of axiological neutrality, according to which assessments of organisational changes should avoid moral and ethical valuation and should focus on the pragmatic aspect of the effects. Of popular metaphors that could describe the functionalist changes, evolution seems to be most accurate. The functionalist current of change management includes publications by many authors from the main current of organisational culture management, including E. Schein, G. Hofstede, C. Handy, T. Deal, A. A. Kennedy and many others.

---

487 M.H. Kavanagh, N.M. Ashkanasy, The Impact of Leadership and Change Management Strategy on Organizational Culture and Individual Acceptance of Change during a Merger, *British Journal of Management*, 2006, 17: S81–S103.

488 W. Boeker, Strategic Change: The Effects of Founding and History, *The Academy of Management Journal*, Vol. 32, No. 3 (Sep., 1989), pp. 489–515.

489 P. Bate, *Strategies for Cultural Change*, Imprint Burlington: Elsevier, 1996.

According to interpretivists, changes take place mostly in the sphere of perception, understanding and interpretation of the organisation itself by its members. Thus, it is not objective but intersubjective through the senses and meanings given to changes by people and spread as part of the social communication. A change is the transformation of individual identities of an organisation's members and collective organisational identities. Within the processes of communication and the social game, spontaneous agreements are formed, consolidating the dominant, stereotypical perception of the process of changes. Thus, the very fact of conducting organisational change, as well as its character, depends solely on the interpretation. The meanings spread can consolidate the perception of the organisational change as evolution, or just the contrary. This is why the process of meaning management, which is often of an unconscious character, is of key importance to change management. Management of meaning can introduce the dominant type of interpretation, which spreads among the organisation's members, at the same time obscuring other ways of understanding changes. The consolidation of stereotypes and agreements concerning organisation also entails problems with the implementation of projects of controlled changes. Planning and implementing changes are entangled in processes of a social game, communication and sensemaking, which are spontaneous and uncontrolled, but often of key significance to the organisation. In the interpretative paradigm, change management is always evaluative – each decision and activity is part of the context of moral and ethical values. Even language, narration and ideas are not axiologically neutral. An appropriate metaphor is the acting, or flow, of the understanding derived from Heraclitus (*panta rei*). The interpretative approach to cultural changes is proposed by numerous authors, especially those functioning in the non-functionalist area, which includes for example: M. J. Hatch, G. Morgan, L. Smircich, J. van Maanen, M. Pacanovsky.

The representatives of Critical Management Studies assume the evaluative axiological orientation. Positive changes lead to the emancipation of disadvantaged social groups, decrease inequalities and the oppressiveness of the organisation, and erase the false awareness. The assumptions of the critical current are radical, and so the change has to be in-depth and revolutionary, even if it is not made with use of the Marxist method of social revolution. Additionally, many CMS researchers note pessimistically that the modern direction of organisational changes often develops negative changes, which deepen inequalities, the dominance of the groups wielding power and false awareness. The proofs of this tendency are supposed to be such elements as the development of neo-imperial practices resulting from the deepening globalisation, a preference for managerial methods which instrumentalise people, and an increase in the significance of the manipulative propaganda of media and marketing. The postulated methods of changing the organisational order are connected with the denaturalisation of managerism's discourse and the deconstruction of notions and structures of power. The techniques of change used include empowerment, parity, the change of language and discourse (towards political correctness) and critical text analyses. According to the critical current authors, positive changes are resisted mostly by the groups wielding power, which face the loss of influence. Thus, barriers to change can be of a conscious character, controlled by the elites of economic and political power, but they can also emerge spontaneously, free of conscious control. Managers rationalise their own instrumentalism and manipulative inclinations with regard to the natural capitalist and organisational order, the lack of possibility of limiting inequalities and their responsibility towards the organisation's owners in terms of its development. One metaphor that could be mentioned here is the Marxist class struggle. The change of the oppressive managerial culture is the subject of deliberations of H. Willmott, M. Alvesson, D. Knights, J. Brewis.

Postmodernists believe that changes are of a subjective and permanent character because they are part of the spontaneous, uncontrolled and unconscious flows of interpretations, narratives, senses and power between different overlapping discourses. A good metaphor for a shapeless change is the root, proposed by Deleuze and Guattari, which crosses in an unpredictable way and attaches itself in random places. In this sense, change cannot by managed, as it is beyond any control. All the methods of managing change are only narratives, rationalisations that can influence the discourse but cannot control it. In the postmodernist understanding, change is made through the discourse and culture, within the multiplicity of meanings and identities of different participants of language and social games. The ephemeral deconstruction method, proposed by J. Derrida, is supposed to lead to a change and rejection of the dominant way of interpreting works or reality, substituting it by the multiplicity of interpretations. Several researchers (S. Clegg, G. Burrell, R. Cooper, B. Czarniawska, M. Kostera and P. Boje) draw on postmodernist thought in their analyses, but rarely call themselves postmodernists.

The concepts of change management differ, depending on the assumed paradigm. The dominant paradigm is the neopositivist-functionalist-systemic approach, including most of the works of modern change management. Interpretivism negated the neopositivist illusion of early functionalists, according to which the processes of change management could be studied with the use of purely objectivist methods, pointing to the social creation of changes[490]. Postmodernism uses the motif of self-emergent, spontaneous and uncontrolled changes that cannot be managed. In this sense, postmodernism can be a supplement to the scepticism about change management, which is characteristic of the critical current. CMS appeared in the 1990s as the last paradigm in management science. In the case of change management, it draws on the concept of emancipation changes, using the methods of the managerial discourse denaturalisation. A comparison of the change management concepts within Burrell and Morgan's four paradigms can be found in Tab. 26.

Looking at the elementary epistemological division within the social sciences, which distinguished the neopositivist paradigm from the paradigms of the social constructivism, one can point to a special understanding of changes within alternative perspectives. This author uses the general term 'social constructivism' to denote paradigms which assume that the organisational reality is constructed (implicitly and explicitly created and constituted) by the active actors taking part in a social game. Thus, we deal with the paradigms of symbolic interactionism, radical structuralism (the critical current) and some elements of radical humanism (postmodernism), as understood by G. Burrell and G. Morgan[491].

Changes within the constructivist paradigms are not objectively existing states, but processes constructed by the perceptions, interpretations and actions of the organisational processes' participants. This means that the understanding of change is closely related to the creation of meanings and senses. L. Smircich described the concept of leadership and the introduction of changes as management of meaning, within which the leader creates and imposes his own organisational vision[492]. Similarly, K. Weick indicated that in order to effectively introduce a strategy of organisational changes, it is necessary to create, implement and transfer new meanings and senses to the participants of the organisational life (sensemaking)[493]. Thus, management of meaning is a process of constructing construction and interpretation based on a series of events,

490 P.L. Berger, T. Luckmann, *The Social Construction of Reality: A Treatise in the Sociology of Knowledge*, Garden City, New York: Anchor Books 1966.

491 G. Burrell, G. Morgan, *Sociological Paradigms and Organizational Analysis*, Heinemann, London 1979.

492 L. Smircich, G. Morgan, Leadership: The Management of Meaning, *The Journal of Applied Behavioral Science* 1982, Vol. 18, 3:257 – 273; L. Smircich, *Organizations as Shared Meaning*, w: 'Organization Symbolism', JAI Press, Greenwich 1983.

493 K.E. Weick, *Sensemaking in organizations*, Thousand Oaks, CA: Sage 1995.

implementing meanings, and then acting in accordance with them in the organisational group[494].

Drawing inspirations from different paradigms, one can propose complementary models of organisational culture changes, accompanied by different organisational methods and techniques (Tab. 27).

The ambiguity of culture and the complexity of its interpretations within different paradigms are the reasons to adopt the position of the epistemological and methodological pluralism. It would mean that the created model of cultural management makes use of the concepts of cultures developed within different paradigms, while the methodology of culture research combines methods consolidated within different cognitive and methodological perspectives.

R. Chin and K. D. Benne proposed a general division of organisational change strategies into three groups: rational/empirical, normative/re-educational and coercive[495]. Rational/empirical strategies are based on the classical assumptions of an idealised model of *Homo sapiens* and the planning school of strategy. People in organisations rely on rational motives in their striving for the fulfilment of their own interests. Thus, an organisation's members are willing to accept changes only when they realise that they will be beneficial to them. The planning school of strategy assumes full rationality of the strategic planning process, postulating the striving for full control over situational variables[496]. In the epistemological sense, the rational-empirical approach to changes is based on the neopositivist-functionalist paradigm. Although normative/re-educational strategies of changes, just like rational-empirical strategies, point to rationality and an orientation towards the individual benefit of people in organisations, they also place great emphasis on the social conditions of all interpretations and activities. Thus, apart from rational motives, a significant role is played by culturally acquired values and norms, meanings, social roles and relationships, cognitive and perceptual orientations[497]. The normative/re-educational approach emphasises the

494 D.A. Gioia, J.B. Thomas, S.M. Clark, K. Chittipeddi, *Symbolism and strategic change in academia: The dynamics of sensemaking and influence*, Organization Science, 1994, 5, pp. 363–383.

495 R. Chin, K.D. Benne, *General strategies for effecting changes in human systems,* In: W.G. Bennis, K.D. Benne, R. Chin (eds), *The planning of change* (4th ed., pp. 22–43). New York: Holt, Rinehart & Winston 1985.

496 H. Mintzherg, *Reflecting on the strategy process*, Sloan Management Review, 1999.

497 R.E. Quinn, S. Sonenshein, *Four general strategies for changing human systems,* In: T.G. Cummings (Ed.), *Handbook of organization development* (pp. 69–78). Los Angeles: Sage 2008.

Tab. 26: Different concepts of change in different management paradigms. Source: Own work.

Paradigms	Neopositivist-functionalist-systemic paradigm	Interpretative-symbolic paradigm	Critical paradigm (radical structuralism)	Postmodernism
Aim of the change	An increase in effectiveness or the cost-effectiveness of the organisation's functioning.	An increase in the awareness and reflection of the organisational actors.	Emancipation of disadvantaged groups in an organisation.	Pointless, a change for the sake of a change.
Positive and negative changes	Positive changes improve organisations and employees, making them more effective (progress), while negative changes mean regress.	Positive changes enrich interpretations and meanings, while the negative limit the discourse.	Positive changes promote equality, while negative changes limit it.	Assessment of changes depends only on the criteria and assumptions of the discourse.
Understanding of the change	Transformation of the organisational system and its sub-systems, leading to a better use of resources and the adjustment to the environment.	Transformation of individual identities of organisation participants and collective organisational identities.	Levelling inequalities in the access to power and resources in organisations and eliminating 'false awareness.'	A constant flow of the discourse and power within different meta-narratives.
Type of change	Evolutionary, continuous, controlled, conscious.	Evolutionary, continuous, uncontrolled, unconscious.	Revolutionary, discontinuous, combining the aspects of control and spontaneity, as well as consciousness and unconsciousness.	Revolutionary, discontinuous, uncontrolled, unconscious.
Subjects of the change	Organisation as a whole, systems, sub-systems, employees.	Organisational actors, organisation as a whole.	Employees subject to power and those wielding power.	People, organisations, narratives.
Methods of the change	Introduction of 'modern' methods of management, such as TQM, reengineering etc.	Introduction of new senses and interpretations to the discourse, e.g. management of meaning.	Denaturalisation and dismantling of the petrified structures of power and making disadvantaged groups more aware.	Deconstruction of discourses and narratives.

(*continued on next page*)

Tab. 26: Continued

Paradigms	Neopositivist-functionalist-systemic paradigm	Interpretative-symbolic paradigm	Critical paradigm (radical structuralism)	Postmodernism
Barriers to the change	Organisational and cultural resistance to changes, being a result of employees' fears and the structural inertia.	Problems with changing the consolidated interpretations and stereotypes.	Conscious and unconscious resistance of those in power and false awareness.	Complete lack of control over changes, which are random and indeterminist.
Assessment of the change	Axiologically neutral.	Inherent part of valuation.	Evaluative.	Evaluative.
Metaphors	Machine, organism, evolution.	Flow, acting.	Class struggle.	Root.

role of cultural processes in change management, and is connected with the evolutionary or resource-based approach to organisational strategy. In the epistemological meanings, this approach can be based on the interpretative-symbolic paradigm or the neopositivist-functionalist. Chin and Benne point to several common features of normative/re-educational strategies:

1. All emphasise the involvement of stakeholders in the process of changes.
2. The key problem of the implementation of changes is not the access to information but culture.
3. Unrealised factors play a significant role in change management.
4. Theories and methods of the behavioural sciences are resources that can be used by stakeholders, especially the agents of changes[498].

The strategies of coercive changes are based on power to a greater extent than the rationalist-empirical, which are oriented towards knowledge, or the normative/re-educational, which relate more to culture. In the epistemological meaning, the strategies of coercive changes can use the critical current (Critical Management Studies, radical structuralism), which explores the topic of the organisational power's oppressiveness[499]. In this sense, the implementation of change is a

498 R. Chin, K.D. Benne, *General strategies for effecting changes in human systems*, In: W.G. Bennis, K.D. Benne, R. Chin (Eds.), *The planning of change* (4th ed., pp. 22–43). New York: Holt, Rinehart & Winston 1985.

499 M. Alvesson, H. Willmott (eds), *Critical Management Studies*, London: Sage 1992.

Tab. 27: Models of cultural changes within different paradigms. Source: Own work.

Paradigm	The essence of changes	The model of changes	The techniques of changes
Neopositivist-functionalist-systemic	Adaptation to the environment	1. Cultural audit 2. Ideal model of culture 3. Identification of the gap 4. Planned changes, controlling	Surveys and questionnaires, interview, focuses, expert panels, observations, documentation analyses, case studies, planned and controlled actions of leaders and agents of changes in the area of strategy, HR management, structure reorganisation, training courses.
	The effectiveness of organisational culture	1. Models of effective culture 2. Evolutionary or revolutionary changes	
Interpretative-symbolic	Management of meaning	1. Creation and consolidation of meanings. 2. Enactment	In-depth interviews, focuses, discourse and text analyses, anthropological case studies, spontaneous actions of leaders and agents of changes in the area of identity and practices change, based on intuition and ad hoc activities.
	Organisational identity change.	Incremental change of the triad: vision – culture – organisational identity.	
Critical current	Criticism of culture's oppressiveness.	1. Deconstruction. 2. Denaturalisation.	In-depth interviews, critical and reflective text analyses.
	Emancipation of organisational culture.	Implementation of emancipation culture.	Empowerment, parity, action research, intervention sociology, actions of leaders and agents of changes in the area of strategy, HR management, structure reorganisation, training courses.
Postmodernism	Cultural deconstruction. Organisational metaphors and paradoxes.	Deepening reflection, distance and irony.	Glossing, metaphorical and paradoxical references to the organisation.

political process, oriented towards power, manifested in the conscious decisions of managers and owners and the unconscious, often concealed processes of the distribution of privileges and power within a hierarchy. Through the processes of power distribution, this current combines the strategic and structural views with the cultural one. Strategic change always brings about structural change, and is closely linked with cultural processes. Because of the control of meanings and 'symbolic violence', culture is a reflection of hierarchy[500].

7.2 Functionalist changed in culture

Change management is mostly based on the systemic and functionalist approaches. This is a result of the pragmatic character of this area of management, the aim of which is to prepare methodologies of making changes to improve organisations, mostly from the point of view of their economic effectiveness.

The general position, based on the neopositivist-functionalist-systemic paradigm, is quite optimistic in terms of changing organisational culture. Most authors believe that culture can be managed or, at east, shaped in a significant way. Thus, a number of concepts and methodologies were created in relation to the implementation of changes in culture and through culture. Some of the authors who regard management through culture as successful include E. Schein, P. Bate, C. Handy, T. Deal and A. A. Kennedy. However, as the research was conducted and the projects of cultural changes implemented, it turned out that steering culture is a very difficult, even impossible undertaking. This issue was raised by the representatives of interpretative, critical and postmodernist paradigms, such as H. Willmott, M. Alvesson, Z. Bauman, G. Burrell, L. Smircich. Numerous practical consulting projects, based on the assumptions of organisational culture management or intercultural management, have failed. Good examples are the breaking of a strategic Daimler-Chrysler alliance and the collapse of a number of companies described by T. Peters and R. Waterman as being based on 'perfect' values[501]. Furthermore, this difficulty in practically steering a culture has forced many functionalist researchers to be more careful in their assessment of the possibility of managing culture. Burman and Evans believe it is not management that influences organisational culture changes, but leadership. Cultural change, especially in the case of organisations with strong organisational cultures, is a difficult, long-term process that cannot be fully controlled[502].

In trying to characterise the functionalist-systemic, 'soft' concepts of management of organisational changes, one can point to several features:

---

500 P. Bourdieu, *Espace social et pouvoir symbolique*, in: *Choses dites*, Minuit, Paris 1987.

501 Peters, Thomas J., Robert H. Waterman, and Ian Jones. 'In search of excellence: Lessons from America's best-run companies.' (1982): 101..

502 R. Burman, A.J. Evans, *Target Zero: A Culture of safety*, Defence Aviation Safety Centre Journal, 2008, pp. 22–27.

1. Their main problems are the social and cultural conditions of change processes, conditioned by all the various kinds of behaviour and interactions in organisations.
2. They can concern the change of organisational culture itself or the change of other aspects of the organisation, made through culture, such as the implementation of a new mission and vision, marketing orientation or implementation of the TQM system.
3. A very broad range of problems that is difficult to study or manage, resulting from the controversial nature of the theory of culture.
4. They are interdisciplinary, which means they are rooted not only in different areas of management, such as organisational behaviour, organisational learning, quality management and strategic management, but also in sociology, social psychology, cultural anthropology, cultural studies and other social sciences and humanities.
5. They are distinguished by a systemic character, which means treating the process of change management as a transformation of the whole organisation, as these two elements are interdependent. Additionally, cultural changes are inseparably connected with the transformation of strategy, structure and other elements of the organisation.

Reflection on the functionalist methods of cultural changes should begin with the more general models, and then move on to the methods and techniques. Analysis of the concept of cultural change in management begins with a classical approach, based on the model of change by K. Lewin, who was a pioneer in the research into the cultural conditions of changes[503]. One popular concept of cultural change, using Lewin's model, was proposed by E. H. Schein. It consists in the implementation of social norms that favour changes and are carried out in three steps: unfreezing, changing, and re-freezing[504]. This approach is still used in management, as it draws attention to the need for the consolidation of changes, and is also not only characteristic of management as it was adapted by Schein to suit organisational changes, having previously been used only with reference to planned changes.

Looking for a general point of reference for cultural change management, it is worth taking inspiration from the works of one of the most eminent

503 K. Lewin, R. Lippitt, R.K. White, *Patterns of aggressive behavior in experimentally created social climates*, Journal of Social Psychology, 1939, 10: 271–301.

504 E.H. Schein, *The Planning of Change*, Holt, Reinhart and Winston, New York 1969, p. 98.

Fig. 10: The typology of reactions to cultural change. Source: Own work.

Change of the organisational culture value		**Acceptance**	**Rejection**
	Acceptance	CONFORMISM	INNOVATION
	Rejection	RITUALISM	REBELION, WITHDRAWAL

functionalists, R. K. Merton. Merton proposed the deviation matrix[505] which – adapted to management – seems to aptly describe the types of social actors' reactions to cultural changes (Fig. 10).

Merton's matrix describes the functionalist concept of the cultural aims' concordance with the institutional means used, understood sociologically. Moving it to the level of management, one can propose an analysis of concordance of the basic organisational culture assumptions with the aims of the planned change. Social actors, stakeholders or subculture members, or even all employees (in the case of changes imposed from the outside) have to make a choice out of five possible options of action. On the one hand, the choice depends on the degree of acceptance of the aims of the change, and on the other, on the acceptance of new values and cultural norms the change entails. From the point of view of those planning the changes, conformism is the appropriate reaction. Conformism here means that the aims of the change are accepted, just as the new values that are gradually internalised. Innovation includes the involvement of social actors (stakeholders), moving towards the rejection of the aims of the change and proposing others. At the same time, stakeholders are aware of the need for a change of the organisational culture values and they accept cultural changes. It is a situation when the social actors put pressure on the decision-makers, in order to correct the set aims of the change, assuming that changes are necessary and positive. Ritualism is an acceptance of the aims of the change, but the social actors maintain the 'old' values. This is a result of the attachment to values and norms from before the change, together with the influence of the petrified organisational culture. After the change, the old values and norms are incompatible with the new aims, which lead to ritualism – detachment of organisational customs from the rational (functional) basis. In practice, this means that some types of collective behaviour are ritually 'enacted', even

505 R.K. Merton, Social Structure and Anomie, American Sociological Review, (1938–10), 3 (5): 672–682; L. Tepperman, J. Curtis, *Principles of Sociology: Canadian Perspectives*, Oxford University Press 2006, Canada, p. 117.

though they are no longer connected with the real aims of the organisation. In consequence, the organisational system is incompatible with the cultural and strategic spheres. These last two reactions stem from the rejection of changes both in the sphere of their aims and values. Such a rejection can take a passive form, which here means a withdrawal from the activities and involvement in the organisational life, or an active form, which is rebellion and creation of resistance to the changes. This brief analysis allows us to apply the matrix to specific cases of change, which should take into consideration diverse responses to the changes, not only from stakeholders, but also from individual, significant organisational actors.

Another important functionalist issue concerning change management is the notion of equilibrium. An organisational system is stable when it is balanced. Each change, by definition, disturbs this balance, and so it is a challenge for the organisational system to create models recovering the balance. Punctuated equilibrium is an example of this concept[506].

The systemic nature of change management through culture can be found in most concepts of organisational learning and development treated as an activity, consisting in the creation and consolidation of positive values and cultural models. Nonaka and Takeuchi developed a model of organisational learning, using the previous concepts of Argyris, Schön and Kim, in which the key role is played by tacit knowledge, which by definition is an element of culture[507]. Cultural models are, by definition, tacit, intuitive and absorbed unintentionally by individuals and communities in the socialisation process. In his systemic concept of changes, P. Senge notes that there are cultural barriers to changes, rooted in organisational values and norms, which can hinder the organisational development. In order to overcome these, it is necessary to conduct research, reflect and understand how the organisation functions[508].

---

506 S.L. Brown, K.M. Eisenhardt, *The Art of Continuous Change: Linking Complexity Theory and Time-Paced Evolution in Relentlessly Shifting Organizations*, Administrative Science Quarterly Vol. 42, No. 1 (Mar., 1997), pp. 1–34

507 I. Nonaka, H. Takeuchi, *The Knowledge Creating Company*. New York: Oxford University Press 1995; C. Argyris, D. Schön, *Organizational Learning: A theory of action perspective*, Reading MA: Addison-Wesley 1978; D.H. Kim, *The Link between Individual and Organizational Learning*, Sloan Management Review 1993, 35 (1): 37–50.

508 P. Senge, *The Fifth Discipline: The art and practice of the learning organization*, Doubleday, New York, 1990.

It is also necessary to coherently combine traditional tools for managing a whole organisation with methods of shaping its organisational culture[509]. Organisational culture should be subject to changes adjusting it to the key changes taking place in the environment, especially in a competitive sector. E. Schein lists several possible negative effects from the lack of cultural changes, which also have an influence on other organisational elements:

1. Limiting the possibility of implementing new strategies – values of the 'old' organisational culture are at odds with the assumptions of the new strategy.
2. Problems in situations where subjects are connected and allied – irrelevance of cultures.
3. Problems with the implementation of new organisational forms, new technologies and structural changes – inconsistency of extant values with the planned changes.
4. Creation of conflicts between groups within organisations – excessive consolidation of subcultures and counter-cultures.
5. Problems with the communications system – different cultural perspective of subcultures within the organisation (lack of the convergence of perception).
6. Problems concerning the secondary socialisation of employees – hermetic cultures limit the possibility of assimilating new organisation members.
7. Lowering the work effectiveness – new cultural forms can lower the effectiveness and efficiency of employees' activities[510].

The development of organisational culture is related with other aspects of management, such as strategic management (mission expresses values), quality management (TQM as a change in the enterprise's philosophy) and human resources management (recruitment, motivation and staff development reflect the organisation's values). However, the organisational culture is not completely comparable will all elements of management[511]. It is the object of intentional modification of values, norms and patterns resulting from them. In consequence, new, coherent, more effective patterns should be created, in specific conditions of the configuration of the organisational culture. Consistent configuration concerns both relationships between the values and subsystems, and the consistency with

509 K. Blanchard, M. O'Connor, *Managing by Values*, Berrett-Koehler Publishers; 1 edition (December 10, 1996).

510 E.H. Schein, *Organisational Culture and Leadership*, John Wiley & Sons, 2004, pp. 30–44.

511 Not all researchers think so f. ex. J.J. Dahlgaard and others. (J.J. Dahlgaard, *Fundamentals of Total Quality Management*, Routledge, 2005, chapter 18).

the context of social culture thatthe organisation functions in. There remains the question of whether such a coherent configuration of values can be effectively developed, and if so, which organisational methods should be applied.

Organisational culture has an influence on the organisation's effectiveness through: (1) impact on individual effectiveness; (2) creation of motivation and involvement; (3) normative control of organisational behaviour and (4) interactions with other organisational subsystems. The shaping of organisational culture leads to the possibility of influencing the directions of its development. The process can be part of planned changes in the area of culture, as well as a continuation and consolidation of the previous directions of culture's development. Many organisational researchers note that it is possible to introduce controlled, intentional, evolutionary, or ever revolutionary changes in organisational culture[512]. In the case of making changes in an organisational culture, all three forms are possible, but the question of the level of control over the changes remains disputable.

Particular care should be taken while determining the possibility of shaping an organisational culture. Changes within cultures are difficult to foresee in the long run. However, it is always possible to find symptoms of changes or new orientations that are being created. In addition, it is possible to make interventions to change the orientation or adjust the cultural values and patterns that are being formed. Nonetheless, such cultural intervention does not guarantee that the desired cultural configuration will be reached.

An especially significant role is played by the shaping of culture in situations when organisations have to make quick changes. In the context of globalisation, with the growing number of economic sectors there is a growing need for organisational change. Culture should not be a barrier to changes, but a catalyst. R. H. Kilmann distinguishes the following stages of directing cultural changes:

- Bringing current norms to the surface,
- Outlining new directions of development,
- Determining new norms,
- Identifying the cultural gap,
- Eliminating the cultural gap[513].

---

512 Warnecke, Hans-Jurgen, and Manfred Huser. 'The Fractal Factory: Revolution in Corporate Culture.' (1993).; K. Blanchard, M. O'Connor, M. J O'Connor, *Managing by Values*, Berrett-Koehler Publisher, 1996, p. 105.

513 R.H. Kilmann, T.Y. Covin, *Corporate Transformation Revitalizing Organization for a Competitive World*, Josey-Bass, San Francisco 1988.

This is an instrumental approach to organisational culture, assuming that it is possible to identify the features of the current culture and the 'ideal' culture[514], which supports the organisation's effectiveness in the given context. Cultural changes can be stimulated, but they cannot be fully controlled, while determining the 'ideal' culture in a very diverse and changeable environment can entail great risks.

T. G. Cummings and C. G. Worley formulated six rules for implementing organisational change, with reference to J. P. Kotter's famous concept[515]:

1. Creating a clear strategic vision that includes the organisation's values.
2. Showing the full involvement of managers, and especially top management, in the process of change.
3. Making changes at the top of the hierarchy and appointing agents of those changes.
4. Adjusting all organisational elements to the changed culture and strategy, as a result of systemic transformations in the organisation's structure and human resources policy.
5. Adapting employees in accordance with new rules, which means appropriate selection and training of new employees, as well as providing those already employed with the conditions and time to transform.
6. Developing ethical and normative sensitivity, as cultural changes always disturb the status quo, and so usually there are those who lose as well as beneficiaries[516]. At this stage, it is especially important to identify the barriers to changes.

There are a number of techniques that can be applied to shape culture, including its consolidation, correction, development and change. The following could be mentioned: (1) redefinition of organisational changes; (2) creation of new normative rules; (3) change of cultural elements; (4) adaptation of artefacts to the core values undergoing change; (5) composition and decomposition of

514 C. f.: R. Hagberg, J. Heifetz, *Corporate culture/organizational culture: understanding and assessment*, http://www.hcgnet.com/html/articles/understanding-Culture, November 10, 2002, pp. 1–5.

515 T.G. Cummings, C.G. Worley, *Organization Development and Change*,,8th Ed., South-Western College Pub. 2004, p. 491 – 492; J.P. Kotter, D.S. Cohen, *The Heart of Change: Real-Life Stories of How People Change Their Organizations*, Harvard Business Press, 2002.

516 T.G. Cummings, C.G. Worley, *Organization Development and Change*, South-Western College Pub, 8 edition, 2004, p. 491.

the mission; (6) designing systems of communication and power; (7) changing the content of job descriptions; (8) meetings, discussions and training of employees; (9) shaping the roles of leaders in the organisation (e.g. as agents of change, role models, heroes, innovators); (10) shaping motivational systems, and (11) changing the selection criteria. These are diverse individual and group techniques, which shape the organisational culture directly (points 1–4) or indirectly (points 5–11). Firstly, the identified values should be redefined, and its final configuration should be 'carefully' assumed. Then, it is necessary to adjust all other elements of culture to the values undergoing changes. At the same time, the changes of culture should be connected with the potential changes in the area of strategy, structure and human resources. The method of cultural intervention assumes evolutionary or revolutionary changes in the organisational culture. Evolutionary changes modify the extant culture, are slower, and do not negate or break the continuum while revolutionary changes are rapid, and often focus on the negation and destruction of the previous cultural configuration. In most cases this entails an in-depth transformation of the organisation, including significant changes within all subsystems and the replacement of the core staff.

In conclusion, it could be said that, as the functionalist claimed, it is possible to shape organisational culture, although the process cannot be fully controlled. The activities of managers and employees can lead to changes within culture. However, the nature of culture is very complex and the directions of its changes can be difficult to predict and plan. In addition, the process of changes in an organisational culture is complicated by other organisational cultural processes, such as power structure, strategy and the influence of changes in the environment.

7.3 Interpretative approach to cultural changes

Analysing the interpretative concepts of organisational changes, one must look at the four significant threads that distinguish this paradigm from functionalism. The first is the identification of organisation with culture, which leads to a conclusion that organisational changes and changes of organisational culture are the same. The second issue is the interpretivist critical approach to the possibility of managing culture. The third concerns the rejection of instrumental and manipulative approaches to organisational culture, and the last is the indeterminist and local understanding of cultural changes.

The interpretative perspective on organisational changes is entangled in cultural changes, resulting from the assumptions of symbolic interactionism, which places cultural meanings and the process of their interpretation in the centre of the paradigm. M. J. Hatch uses the notion of cultural dynamics, noting that the assumption of an interactionist perspective greatly extends the concept of E. Schein's organisational culture by the area of manifestation, implementation, symbolisation and interpretation[517]. This is a cultural transformation which takes place spontaneously, although it can also be used as a method of studying planned changes. According to the assumptions of social constructivism, organisational changes are phenomena that occur only within social relationships between people, and in the processes of creating, negotiating and agreeing on meanings. The interpretative-symbolic paradigm analyses cultural changes from the micro perspective, looking for their mechanisms in the interactions between social actors. Thus, changes are not individual processes that take place in social macrostructures, but are located at the mezzo level, in the relationships between social actors. Interpretivists treat organisational culture as a root metaphor, and identify it with the organisation itself[518]. This is why, contrary to functionalism, in this paradigm it is pointless to distinguish culture from other subsystems (strategy, organisational structure etc). Organisation is, by definition, permanently cultural, and so, in the case of symbolic interactionism paradigm, organisational changes and the changes to organisational culture are the same.

The position of interpretivists is sceptical about the possibility of managing organisational culture. Most authors emphasise that culture develops spontaneously and cannot be controlled, as it is set within complex interactions. These interactions include numerous social actors, diverse communication processes, negotiation, and the creation of status and power relationships. A great number of them are carried out intuitively and are not subject to full conscious control. Following such arguments, a large part of interpretivists rejected cognitive and pragmatic optimism, characteristic of functionalists. According to most interpretivists, one can get to know culture but it is virtually impossible to steer it[519].

---

517 M.J. Hatch, *The Dynamics of Organizational Culture*, 'Academy of Management Review', no. 18, 1993, pp. 657–693.

518 L. Smircich, *Studying Organizations as Cultures*, in: G. Morgan, *Beyond Method: Strategies for Social Research*, Beverly Hills-London-New Delhi 1983, pp. 160–172.

519 L. Smircich, *Concepts of Culture and Organizational Analysis*, Administrative Science Quarterly: 28(3), 1983, pp. 160–172.; M. Rosen, *Coming to the Terms with the field: Understanding and doing organisational ethnography*, 'Journal of Management Studies', no. 28, 1991, pp. 1–24.

Furthermore, interpretivists oppose the instrumentalisation of cultural issues in management, similarly to other representatives of alternative paradigms (based on social constructivism). Culture should not be treated as a tool for manipulating employees[520]. From the interpretivist point of view, the instrumentalisation of the approach to organisational culture, characteristic of many functionalist concepts, is not only unethical, but also ineffective in cognitive, methodological and pragmatic terms.

The determinist and Universalist understanding of cultural change is inherent in the basic assumptions of the NFS paradigm. This means that culture can be analysed by placing it in a causative model, which offers diagnostic possibilities and a predictive power. The interpretative approach to cultural changes contrasts with the functionalist, and is based on the indeterminist and local perspectives. Indeterminism says that the directions of cultural changes are unpredictable in the long run and that, in consequence, one should avoid prognoses and focus on diagnoses. On the other hand, the local approach to cultural change assumes that generalisation models are pointless, as they lose the uniqueness of a given culture. This is why interpretivists focus instead on in-depth research into individual cases.

The most important concepts of cultural change management within the interpretative-symbolic paradigm include sensemaking, enactment, management of an organisation's identity and the management of meaning. The concept of organisational identity was described in the chapter concerning the interpretative understanding of culture, and focuses on sensemaking and management of meaning.

The concept of sensemaking was proposed in the 1970s by K. Weick and became the subject of interest of such interpretivists as M. J. Hatch, L. Smircich, G. Morgan, A. D. Brown and others[521]. It seems that this is the most popular concept of management located within the interpretative-symbolic paradigm, which is confirmed by the large number of times Weick's book has been quoted from (more than 16,000 according to Google Scholar). The essence of this concept is that organisational reality is socially constructed through interpretations, perceptions, intentions and emotions of social actors. Thus, organisation is a network of meanings which create the collective identity, but at the same time it

520 Hatch, Mary Jo, and Ann L. Cunliffe. *Organization theory: modern, symbolic and postmodern perspectives*. Oxford university press, 2012., p. 233.
521 K.E. Weick, *Sensemaking in organizations*,, Thousand Oaks, CA: Sage 1995.

includes a multiplicity of individual and group identities (subcultures)[522]. This vision of organisation locates culture, interpretatively understood as a root metaphor, in the centre of the managerial discourse. Organisation equated with organisational culture is created and maintained based on a kind of 'acts of faith' because people identify it as a real entity, and conduct their activities in accordance with the interpretations they make. Organisational actors play their roles, creating identity in terms of the social order, consolidating it by activities, the aim of which is to build or question a consensus[523]. Social activities, through which identity is constructed, include dialogues with others and the creation of narratives[524]. When interpreting the organisational reality, people tend to assume simple solutions, based on implicitly accepted 'interpretative keys', often shared by organisation members[525], such as popular metaphors, stereotypes, archetypes, paradoxes and antinomies. This is a pragmatic approach, in which the credibility of the solutions assumed is more important than their precision[526]. According to Weick, this ambiguity and entanglement in interpretation is a fundamental feature of the organisational world. A change in the organisational identity, as well as individual and collective identities connected with it, is a permanent correlation[527]. Organisational actors interpret their own roles and social identities through the activities of others, and at the same time, try to shape the perception of others, consolidating their own, idealised image[528]. This feedback is a source of incremental cultural change, at the level of the whole organisation

---

522 K.E. Weick, *Sensemaking in organizations,*, Thousand Oaks, CA: Sage 1995; S. Maitlis, *The social processes of organizational sense making*, Academy of Management Journal, 2005, 48(1): 21–49.

523 J. Bruner, *The narrative construction of reality*, Critical Inquiry, 1991, 18: 1–21.

524 M. Abolafia, *Narrative construction as sensemaking*, Organization Studies, 2010, 31(3): 349–367.

525 A. D. Brown, P. Stacey, J. Nandhakumar, *Making sense of sensemaking narratives*, Human Relations, 2007, 61(8): 1035–1062.

526 K.E. Weick, *Sensemaking in organizations,*, Thousand Oaks, CA: Sage 1995., p. 61; R. Dunford, D. Jones, *Narrative in strategic change*, Human Relations, 2000, 53: 1207–1226; G. Currie, A. Brown, *A narratological approach to understanding processes of organizing in a UK hospital*, Human Relations, 2003, 56: 563–586.

527 A. Thurlow, J. Mills, *Change, talk and sensemaking*, Journal of Organizational Change Management, 2009, 22(5): 459–579. M.G. Pratt, *The good, the bad, and the ambivalent: Managing identification among Amway distributors*, Administrative Science Quarterly, 2000. 45: 456–493.

528 L.A. Isabella, *Evolving interpretations as change unfolds: How managers construe key organisational events*, Academy of Management Journal, 1990, 33(1).

(organisational culture), the collective identities (subcultures) it is made of and individual identities of organisational actors.

An important problem of perceiving the cultural change is retrospection and the creation of collective memory[529]. Organisational identity, according to A. Albert and D. A. Whetten's criteria, crystallises through the sense of temporal continuity[530]. This is related to the intersubjective process of creation of an organisation's collective memory, which is a kind of a narrative about the origins and development of the organisation, created by its members, and often also by other stakeholders. Thus, cultural changes can be made in two ways. The first includes incremental, evolutionary and slow changes, which are not perceived by the organisational actors as changes. The other type includes cultural transformation that is visible to the organisational actors, and in many cases even stimulated by them. Naturally, the directions of such changes cannot be controlled, as they are made spontaneously. The cultural changes are reflected in the emerging and changing narratives, which appear spontaneously, but should be a projection of the transformations taking place[531].

The world's literature offers much research and numerous concepts of change, culture and organisational identity using sensemaking. The most significant examples of such research are focused on strategic change management through sensemaking and sensegiving, achieving greater effectiveness and reducing the effects of crises, implementing changes by middle-level managers, and resisting changes.

1. Sensemaking and sensegiving can be used as methods for making strategic changes, in which managers become the creators and propagators of new meanings that are of key importance to the organisation. The research here includes a study on change at a public university, carried out in several stages, described as envisioning, signalling, re-visioning and energising[532].

529 T.J. Watson, *Managerial sensemaking and occupational identities in Britain and Italy: The role of management magazines in the process of discursive construction*, Journal of Management Studies, 1998, 35(3): 285–301.

530 S. Albert, D.A. Whetten, *Organizational Identity*, in: 'Organisational Identity. A Reader', red. M.J. Hatch, M. Schultz, Oxford University Press, Oxford – New York 2004, p. 90.

531 G. Currie, A. Brown, *A narratological approach to understanding processes of organizing in a UK hospital*, Human Relations, 2003, 56: 563–586.

532 D.A. Gioia, K. Chittipeddi, *Sensemaking and sensegiving in strategic change initiation*, Strat. Mgmt. J., 1991, 12: 433–448. doi: 10. 1002/smj. 4250120604.

This concept was presented by D. A. Gioia and J. B. Thomas as sensemaking in strategic changes through the management of identity and organisational image[533].

2. Using sensemaking in order to achieve greater effectiveness in the process of evolutionary change. Research was carried out in 156 hospitals and serves as an example of methodological pluralism, which is the combination of quantitative and qualitative methods[534].
3. Implementation of change is often crucial in the case of a crisis in the organisation. Noting that processes of analysis and reflection on the effects of crisis, conducted by managers, can deepen the crisis, K. Weick proposed a concept of interpretative change (enactment), easing the effects of the crisis[535].
4. Changes during a crisis can lead to development, thanks to the creation of an organisational creativity model making use of the sensemaking concept[536].
5. Change management should use sensemaking mostly among middle-level managers, who would become the agents of the change[537]. In his study of a clothing enterprise, L. Rouleau analysed the process of implementing changes with the use of sensemaking among middle-level managers.
6. Strategic change management has unpredictable effects, being a consequence of interpretations that are beyond the control of those who implement changes. Managers, especially at the middle level, can shape these interpretations and thus facilitate the change process[538].

---

533 D.A. Gioia, J.B. Thomas, Identity, *Image, and Issue Interpretation: Sensemaking During Strategic Change in Academia*, Administrative Science Quarterly Vol. 41, No. 3 (Sep., 1996), pp. 370–403

534 J.B. Thomas, S.M. Clark, D.A. Gioia, *Strategic Sensemaking and Organizational Performance: Linkages among Scanning, Interpretation, Action, and Outcomes*, The Academy of Management Journal Vol. 36, No. 2 (Apr., 1993), pp. 239–270

535 K.E. Weick, *Enacted sensemaking in crisis situations*, Journal of Management Studies, 1988, 25: 305–317.

536 R. Drazin, M.A. Glynn, R.K. Kazanjian, *Multilevel Theorizing about Creativity in Organizations: A Sensemaking Perspective*, The Academy of Management Review, Vol. 24, No. 2 (Apr., 1999), pp. 286–307

537 L. Rouleau, *Micro-Practices of Strategic Sensemaking and Sensegiving: How Middle Managers Interpret and Sell Change Every Day*, Journal of Management Studies, 2005, 42: 1413–1441.

538 J. Balogun, G. Johnson, *From Intended Strategies to Unintended Outcomes: The Impact of Change Recipient Sensemaking*, Organization Studies, November 2005; vol. 26, 11: pp. 1573–1601.

7. Another example of the use of sensemaking to implement new organisational meanings, with the use of paradoxes, is the study of the Danish Lego company by L. S. Lüscher, M. W. Lewis[539].
8. Sensemaking can also be used to reduce the barriers to the implementation of organisational changes by using the agents of change[540].
9. P. S. Weber and M. R. Manning propose applying sensemaking and the technique of creating causative maps to the implementation of planned organisational changes[541].
10. Sensemaking can be applied to changes in human resources, for example to analyse a manager's change processes[542] or the adaption of new employees to the organisational culture[543].

These are only 10 examples of how to use the sensemaking concept in management science. Today, this is one of the most important areas of reflection on organisational culture, based on the interpretative-symbolic paradigm.

Enactment is one of K. Weick's ideas, and is closely related to sensemaking. Unfortunately, it is also as difficult to translate as 'sensemaking'. In legal terms it means 'coming into force' or 'enforcement', but on the other hand it also means 'acting on a stage', 'presenting', and 'dramatic interpretation'. K. Weick plays on this ambiguity, using the term as an establishment of an interpretation (a creation of a consensus around an organisational meaning, which is a kind of enforcement), and at the same time, as a social game which implements this interpretation through action[544]. The enactment concept is a presentation of different ways of maintaining the continuity of organisational identity and the organisational

539 L.S. Lüscher, M.W. Lewis, *Change and Managerial Sensemaking: Working through Paradox*, The Academy of Management Journal, vol 51 no. 2, 2008, pp. 221–240.

540 J.D. Ford, L.W. Ford, A. D'Amoto, *Resistance to Change: The Rest of the Story*, Academy of Management, Volume 33, Number 2 / April 2008, pp. 362–377.

541 P.S. Weber, M.R. Manning, Cause Maps, Sensemaking, and Planned Organizational Change, Journal of Applied Behavioral Science June 2001 vol. 37 no. 2 227–251

542 R.P. Gephart, Jr, *Succession Sensemaking and Organizational Change: A Story of a Deviant College President*, Journal of Organizational Change Management, 1991, Vol. 4 Iss: 3, pp. 35 – 44

543 M.R. Louis, *Surprise and Sense Making: What Newcomers Experience in Entering Unfamiliar Organizational Settings*, Administrative Science Quarterly, Vol. 25, No. 2 (Jun., 1980), pp. 226–25

544 K.E. Weick, *The Social Psychology of Organizing*, New York: McGraw-Hill 1979; K.E. Weick, *Enacted sensemaking in crisis situations*, Journal of Management Studies, 1988, 25: 305–317.

roles of the interested parties. People within the organisation are the creators of their own identity and the organisational identity through the enforcement of the interaction chains, the acceptance of norms of appropriate behaviour and the creation of routines (e.g. customs, rituals)[545]. Thus, enactment is a concept of the analysis of the organisational culture dynamics, which uses the organisational anthropology and storytelling[546]. Enactment is sometimes used in the analysis of organisational identity and culture[547].

An example of the evolution of the sensemaking idea is the management of meaning. Management of meaning was popularised by G. Morgan and L. Smircich in relation to the analysis of the leadership process. The actions of organisational leaders are analyses from the point of view of symbolic interactionism, while the leadership process was presented as:

- Creation of the cognitive framework by leaders (drawn from E. Goffman's framework analysis),
- Interpretation of the situation by the leader and other organisational actors (with use of the figure-ground concept, drawn from gestalt psychology),
- The meaning and action (combining the interpretative and gestalt perspectives).

Organisational managers, following their own interpretations, aims and narratives, implicitly or explicitly create the concepts of the organisation's development. Their key elements are significant, often new meanings, which leaders try to communicate to the employees and other organisational actors. This managerial process is part of the creation of a vision of the organisational reality through narratives, and, as each communications process, this is a complex interaction. The vision of the organisational reality, promoted by the leader, is accompanied by counter-visions, created by the opposing subcultures. Thus, organisational leadership is a symbolic activity, carried out consciously and unconsciously, reminiscent of a complex game of social actors. The methods of its study include organisational ethnography, making use of case studies, framework analysis, as well as other, interpretative methods of cultural management

545 E.M. Eisenberg, H.L. Goodall, *Organizational Communication: Balancing creativity and constraint,* (2nd ed.) New York: St. Martin's Press 1997.

546 L.L. Putnam, *Negotiating as organizing: Two levels within the Weickian model,* Communication Studies, 1989. 40, 249–257.

547 S.M.B. Thatcher, X. Zhu, *Changing Identities in a Changing Workplace: Identification, Identity Enactment, Self-Verification, and Telecommuting,* The Academy of Management Review, Vol. 31, No. 4 (Oct., 2006), pp. 1076–1088

described below. In its symbolic aspect, the leadership process is especially visible during crises, which was described by Morgan and Smircich[548]. As the key elements of management of meaning are meanings, this is a concept occupying the focal point of the cultural current in management. Most concepts, created based on the management of meaning, relate all kinds of change processes[549].

Concepts located within the symbolic interactionism paradigm of the management of identity and organisational culture, such as sensemaking, enactment, organisational identity management and management of meaning, are reflected in the interpretative methods of research into organisations. The interpretative methodology of research into cultural change is of a qualitative character, although it is not orthodox. Instead, it focuses on the methods of in-depth, individual and non-representative research, which allows us to understand cultural changes, but not to measure them. On the other hand, interpretivists usually assume methodological pluralism, postulating the use of numerous different research methods. Moreover, there is no agreement between researchers oriented towards symbolic interactionism as to the assessment of the quantitative methodology. Some researchers are completely open and believe that a compilation of qualitative and quantitative methods leads to creative research results. Other authors think that we should use only qualitative methods, because research compiling both approaches gives contradictory or disproportionate results. This author is in favour of the open, multi-pragmatic approach and I believe that even disproportionate and contradictory research results can be a source of interesting interpretations for researchers.

The methodology of interpretative research into cultural changes in management has several characteristic features, all related to the paradigm. This is because the methodology is:

1. Qualitative – it focuses on understanding (hermeneutic), in-depth, non-representative research which does not make it possible to measure results,
2. Idiographic – it gives individual descriptions and no possibility to generalise,
3. Of an emic type – it conducts individual, local research, making use of a 'thick description' and popular categories of subjects.

548 L. Smircich, G. Morgan, *Leadership: The Management of Meaning*, The Journal of Applied Behavioral Science 1982, Vol. 18, 3:257–273.

549 B. Czarniawska, *The management of meaning in the polish crisis*, Journal of Management Studies, 1986, 23: 313–331.

Analysing the multiplicity of methods used for the analysis of cultural changes from the interpretative-symbolic perspective, it can be seen that there are numerous diverse methods. The most important are the methods of organisational anthropology (organisational ethnology), which are field methods based on the assumptions that subjects are studied in their natural environment.

The classical anthropological method is commonly used, which consists in all kinds of observation (participatory, non-participatory, overt and covert). Furthermore, unique anthropological methods have been developed, such as shadowing, which is used in research into cultural changes in management. This method consists in observation and passive participation in the subject's work for a longer period (several days or weeks)[550].

The second interpretative method most often used is the interview, which is always of an in-depth and open character. In this case, organisational anthropology draws on the experiences of cultural anthropology, conducting research in the form of in-depth and biographical interviews. Apart from individual interviews, the methodology of group focus interviews is also developed. This was created within functionalism, and then adapted by interpretivists. The assumption of group interviews is the understanding of activities in a social context, where they acquire their intersubjective aspect and a group influence is revealed[551].

The third large group of interpretative methods takes from language studies (spoken and textual) and includes conversational, narrative, metaphorical and discursive methods, as well as qualitative text analyses. The assumption of conversational analyses, stemming from ethnomethodology, is the interpretation of the course of natural interactions that take place in everyday life. This is a cultural perspective that changes on a micro scale, including the communication and interactions between individuals. These are expressed by, amongst others, sequences of utterances, preferred types of utterances and ways of restoring dialogue[552]. Currently, this method is often used with the support of specialist computer software[553]. The narrative inquiry is based on the interpretation of the ways people give meaning to the social reality by creating narratives. The research

---

550 B. Czarniawska, *The management of meaning in the polish crisis*, Journal of Management Studies, 1986, 23: 313–331.

551 R.K. Merton, M. Fiske, P.L. Kendall, *The Focused Interview. A Manual of Problems and Procedures*, The Free Press, Glencoe, Illinois 1956.

552 H. Sacks, Lectures on Conversation, Volumes I and II, Edited by G. Jefferson with Introduction by E.A. Schegloff, Blackwell, Oxford 1992.

553 J. Sidnell, T. Stivers (eds.), *Handbook of Conversation Analysis*, Boston: Wiley-Blackwell 2012; J. Sidnell, Conversation Analysis: An Introduction, London: Wiley-Blackwell

and pragmatic technique, used within the narrative current is storytelling, which can improve the cognition of organisational culture[554] or management[555]. D. A. Jameson described how storytelling could be used by managers to interpret the organisational world, resolve conflicts and enhance creative thinking[556]. Other authors believe that the role of storytelling is to build identity and the organisation's image[557]. Metaphorical analysis, created by G. Morgan[558], is similar to narrative inquiry. It is based on the assumption that metaphors are fundamental categories for the interpretation of the world by the human mind[559]. By comparing organisational culture and its changes to other, better-understood processes and objects, it is possible to understand its complexity better. Therefore, organisational culture is compared by functionalists and interpretivists to such objects as glue, glasses, temple, dance, text, language, religion and many others. An interesting connotation, related to the narrative approach, is the fact that much research has been conducted within the neoevolutionary approach, proving that the human cognitive apparatus is especially well prepared to process and remember narratives and metaphors.

The methods of linguistic studies also include text analyses, which are quite heterogeneous and include qualitative techniques, which are often supported by quantitative techniques. Qualitative text analyses can take different forms:

- Conversational analysis, drawing inspirations from ethnomethodology,
- Content analysis, which has both interpretative and functionalist contexts[560],
- Critical and reflective reading – part of the critical paradigm.

Interpretative text analyses draw inspirations from hermeneutics, which is a philosophical method of reaching to the text meaning. They sometimes use the

---

2010; C. Antaki, *An introductory tutorial in Conversation Analysis*, 2002, Online at <http://www-staff.lboro.ac.uk/~ssca1/sitemenu.htm>, 2012.

554 B. Czarniawska, *A Narrative Approach to Organization Studies*, Qualitative Research methods Series Vol. 43. Thousand Oaks, Ca; Sage 1998.

555 S. Denning, *The Leader's Guide to Storytelling: Mastering the Art & Discipline of Business Narrative*, Jossey–Bass, San Francisco 2005.

556 D.A. Jameson, Narrative Discourse and Management Action, *Journal of Business Communication*, 2001, 38 (4), p. 476–511.

557 G. Lury, *Brand Strategy*, 2004, Issue 182, p. 32; C. Huang, *Advertising Age*, Volume 80, Issue 40, p. 13

558 G. Morgan, *Images of Organization*, Thousand Oaks, CA: Sage Publications, 1997.

559 G. Lakoff, M. Johnson, *Metaphors we live by*, Chicago University Press, Chicago 1980.

560 K. Krippendorff, *Content Analysis: An Introduction to Its Methodology*, 2nd edition, Thousand Oaks, CA: Sage 2004.

assumptions of phenomenology, looking for the text meaning as such (eidetic)[561]. Critical and postmodernist approaches to text analyses are often based in interpretivism, but are located within other paradigms[562]. Still, the classification of paradigms in relation to text analysis is ambiguous. For example, M. A. Janson proposes distinguishing three paradigms: positivist, linguistic and interpretative[563]. The interpretative approach to text analysis in the organisational discourse always refers to the description of culture, which is usually considered in micro scale, as social activities that are reflected by an ambiguous network of meanings and symbols[564]. Text analyses are broadly used as a research method and technique, being an element of a broader method, one example of which is case study. Some of the problems in researching culture and change management are leadership through culture[565], textual culture interpretation[566], theory of structuration and agency[567], relationships between text and conversation[568], or even a textual approach to accounting[569].

Case study is not only a technique, but also an extensive research methodology that can be located within different paradigms of the social sciences[570].

---

561 R. Ingarden, 'Theory of Knowledge as Phenomenology of the Essence of Cognitive Experiences and Their Correlates', transl. A. Szylewicz, *Aletheia: An International Journal of Philosophy*, t. 4: *Epistemology and Logic*, Bern: Lang 1988, pp. 1–106.

562 B. Czarniawska, *Writing Management. Organizational Theory as a Literary Genre*, Oxford: Oxford University Press. 1999.

563 M.C. Lacity, M.A. Janson, Understanding Qualitative Data: A Framework of Text Analysis Methods, *Journal of Management Information Systems*, Vol. 11, No. 2 (Fall, 1994), pp. 137–155

564 B. Czarniawska, *A Narrative Approach to Organization Studies*, SAGE, 1997.

565 M.F. Nielsen, Interpretative Management in Business Meetings Understanding Managers' Interactional Strategies through Conversation Analysis, *Journal of Business Communication* January 2009 vol. 46 no. 1 23–56.

566 M.H. Browns, J.J. McMillan, Culture as text: The development of an organizational narrative, *Southern Communication Journal*, Volume 57, Issue 1, 1991.

567 R.D. McPhee, *Text, Agency, and Organization in the Light of Structuration Theory*, *Organization* May 2004 vol. 11 no. 3 355–371.

568 J.R. Taylor, F. Cooren, N. Giroux, D. Robichaud, *The Communicational Basis of Organization: Between the Conversation and the Text, Communication Theory*, 1996, 6: 1–39.

569 R.J. Boland Jr., Beyond the objectivist and the subjectivist: Learning to read accounting as text, *Accounting, Organizations and Society*, Volume 14, Issues 5–6, 1989, Pages 591–604.

570 R. Gomm, M. Hammersley, P. Foster (eds.), Case study method: Key texts, key issues, London: Sage 2000.

However, it is worth noting that the increase in its popularity comes from development of the interpretative-symbolic paradigm[571], and that this is a very popular method in management science. The spread of case study in management had its sources in the practical orientation of our science. At first, case study was used as an educational method by Harvard Business School[572], then it became the key consulting method, but only after the interpretative approach gain significance, it became popular in science. Interpretative case study is subject to the analyses of organisational anthropology, ethnomethodology, the dramatic approach and other currents of qualitative research, with the aim to study a broad range of managerial problems, from identity and culture[573], through strategy and organisational change[574], to accounting[575], SME management[576] and marketing and information systems[577]. In the case of organisational anthropology, the dominant methods of research are cultural studies of organisations. They often concern the dynamic approach to organisational culture, which involves planned or

---

571 M. Wieviorka, Case studies: history or sociology?, In: C.C. Ragin, H.S. Becker (Eds), *What is a case? Exploring the foundations of social inquiry*, New York: Cambridge University Press 1992.

572 M.P. McNair, The Case Method at the Harvard Business School: Papers by Present and Past Members of the Faculty and Staff, New York: McGraw-Hill 1954, pp. 139; R. Corey, Case Method Teaching, Harvard Business School 9–581–058, Rev. November 6, 1998.

573 J.E. Dutton, J.M. Dukerich, Keeping an Eye on the Mirror: Image and Identity in Organizational Adaptation, *The Academy of Management Journal*, Vol. 34, No. 3 (Sep., 1991), pp. 517–554.

574 W.J. Orlikowski, CASE tools as organizational change: investigating incremental and radical changes in systems development, MIS *Quarterly*, Volume 17 Issue 3, September 1993; A.M. Pettigrew, Contextualist research and the study of organisational change processes, In: E. Munford et al. (Eds.), *Research methods in information systems*, New York: North Holland 1985.

575 M.-L. Kakkuri-Knuuttilaa, K. Lukkab, J. Kuorikoskic, Straddling between paradigms: A naturalistic philosophical case study on interpretive research in management accounting, *Accounting, Organizations and Society*, Volume 33, Issues 2–3, February–April 2008, Pages 267–291; M. Järvenpää, Making Business Partners: A Case Study on how Management Accounting Culture was Changed, *European Accounting Review*, Volume 16, Issue 1, 2007.

576 N. Costello, Learning and Routines in High-Tech SMEs: Analyzing Rich Case Study Material, *Journal of Economic Issues*, Vol. 30, No. 2 (Jun., 1996), pp. 591–597.

577 G. Walsham, T. Waema, *Information systems strategy and implementation: a case study of a building society*, ACM Transactions on Information Systems (TOIS), Volume 12 Issue 2, April 1994, p. 150–173.

spontaneous cultural changes. The most important authors concerned with such research are G. Morgan, M. G. Hatch, M. J. Hatch, L. Smircich, J. van Maanen and many others. In most cases, the subjects of case study are entire organisations, although there are also studies focusing mostly on people (employees, managers, leaders), smaller organisational units (departments, sections, teams), and even interactions (organisational situations, events). The choice of cases is, by definition, intentional and can be based on one of the three models: key cases, untypical cases, local cases. Key cases here mean the choice of the most important entity, for example the dominant enterprise in a given sector. The model of untypical choices entails selecting entities that are largely different from typical cases, for example a private company in a sector dominated by public organisations. The choice of cases based on local knowledge is part of the deliberate limitation of the selection model to an entity or entities (in the case of comparative analyses), which are more familiar to the researcher or in the case of which it is possible to conduct more in-depth research[578].

Interpretative case study has several characteristic features, distinguishing it from the case study located within the neopositivist-functionalist-systemic paradigm (Table 33).

1. A case study is an interpretative method allowing us to understand individual[579], difficult to capture, covert, and often unique aspects of an organisation, which cannot be the basis for the development of a model used for generalisation. This method is classified as qualitative, although it can also be based on quantitative data analysis, or even take the form of quantitative research[580]. It is worth drawing the attention to the promising attempts at combining case study with other research methods, including the quantitative[581].

---

578 B. Flyvberg, Case Study, In: N.K. Denzin, Y.S. Lincoln. eds. *The Sage Handbook of Qualitative Research*, 4th Edition. Thousand Oaks, CA: Sage 2011, Chapter 17, pp. 301–316.

579 B. Flyvberg, *Case study*, In: N.K. Denzin, Y.S. Lincoln. eds. *The Sage Handbook of Qualitative Research*, 4th Edition. Thousand Oaks, CA: Sage 2011, Chapter 17, pp. 301–316.

580 G. Thomas, A typology for the case study in social science following a review of definition, discourse and structure, *Qualitative Inquiry*, 2011, 17, 6, 511–521.

581 G.G. Gable, Integrating case study and survey research methods: an example in information systems, *European Journal of Information Systems*, 1994. 3(2), pp. 112–126; S. Modell, Triangulation between case study and survey methods in management accounting research: An assessment of validity implications, *Management Accounting Research*, Volume 16, Issue 2, June 2005, Pages 231–254.

2. The subject of study is usually the whole organisation, including its culture, identity, practices and interactions. It is usually treated dynamically as a process, transformation, and so an incremental change.
3. Case studies are the most important research method in the case of culture and changes. Organisational culture, and the culture's influence on the organisation, are perceived mostly on the micro scale through social practices (interactions, discourse, social games). This is why cultural research often focuses on organisational identities, both collective and individual. Case studies inspired by interpretivism strive for a dynamic approach, capturing the meaning of the changes and transformations taking place. This concerns organisational changes, mostly spontaneous but planned as well, which – from the interactionist perspective – can never be controlled. The concept of including culture in the process of changes stems from the negation of the functionalist approach in the classical cultural anthropology and sociology, which preferred static descriptions, oriented towards the status quo, permanence, functionality and a systematic nature of social practices.
4. The assumptions include pluralism and methodological triangulation. The methodology of research can even be based on methodological eclecticism (bricolage), so the multiplicity of research techniques is needed, which can give contradictory or disproportionate descriptions.
5. Researchers should strive for the position of insider, submerged in the culture, who also understands it intuitively. Valuation and involvement are valued. Subjectivism is not a problem.
6. By definition, case study of one case dominates, and its analysis is of an in-depth, explorative character.
7. The data most often used is qualitative, descriptive, subjective or intersubjective; its source is the communication with subjects and it is gathered with the use of anthropological techniques, such as free-form interviews, group interviews, participant and non-participant observations, discourse and text analyses.
8. Just like in the case of other interpretative methods, self-analysis and a description of cases known from personal experience are possible. Subjectivism and involvement are here accompanied by an in-depth knowledge of the case, e.g. an organisation in which the researcher worked.

Other methods characteristic of different currents of understanding culture include intervention sociology, frame analysis and the breaching experiment, which is almost never used in management. These are approaches to the analysis of changes in cultural processes, but so far, their application in research

Tab. 28: Case studies in management: The interpretative-symbolic paradigm vs. the neopositivist-functionalist-systemic paradigm. Source: Own work.

	Interpretative-symbolic paradigm	**Neopositivist-functionalist-systemic paradigm**
Method understanding	Striving for an understanding of the meaning of a people's and an organisation's activities.	Causative explanations of a people's and an organisation's activities.
Research aims	Interpretation of meaning, sense of individual cases, which are unique and cannot be generalised.	Finding explanations of individual cases that become models for generalisation in representative research.
Dominant research subjects	Organisation, identity and organisational culture, interactions, communication, people.	All structural elements of the organisation and functional elements of management.
Methodological assumptions	Methodological pluralism Methodological triangulation	Fundamentalism or methodological pluralism
Researcher's position	Insider, involved, does not strive for axiological neutrality.	Outsider, distanced, free of valuation.
Dominant research type	Individual, explorative, in-depth case study.	Explanatory, individual case study or comparative case analyses.
Preferred data type	Qualitative, descriptive, subjective or intersubjective.	Qualitative, analytical, objective or quasi-objective.
Role in management	The key method, used in all currents. A research, consulting and educational method.	Method used less often than survey and statistical methods. An educational, consulting and research method.
Research techniques	Organisational anthropology (interviews, observations, text and discourse analyses).	Analyses of quantitative and qualitative data, using documentary methods, surveys and observations.
Significance for cultural research	The most important method of research into organisational culture and culture in management.	An important research method, but cross-cultural comparative studies, using the survey method, are equally important.
Significance for research into change management	The most important method of research into organisational changes, mostly spontaneous but planned as well.	One of numerous methods of research into organisational culture, mostly planned but spontaneous as well. Studies based on quantitative data dominate[a].
Practical significance	Large, it is used for the purpose of consultancy and education.	Large, it is used for the purpose of education and consultancy.

Tab. 28: Continued

	Interpretative-symbolic paradigm	Neopositivist-functionalist-systemic paradigm
Chosen researchers using this method	G. Morgan, M. G. Hatch, M. J. Hatch, L. Smircich, J. van Maanen	G. Hofstede, A. Trompenaars, C. Hampden-Turner, C. Handy R. House, E. Schein

[a] S. Guha, V. Grover, W. J. Kettinger, J. T. C. Teng, J, *The impacts of business process change on organizational performance*, Journal of Management Information Systems - Special section, Volume 14 Issue 1, June 1997, pp. 119–154.

within management science has been very limited. The intervention method is based on the constructivist assumption concerning the creation of social movements, institutions, organisations and the whole society[582]. This methodology, mostly used to study social movements, assumes the involvement of a team of researchers in the process of creating the group identity[583]. Observations, interviews, shadowing meetings are supposed to bring out the essence of community, and to influence the process of its creation and crystallisation. This is the assumption of a researcher submerged in their studied social group, who is at once involved and occupying a place on the borderline between outsider and insider.

Frame analysis was proposed as a research method in 1974, in E. Goffman's book *Frame Analysis: An Essay on the Organisation of Experience*[584]. A 'frame analysis' can be understood as an interpretation of a text or a communications process, which brings out the subjective understanding of a situation. In other words, a 'frame' includes the rules managing discourse and communication, understood as hidden rules or concepts managing our process of interpreting the social reality[585]. Framing means choosing certain aspects of perceivable

582 A. Touraine, *The Self-production of Society*, Chicago: The University of Chicago Press 1977; A. Touraine, *La voix et le regard*, Seulil, Paris 1978.

583 A. Touraine, *The Voice and the Eye: An Analysis of Social Movements*, Cambridge: Cambridge University Press 1981.

584 E. Goffman, Frame Analysis: An Essay on the Organization of Experience, New York, NY et al.: Harper & Row 1974.

585 T. Gitlin, *The Whole World Is Watching: Mass Media in the Making and Unmaking of the New Left*, Berkeley, CA, Los Angeles, CA & London, U.K.: University of California Press 1980, p. 6.

reality and making them more visible in a text and discourse, in order to reveal special problems with definition, causative explanations, moral assessment or treatment[586]. The research techniques used are derived from sociolinguistics, discursive analysis and critical rhetoric[587], and they concern studying media, social movements[588], problems of organisation and management[589]. In the case of the research into change and organisational culture, they are used in the concepts of symbolic organisational transformation through 'management of meaning' and 'management of impressions'[590]. Other areas of management related to culture, which use the methods of frame analysis, include cultural diversity[591], change management[592], organisational conflicts and negotiation[593], knowledge management[594], organisational and managerial identity[595], organisational

---

586 R.M. Entman, Framing: Toward Clarification of a Fractured P*aradigm*, *Journal of Communication* 43 (4), 1993, p. 51.

587 J.A. Kuypers, *Framing Analysis From a Rhetorical Perspective*, P. D'Angelo, J.A. Kuypers, eds., Doing News Framing Analysis, Routledge, 2010.

588 D.A. Snow, R.D. Benford, Ideology, Frame Resonance, and Participant Mobilization, *International Social Movement Research*, 1988, 1: 197–217.

589 R.D. Heimovics, R.D. Herman, C.L. Jurkiewicz, Executive Leadership and Resource Dependence in Non-profit Organizations: A Frame Analysis, *Coughlin Public Administration Review*, Vol. 53, No. 5 (Sep.–Oct., 1993), pp. 419–427

590 L. Smircich, G. Morgan, Leadership: The Management of Meaning, *The Journal of Applied Behavioral Science* 1982, Vol. 18, 3:257 – 273; S.J. Grove, S.P. Fisk, *Impressions Management in Organizations*, Routlege 1989.

591 W.E.D. Creed, J.A. Langstraat, M.A. Scully, A Picture of the Frame: Frame Analysis as Technique and as Politics, *Organizational Research Methods* January 2002 vol. 5 no. 1 34–55

592 R.L.M. Dunbar, R. Garud, S. Raghuram, A Frame for Deframing in Strategic Analysis, *Journal of Management Inquiry* March 1996 vol. 5 no. 1, 23–34.

593 R.L. Pinkley, G.B. Northcraft, Conflict Frames of Reference: Implications for Dispute Processes and Outcomes, *The Academy of Management Journal*, Vol. 37, No. 1 (Feb., 1994), pp. 193–205; S.J. Downing, Learning the Plot: Emotional Momentum in Search of Dramatic Logic, *Management Learning* March 1997 vol. 28 no. 1, 27–44.

594 F. Blackler, Knowledge and the theory of organizations: organizations as activity systems and the reframing of management, *Journal of Management Studies* Volume 30, Issue 6, pages 863–884, November 1993; M. Bonifacio, P. Bouquet, P. Traverso, *Enabling Distributed Knowledge Management: Managerial and Technological Implications*, Novatica and Informatik/Informatique, III(1), 2002.

595 K. Rodham, Role Theory and the Analysis of Managerial Work: The case of occupational health professionals, *Journal of Applied Management Studies*, Volume 9, Issue 1, 2000.

image[596] and public management[597].

The grounded theory is used in management science mostly within research into organisational culture, cultural changes and work processes[598]. The methodology is qualitative, so it focuses on an in-depth, non-mass and non-orthodox process of acquiring knowledge, mostly through direct contact with the research subject[599]. The emergence of theories and hypotheses assumes that the researcher understands local categories and uses the subject's language and cognitive network, so he does not impose his own perspective, but discovers the one used by the subject[600]. The research process postulates cognitive openness, local approach, pluralism in relation to the choice of data selection techniques, research triangulation. The researcher should not have too many pre-conceptualisations, i.e. he should try to begin the research from a position of *tabula rasa*, without any previous readings or theoretical constructs. It is crucial to understand colloquial and local categories used by the subject, which is possible after getting to the practices, interactions and social situations (incidents). Research into the processes of cultural changes is oriented towards the processual approach, with use of the category of organisational identity or reference to the sphere of organisational behaviour. There are numerous examples of such research in the world's literature[601].

---

596 R. Whitea, D. Hansonb, Corporate self, corporate reputation and corporate annual reports: re-enrolling Goffman, *Scandinavian Journal of Management*, Volume 18, Issue 3, September 2002, Pages 285–301.

597 P. Shrivastava, I.I. Mitroff, *Enhancing Organizational Research Utilization: The Role of Decision Makers' Assumptions, The Academy of Management Review*, Vol. 9, No. 1 (Jan., 1984), pp. 18–26.

598 C. Goulding, *Grounded Theory: A Practical Guide for Management*, Business and Market Researchers. London: Sage 2002.

599 P.Y. Martin, B.A. Turner, Grounded Theory and Organizational Research, *The Journal of Applied Behavioral Science*, vol. 22, no. 2, 1986.

600 B. Glaser, A. Strauss, Anselm, *The Discovery of Grounded Theory: Strategies for Qualitative Research*, New York: Aldine de Gruyter 1967; U. Kelle, *'Emergence' vs. 'Forcing' of Empirical Data? A Crucial Problem of 'Grounded Theory' Reconsidered*, Forum Qualitative Sozialforschung / Forum: Qualitative Social Research, 6(2), Art. 27, 2005.

601 B.A. Turner, The use of grounded theory for the qualitative analysis of organizational behaviour, *Journal of Management Studies*, 1983, 20: 333–348; L.D. Parker, B.H. Roffey, Methodological Themes: Back to the Drawing Board: Revisiting Grounded Theory and the Everyday Accountant's and Manager's Reality, *Accounting, Auditing & Accountability Journal*, 1997, Vol. 10 Iss: 2, pp. 212 – 247; A. Bryant, K. Charmaz, *The Sage Handbook of Grounded Theory*, London Sage.

The process of research in the grounded theory consists of four stages, although it is flexible and allows for a return to any of the stages, as needed. The first stage is coding, which aims to find the roots of the cognition of the processes used by the subjects. In the coding stage, all available techniques for acquiring data should be employed, such as interviews, observations, as well as all originally available, and then secondary written and documentary materials, as well as expert panels, group interviews, consultations etc. This stage postulates open, selective or cross coding, with the purpose in finding the relationships between primary categories, drawn directly from the data. The second stage is called conceptualisation and aims at grouping codes acquired from the empirical material which have a similar, repeatable pattern, into broader categories. The third stage of the research is categorisation, which is a move from the inductive approach to the inductive-deductive, which includes generalisations and relationships between the variables. The last stage is theorising, being a synthesis of the research conducted, which allows for formulation of an explanatory theory[602].

Analysing the methodology of the interpretative change in organisational culture, one can draw several conclusions. Firstly, interpretative research into cultural changes is an extensive, diverse methodological area, based on common cognitive assumptions. It includes methods which belong to the symbolic interactionism paradigm only (such as ethnomethodology and frame analysis), and other methods, which draw inspirations from interpretivism, trying to combine paradigms (e.g. the grounded theory or case study). These common cognitive assumptions include interactionist and constructivist understanding of culture, idiographic vision of practicing science (emic), treating culture as a root metaphor of an organisation, axiological involvement of researchers, anthropological methodology based on 'thick descriptions' of culture.

Secondly, the applications of the interpretative methodology in the research into organisation and management are vast and are becoming more and more significant. The importance of postmodernism is decreasing, and so the most important alternative paradigms of culture are interpretivism and Critical Management Studies.

Thirdly, interpretative research into cultural changes in management includes a wide range of problems that are analysed with the use of sophisticated

602 A. Strauss, J. Corbin, *Basics of Qualitative Research: Grounded Theory Procedures and Techniques*, Sage, 1990.

methodological tools. Important problems of interpretative management of cultural changes in organisations include:

- Dynamic approach to organisational culture in the process of its manifestation and permanent transformation[603],
- Change management through sensemaking and management of meaning[604],
- Organisational learning understood as a change[605],
- Relationships with the organisation's effectiveness[606],
- Relationships with strategic management[607],
- Reorganisation and restructuring of the organisation[608],
- The issue of time in change management[609],
- Studies of longitudinal change[610],
- The characteristic of cultural changes in different types of organisation[611],

---

603 M. J Hatch, The Dynamics of Organizational Culture, *Academy of Management Review*, Vol. 18, No. 4 (Oct., 1993), pp. 657–693

604 L.A. Isabella, Evolving Interpretations as a Change Unfolds: How Managers Construe Key Organizational Events, *The Academy of Management Journal*, Vol. 33, No. 1 (Mar., 1990), pp. 7–41; S.G. Harris, Organizational Culture and Individual Sensemaking: A Schema-Based Perspective, *Organization Science*, Vol. 5, No. 3 (Aug., 1994), pp. 309–321

605 J.S. Brown, P. Duguid, Organizational Learning and Communities-of-Practice: Toward a Unified View of Working, Learning, and Innovation, *Organization Science*, Vol. 2, No. 1.

606 J.D. Ford, David A. Baucus, Organizational Adaptation to Performance Downturns: An Interpretation-Based Perspective, *The Academy of Management Review*, Vol. 12, No. 2 (Apr., 1987), pp. 366–380.

607 G. Johnson, *Rethinking incrementalism*, Strategic Management Journal, 9, 75–91 (1988).

608 J.M. Bartunek, Changing Interpretive Schemes and Organizational Restructuring: Th Example of a Religious Order, *Administrative Science Quarterly*, Vol. 29, No. 3 (Se 1984), pp. 355–372.

609 K.E. Weick, R.E. Quinn, Organizational Change and Development, *Annual Revi Psychology*. Vol. 50: 361–386 (Volume publication date February 1999).

610 A.M. Pettigrew, *Longitudinal Field Research on Change: Theory and Pr* Organization Science, Vol. 1, No. 3, Special Issue: Longitudinal Field R Methods for Studying Processes of Organizational Change (1990), pp. 267–

611 J. Mahler, Influences of Organizational Culture on Learning in Public *Journal of Public Administration Research and Theory*, 1997, 7(4): pp. 519 Tierney, Organizational Culture in Higher Education: Defining the Ess *Journal of Higher Education*, Vol. 59, No. 1 (Jan.–Feb., 1988), pp. 2–21.

- Empowerment as a tool of cultural changes[612],
- The use of archetypes in cultural change management[613],

To sum up, the interpretative approach to cultural change in the organisation is a fundamental problem of symbolic interactionism. Thus, a number of concepts of organisation and management exploring this approach have been created. It seems that it would be good to transfer these managerial experiences to Poland, especially since as the world's literature shows, there are many applications of interpretivism, and the importance of this paradigm increases.

7.4 Emancipatory cultural changes

The emancipation project is a methodological element that is integrally related to the criticism of instrumentalism and oppressiveness of organisational culture. Critical assessment should lead to a change. The aim of the emancipation project is to change the unjust order, and not to increase the cost-effectiveness or efficiency of the organisation's activities. Although the aspects of cost-effectiveness and organisational efficiency also have to be taken into consideration when implementing changes. The conflicting interests, limitations to subjectivity and dehumanisation aspects of management revealed should be analysed, which should lead to the decrease in the influence of false awareness. The emancipation project should lead to a greater participation of disadvantaged groups in the power structures and the decision-making process. Thus, the project of changes should include an increase of the employee participation in the managerial ructures and the development of the organisational democracy. Guaranteeing ore just, sustainable division, which would take into consideration the dis- ntaged groups, is equally important. This should be part of a change of the f remuneration, motivation and development of employees, i.e. the com- tem of human resources management in the organisation. Naturally, ections of this change include greater organisational equality and jus- change in the managers' and employees' awareness. The process of emancipation changes should develop a new organisational cul- owards employee subjectivity, justice and equality. The creation of

---

Velthouse, Cognitive Elements of Empowerment: An 'Interpretive' Task Motivation, *The Academy of Management Review*, Vol. 15, . 666–681.

nings, *Organizational Design Types, Tracks and the Dynamics* nization Studies July 1988 vol. 9 no. 3, 293–316.

this new culture has to be part of key structural and strategic changes, oriented towards the humanisation and emancipation of disadvantaged groups. The necessary changes concern mission, strategic aims, organisational structure, values, norms and management systems. Furthermore, it is important to pay attention to the limited control over cultural changes arising from the fact that besides the formal culture which is controlled by the organisation, there is a 'clandestine circulation' of informal culture. This is why the last stage of a cultural change is its consolidation, corresponding to the re-freezing stage of K. Lewin's model of social changes. Consolidation should mean the acceptance of emancipation values as key for organisational culture and identity. Employees should maintain, develop and enhance the emancipation and participatory practices in the organisation. Additionally, they should learn the reflective and critical view of organisational practices, in order to develop the organisation's humanisation and to prevent R. Michels' iron law of oligarchy – a tendency for bureaucracy to lay claim to the entire organisational power[614].

The concept of cultural changes proposed here is a result of the assumption also adopted by critical researchers, according to which culture is a root metaphor for management or even the metaphor of organisation[615]. Thus, cultural changes are changes of the whole organisation, including its strategy, organisational structures, management models and styles, and management systems.

The proposal to study culture and implement emancipation change from the perspective of the critical current can be presented in eight stages (Tab. 29), which combine aspects of critical analysis (stages 1–4) with the emancipation project (stages 5–8):

All organisational changes are resisted, so in the case of radical changes that disturb the status quo, resistance can be especially strong to a project of transformations that violates the interests of groups wielding power. In practice, this is often a revolutionary change, because groups wielding power will not limit it selflessly. Thus, cultural change under the critical approach quite often takes a progressive, evolutionary form. If, for example, because of criticism of organisational culture, it is possible to introduce some aspects of the work humanisation or to limit the oppressiveness and exploitation, we can talk about a gradual change. It is important not to limit the critical research to descriptive

614 R. Michels, *Political Parties: A Sociological Study of the Oligarchical Tendencies of Modern Democracy*, 1915, [in:] www.http://socserv.mcmaster.ca/econ/ugcm/3ll3/michels/polipart.pdf, (08. 08. 2012).

615 M. Alvesson, *Understanding Organizational Culture*, London: Sage, 2002

Tab. 29: Changes in organisational culture within the critical paradigm. Source: Own work.

Description	Stage, methods and techniques	Effects
1. Denaturalisation of the extant culture	Critical stage Interviews, discourse analyses, observations	Distorted sense of organisational obviousness, naturalness and justice among the employees
2. Exposing the cultural patterns maintaining the status quo	Critical stage Interviews, discourse analyses, observations	Realising and recognising rationalisations and myths used by power
3. Discovering the ideology, indoctrination and false identity	Critical stage Interviews, discourse analyses, observations	Knowledge of manipulative social engineering used against organisation's employees and customers
4. Revealing the aspects of symbolic violence	Critical stage Interviews, discourse analyses, observations	Making employees aware of the mechanism, system and tools of organisational control
5. Planning and implementing an increase in employee participation and organisational democracy	Emancipation stage Change of the mission, strategy, management models and style Education and training	Implementing a new strategy, taking into consideration the aspects of humanisation and emancipation
6. Changing the system of human resources management and organisational structures	Emancipation stage Change of the organisational structures and the system of HR management Education and training	Implementing a new structure, taking into consideration greater humanisation, employee participation and emancipation
7. Creating an emancipation culture	Emancipation stage Change of the cultural values and patterns Education and training	Implementation of a new culture, the core values of which include employee subjectivity, justice and equality
8. Consolidating the emancipation culture	Emancipation stage Management of meaning and organisational identity Education and training	Active involvement of the employees in the development of the emancipation culture

aspects, but use them to implement real emancipation changes in organisations. The subject literature already identifies such cases, which are often related to the public sector[616].

Critical researchers strive for the propagation of emancipation models of organisational culture, which is supposed to develop thanks to the criticism of the oppressive managerial practices and the greater awareness of employees. The applied techniques of change management include mostly critical managerial education and communications tools[617]. Thanks to the implementation of the emancipation project, the models of culture understood instrumentally, which dominate today, are supposed to evolve towards greater humanisation. The barrier that needs to be overcome is the interest of the groups exercising power and deriving the greatest benefits from the organisation's functioning, including managers, owners and entrepreneurs.

7.5 The metaphorical research method in organisational culture

The metaphorical method of organisational culture analysis is located within the humanist discourse. Apart from metonymy, parable and synecdoche, metaphor is a rhetorical figure used in literature, which has been described and analysed by philologists and linguists[618]. On the other hand, metaphor is a cognitive tool, which uses analogies and images to compare complex, abstract objects and processes with other, simpler or better understood[619].

In management, metaphors have been used since the beginning of its existence, but the analytical scientific reflection on the cognitive value of metaphors in research into organisations developed with the cultural current[620]. The end of the 1970s and the beginning of the 1980s saw rapid development of the concepts of organisational culture and culture in management. A number of comparative

616 H. Willmott, *Renewing Strength: Corporate Culture Revisited*, Management, Vol. 6, No. 3, 2003, 73–87.

617 S.A. Deetz, Critical Interpretive Research in Organizational Communication, Western *Journal of Speech Communication*, Volume 46, Issue 2, 1982, pages 131–149.

618 M. Black, *More about metaphor*, in: 'Metaphor and Thought', red. A. Ortony, Cambridge 1979.

619 D. Davidson, *What Metaphors Mean*, Reprinted in Inquiries Into Truth and Interpretation, 1984, Oxford, Oxford University Press 1978.

620 Z. Kövecses, *Metaphor in Culture: Universality and Variation*, Cambridge University Press, 2005.

cross-cultural studies, anthropological analyses of culture and bestsellers aimed at managers have contributed to the increase in the interest in values and culture within management science. In *Images of Organisation*, G. Morgan presented possibilities of applying metaphors to the studies of organisational and managerial issues. One of many metaphors Morgan described is the comparison of an organisation to a culture, which according to Morgan is one of the most creative references. Since this pioneer publication, metaphorical analysis has spread within the management science discourse and it is now quite commonly used, both as a tool for the creation of a theory of organisation and its culture, and as a management method.

Metaphorical thinking is a useful way of interpreting organisation, permanently interwoven with the cognitive process in management. Metaphors are a part of language, so their change entails a transformation of the ways of thinking and speaking, and in consequence, organisational activities. Depending on the approach assumed, metaphors can be perceived as a useful technique or a basis for understanding the organisation. However, it has to be noted that the use of metaphors should not be completely free. Metaphorical thinking leads to certain trails, points to concealed features of the studied object, provokes creative thinking, but it is pointless to thoroughly identify the object described with the metaphor. Applying and discovering a quasi-metaphorical process in the interpretations of management should lead to a better understanding of the organisational life[621].

Organisational culture is often interpreted as a metaphor and described with the use of metaphors. In the Morganian understanding, culture was the metaphor of the organisation itself. As the cultural current in management developed, more metaphors describing organisational culture appeared. There is a clear distinction between representatives of different paradigms, who view culture in different ways.

Functionalism is dominated by metaphors of organisational culture, understood as a method of integrating the organisation, combining its key values, management philosophy and development directions. Thus, functionally interpreted organisational culture can be compared to 'social glue', 'clan', 'resource' or 'compass'[622]. The ideal is a cohesive, strong and integrated organisational culture,

621 C.f.: C.M. Schmidt, *Metaphor and Cognition: A Cross-Cultural Study of Indigenous and Universal Constructs in Stock Exchange Reports*, Intercultural Communication, ISSN 1404–1634, 2002, issue 5, http://www.immi.se/intercultural/.

622 M. Alvesson, *Understanding Organizational Culture*, London: Sage 2002, pp. 16–41.

which holds the whole organisation together (the 'glue'). Thus, it can also be a source of employee identification with the organisation, resulting in their loyalty, the sense of a positive internal image and unity around the aims and values determined ('clan'). Culture is subject to control and steering, depending on the organisation's and managers' needs. Therefore, according to functionalists, it is a tool allowing for achievement of higher work effectiveness and the greater involvement of the employees by stimulating the social and emotional potential of the organisation ('resource'). Apart from that, organisational culture determines the direction of the organisation's development, expresses its aims and values, and is a kind of organisational credo ('compass'). Organisational culture is supposed to be the organisation's philosophy, the strength of which is its conscious and unconscious influence.

In the case of non-functionalist paradigms, metaphors of organisational culture and the organisation itself are practically the same. If we assume the root metaphor, according to which organisation does not *have* a culture but *is* a culture[623], any comparison of an object to the organisation is a comparison to its organisational culture. The most common metaphors for organisations, and so organisational culture, include comparisons to a temple, theatre, text, language, work of art, acting and drama, flow, autopoiesis and brain. The metaphors of temple, theatre and language are used mostly by L. Smircich, M. J. Hatch and B. Czarniawska-Jorges to describe the interpretative and symbolic aspects of organisation[624]. The metaphor of acting, drama and a work of art was drawn from E. Goffman, who was one of the creators of symbolic interactionism. Treating organisation and organisational culture metaphorically as a brain or flow and autopoiesis was proposed by G. Morgan. Interpretative metaphors focus on comparing culture to complex social processes or entities (the brain). In the cognitive sense, they could be accused of a limited power of interpretation and explaining reality, as they explain managerial processes that are difficult to interpret, using equally complex entities, such as language, brain and social processes. On the

623 L. Smircich, Studying Organizations as Cultures, in: G. Morgan, *Beyond Method: Strategies for Social Research*, Beverly Hills-London-New Delhi 1983, pp. 160–172.

624 M.J. Hatch, M.S. Schultz, Scaling the Tower of Babel: Relational Differences Between Identity, Image and Culture in Organizations, in: *The Expressive Organisation: Linking Identity, Reputation and the Corporate Brand*, Oxford University Press, Oxford 2000; L. Smircich, Organizations as Shared Meaning, in: *Organization Symbolism*, JAI Press, Greenwich 1983; B. Czarniawska, *Writing Management. Organizational Theory as a Literary Genre*, Oxford: Oxford University Press. 1999.

other hand, interpretative metaphors focus on pointing to individuality and uniqueness of management, understood as a complex social process, which is characteristic of this current.

Many cultural and organisational metaphors are spread in the CMS current, reflecting the essence of the oppressiveness and inequality, as seen from the critical perspective. The most popular metaphors include the comparisons of the organisation to mental prison, a tool of domination and repression, political system, ideology and totalitarianism, war, battle and Panopticon[625]. 'Mental prison' is a metaphor proposed by G. Morgan, mostly describing the obsessive, repressive and self-censoring aspects of the human psyche[626]. Describing culture as a 'tool of dominance and repression' is commonly and literally used in the critical current to describe the negative aspects of cultural control. In the case of the metaphors of ideology, war and Panopticon, the situation is similar. According to the CMS representatives, organisational culture is a source of ideological false awareness, symbolic violence, conflicts and fights of social groups, inherent in the system. The Panopticon is a historical metaphor drawn by M. Foucault from J. Bentham, based on the ideal of control and invigilation[627]. Following H. Willmott and M. Alvesson, M. Zawadzki proposes a metaphorical understanding of organisational culture as an emancipation tool[628]. The metaphors of the critical current are rather one-sided and ideological, as they focus on two aspects of organisation, namely repressiveness and control. Thus, focusing on these aspects of management, these comparisons sometimes obscure positive aspects, although they reflect the essence of the radical structuralism current.

The postmodernist understanding of an organisation is generally of a metaphorical character, and so most of its ideas and theories have more of a metaphorical and analogous, rather than literal nature. This is related to the postmodernist references to the Wittgensteinian 'language game' and 'linguistic breakthrough', as well as literary, artistic and textual roots of this current. Root is one of the earliest metaphors of culture, used by postmodernists to describe a shapeless,

625 M. Alvesson, 'The Play of Metaphors,' in J. Hassard and M. Parker (eds) *Postmodernism and Organizations*, London: Sage, 1993b.

626 Morgan, Gareth, Fred Gregory, and Cameron Roach. 'Images of organization.' (1997).

627 M. Foucault, *Power Knowledge Selected Interviews & Other Writings*, Random House, New York 2000.

628 M. Alvesson, *Understanding Organizational Culture*, London: Sage 2002, pp. 16–41; M. Alvesson, 'The Play of Metaphors,' in J. Hassard and M. Parker (eds) *Postmodernism and Organizations*, London: Sage, 1993b.

tangled and unpredictable –from the point of view of the growth point – entity[629]. Simulacra and matrix reflect the essence of the postmodern hyper-reality, within which the essentialist notion of sense and truth disappears. Cultural processes are games, simulations and subsequent veils, behind which there is no core of the reality or truth[630]. The metaphors of a supermarket, collage and group happening reflect the understanding of culture as an eclectic, indeterminist and unpredictable entity, which can sometimes be internally contradictory and develop spontaneously. Most postmodern metaphors are exploited mostly in their literal meaning, not the cognitive meaning. Postmodernists, occupying a position of radical humanism, believe that literature helps to understand the world better than science. This type of thinking leads to excessive attachment to popular metaphors of culture, which are treated uncritically and sometimes overexploited. For example, Z. Bauman wrote a number of publications concerning fluid culture and modernity, which contain only unsystematic observations and no empirical research[631].

Thus, metaphors can be ascribed to a specific way of thinking, as part of a specific paradigm. This means that the way a metaphor is interpreted emphasises its assumptions and brings to mind associations and images rooted within different cognitive perspectives (Tab. 30).

The proposed metaphors of organisational culture fall within Burrell and Morgan's four paradigms, although it is worth noting that many of them, depending on the interpretation, can be located in different paradigms[632]. This is one of the features of metaphorical thinking, indicating that the cognitive and pragmatic functions of a metaphor depend only on the way it is interpreted. For example, the metaphor of an organisation as a brain can take a functionalist character, if we assume a computational theory of mind. Organisation is thus based on learning and processing information. However, if we assume that brain is an organ of perception, interpretation and understanding of the world, then the emphasis is put on the reflective aspects and the metaphor can be located within the discourse of symbolic interactionism. Similarly ambiguous metaphors located in different paradigms are, again, the metaphors of temple, text and language.

---

629 G. Deleuze, F. Guattari, *Anti-Oedipus*, Trans. R. Hurley, 1972.

630 J. Baudrillard, *Symulacra and Simulation*, University of Michigan Press, Ann Arbor 1994.

631 Z. Bauman, *Liquid fear*, Polity, 2006.

632 G. Burrell, G. Morgan, *Sociological Paradigms and Organizational Analysis*, Heinemann, London 1979.

Tab. 30: Metaphors within paradigms. Source: Own work, my proposals for metaphors are in bold.

Neopositivist-functionalist-systemic paradigm (NFS)	Critical current (radical structuralism, Critical Management Studies, CMS)
Social glue	Political system
Clan	Ideology and totalitarianism
Resource	War and battle
Compass	Prison
	Panopticon
A shooting range and labyrinth	Emancipation tool
Compulsive neurosis	**Castle of fear**
	Paranoia
Interpretative-symbolic paradigm	**Postmodernism (radical humanism)**
Acting, theatre, drama	Temple
Religion and a temple	Performance and happening
Flow, transformation, autopoiesis	A work of art
Brain	Root
Text and language	Collage
Chameleon	Russian dolls
	Matrix and simulacra
Masquerade	**Hall of mirrors**
Schizophrenia	**Autism**

The proposed list of metaphors includes: those that are strongly rooted in the managerial discourse (glue, clan, resource, theatre, language, prison); those present in the discourse but not widespread (a work of art, collage, chameleon, Russian nesting dolls); those drawn from the discourse of other humanist and social sciences (Panopticon, root, simulacra and matrix), and those which are completely new (a shooting range and labyrinth, compulsive neurosis, arrogance etc). The last group of two metaphors in the table is an ironic illustration of the thesis concerning the interpretative character of a metaphor. Interpreting an object in an appropriate way, one can compare it to any other object, which is a result of the nature of language and our cognitive apparatus. For example, culture can be compared to funfair attractions, or even mental disorders and emotions. Organisational culture interpreted as 'a shooting range and labyrinth' is of a purposeful character and has one effective solution, leading to success. When associated with the 'castle of fear', it refers to the dark side of the human nature. In the case of a 'masquerade', it brings to mind a multiplicity of organisational roles and identities. When seen as 'a hall of mirrors', it can provide multiple, distorted images. In the case of the metaphors of cultural processes as mental disorders, it is easy to find points of reference. Organisational culture within the NFS paradigm can be ironically interpreted as obsessive thoughts about the striving for cognition and managerial perfection, manifested in 'compulsive actions' such as the obsessive search for methodological perfection, the one, perfect scientific method of cultural cognition and management. Within the paradigm of the critical current (CMS), organisational culture sometimes reminds of a paranoid vision, which is based on obsessive delusion. Thus, culture is a tool of repression, 'false awareness', psycho-manipulation and social engineering, the aim of which is to control and exploit employees. If the environment is uncritical of such obsessive delusions, they can lead to paranoia, induced among seemingly healthy members of an organisation. Within the paradigm of symbolic interactionism, organisational culture can be compared to schizophrenic psychosis. Culture as a 'schizophrenia' is manifested by a split (Greek *schisis*) between emotion and thought, which leads to an increase in reflection, unfortunately accompanied by permanent dysfunction. Finally, the postmodern 'autism' of organisational culture can be interpreted as managerial discourse enclosed in a world of its own experiences.

The metaphorical method is commonly used for studying and changing organisational cultures. Its unquestionable advantages include reflection and openness, which is why it is a non-orthodox and creative method, especially useful in the case of studying and understanding such a complex and ephemeral phenomenon as organisational culture. On the other hand, the use of metaphor in cultural studies in management faces a number of limitations.

1. It is a reflective, non-structured and non-standard method, which limits its applications to creative aspects rather than systematic analyses and measurements. Besides, metaphors are only used in qualitative and interpretative research.
2. The presented analysis of 'new metaphors' (culture as a 'funfair', 'mental disorders') points to the dangers of such interpretations of reality. Freedom of comparisons can lead to a complete loss of their cognitive function, replaced by a creative function related to imagination and association[633].
3. How to distinguish metaphors from literal meanings? Language itself is metaphorical, something people don't even really notice. Is 'resource' a metaphor?

633 C. Oswick, P. Jones, Beyond Correspondence? Metaphor in Organization Theory, *Academy of Management Review* 2006, 31(2): 483–485.

Writing here that the metaphor of 'resource' is used to start up employees' potential, it is necessary to use two further metaphors. 'Starting up' is a mechanistic metaphor, comparing the beginning of human activity to starting a device or a machine, while 'potential' is a notion drawn directly from physics.
4. In some cases, it is difficult to locate the metaphor in only one paradigm, as everything depends on the interpretation. The meaning of metaphors can be quite fluid. For example, 'organisational glasses', although originally used within the functionalist paradigm, later became a method of interpreting organisational culture within other paradigms. 'Organisational glasses' are also an interpretative metaphor, because culture is identified with the perception of reality. 'Black organisational glasses' could be the cultural perception of reality as seen by the critical current.
5. Identifying organisational culture with the whole organisation, characteristic of non-functionalist paradigms, broadens the sphere of comparisons, which in consequence become very general and vague.

Naturally, the presented essence and problems of the metaphorical approach to organisational culture do not exhaust the complexity of these issues. Many other metaphors of culture used in research and managerial education could be mentioned. For example, M. J. Gannon proposes a metaphorical understanding of organisational culture as a computer, tree, whale, genetic pool, rainbow, prism, school, skyscraper and filter[634]. Another problem is the multiplicity of proposals and lack of agreement as to the canon of the metaphorical method in management.

The metaphorical approach to organisational culture described is used in research, as well as managerial and advisory practices around the world[635]. However, the knowledge of the metaphorical idea and method is not widespread among Polish researchers, much less managers.

634 M.J. Gannon, *Cultural Metaphors: Applications and Exercises*, Internet.

635 M.J. Gannon, *Integrating Context, Cross-Cultural Dimensions, and Cultural Metaphors in Management Education and Training*, Paper presented at the Biennial International Conference of the Western Academy of Management, Istanbul, Turkey, June 28–July 2, 1998.

Summary

The theory of culture in management and the attempt to present ways of studying its changes, as described in this book, indicate that there are multiple diverse concepts. The complexity of the theory is a derivative of problems related to the notion of culture, which are vast, ambiguous and difficult to operationalise. The multiplicity of the concepts results from the fact that researchers assume different paradigms, and in consequence, their initial assumptions lead to diametrically different descriptions of culture, the process of its changes and its management methods. This is why resolving the problems of cultural research in management depends, to a large degree, on research progress and the development of methods for studying culture. This work presented the concept of a broad multi-paradigmatic approach, combining different cognitive perspectives, drawn from the social sciences and the humanities.

One solution to the problem of multiplicity of concepts of organisational culture could be the assumption of multi-paradigmatic analysis. We have been educated in accordance with paradigms and the epistemic and methodological ideals of our chosen scientific disciplines. But theoreticians and actual managers have different intellectual backgrounds. Some followed the path of economic education, some of managerial education, and some of technical, scientific, social, artistic or humanist education. Our professional and educational paths have shaped our cognitive networks, which include values, norms and models of 'scientificity' and 'usefulness'. Thus, we have built coherent interpretations of notions, harmonising with our cognitive networks, acquired in the socialisation process. Of course, this is not determinism, as there is no agreement as to the paradigm within numerous scientific disciplines, especially the humanities and social sciences. Besides, education is overlapped by the filter of professional and life experiences, which can correct, and sometimes radically change the original orientation, stemming from education. The notion of organisational culture is also influenced by analogies and metaphors of understanding culture, as such.

So what are the existing pre-judgments about organisational culture? Most of all, it is coherence with the thinking drawn from exact, technical and economic sciences, which often treats organisational culture in analytical and operationalist terms. This means a tendency to accept the possibility of separating organisational culture from other organisational elements, such as strategy and structure, the possibility of managing and predicting the directions of the culture's development and acceptance of the need for precise definition and measurement. Generally speaking, this is a tendency to interpret organisational culture within the functionalist paradigm. Apart from that, there are many cases of scepticism about the cognitive value of the concept of organisational culture. On the other hand, representatives of the social sciences and humanities are more often moving towards an understanding of organisational culture in accordance with the interpretative-symbolic paradigm, radical structuralism and even radical humanism. In such cases, organisational culture is a root metaphor for an organisation as a whole, without the possibility to separate structure and strategy. There is a greater awareness in terms of the inevitability of ambiguity and the incoherence of the organisational culture's research results. Usually there is less faith in the possibility of operationalising, managing and controlling organisational culture. The influence of education (or, more generally, intellectual background) can be supplemented with the harder-to-capture influence of professional and life experiences, which determine our beliefs, consolidating some and eliminating others. In terms of organisational culture, experience shapes our deepest beliefs and intuition about the possibility of wielding influence on people, their behaviour and systems of values. In consequence, we move closer to a more universalist and scientistic understanding of organisational culture, or we are oriented towards the relativism and ambiguity of these concepts. Understanding culture as such is also important, as it is a kind of model for the understanding of organisational culture. If culture is interpreted unambiguously, mostly as a civilisation, including its technological and material aspects, as well as other measurable values, then there is a preference for functionalist-structuralist approaches to organisational culture. In most cases, awareness of the ambiguity of the understanding of culture and its contentious nature leads to the implicit or explicit assumption of non-functionalist paradigms.

Many authors try to understand the essence of organisational culture using metaphors, analogies, paradoxes and symbols. The idea of culture as a metaphor for an organisation as a whole was first proposed by G. Morgan, and has been used by many other authors since then (including Smircich, B. Czarniawska)[636]. Organisational culture is described metaphorically as the organisational glue, a mental programme, theatre, social happening or even text. Models and typologies of organisational cultures, proposed by such researchers as T. Deal,

---

636 L. Smircich, Organizations as Shared Meaning, in: *Organization Symbolism*, JAI Press, Greenwich 1983, pp. 55–65.; B. Czarniawska, *Writing Management: Organization Theory as a Literary Genre*, The University of Chicago Press, Chicago-London, 1997.

A. Kennedy and C. Handy[637] are full of such symbols. The symbol of a cobweb, analogies to Greek gods, comparisons to social roles (e.g. machos) are just some of the rhetorical figures commonly used by researchers of organisational cultures. These symbols allow them to aptly, synthetically describe the dominant outline of a given cultural configuration. Further, a metaphorical understanding of organisational culture is in accordance with the spirit of humanities, and especially hermeneutics. Most of all, this is an explanation and interpretation of meaning, even if it is ambiguous, as well as a clear use of the art and essay-writing apparatus to interpret social reality. According to many researchers, mostly interpretivists, organisational culture management is not only based on scientific rules and methods, but is also an art[638]. One can point to its intuitive nature, the role of covert knowledge and creativity in the management of such an ephemeral organisational sphere as a culture. We are submerged in our own cultures, we feel them, interpret them and function within them reflectively, out of habit. In both cases, we use intuition based on covert knowledge and experience. This allows us to make decisions, convince others of them and implement them with the necessary determination. As most interpretivists and postmodernists believe, the sphere of cultural management eludes control and its predictive power is low, as within it we are dealing with creativity and the shaping of social reality, rather than the social engineering associated with determinism and algorithms of action.

The shaping of organisational culture entails axiological, aesthetic and praxeological aspects. It is an evaluative activity, including ethical and moral content. The building of an organisation's identity around certain values has an effect on all of its stakeholders. It is crucial to answering questions about the development of values and norms, which take into consideration social responsibility, orientation towards sustainable development and subjective treatment of employees and other stakeholders.

The axiology of organisational culture is related to the implementation of the idea of 'good', while aesthetics focuses on art and the idea of 'beauty'. Aesthetics is of key significance to the understanding of culture, which is part of the process of creating beauty or its antithesis. Thus, it is difficult to assume that a derivative

637 T.J. Peters, R.H. Waterman, *In Search of Excellence: Lessons from America's Best-Run Companies*. New York: Harper & Row, 2004, W. Ouchi, Markets, Beaucracies and Clans, *Administrative Science Quarterly*, no. 25, 1980, pp. 129–141.

638 Por. *Text/Work. Representing Organization and Organizing Representations*, ed. S. Linstead, Routledge, London 2003.

of culture – organisational culture – could be completely devoid of aesthetic ideals. The aesthetic threads, although still marginal in management, are more and more often applied to organisational culture. Organisational anthropology is also increasingly often the basis for documentary texts, forming a kind of organisational literature. The creation of organisational stories, role-play scenarios and performances are also used for cultural diagnosis[639].

The praxeology of organisational culture focuses on analysis of organisational culture from the point of view of the activity's effectiveness. It is related to the practical character of the issues, which can distinguish research into organisational culture from cultural analyses as such. Cultural studies do not have to be praxeologically oriented, unlike research into organisational culture – at least the research being subject to management science.

639 J.S. Brown, S. Denning, K. Groh, L. Priska, *Storytelling in Organizations. Why Storytelling Is Transforming 21st Century Organizations and Management*, Elsevier Butterwoth-Heinemann, Oxford, 2005.
M. Rosen, Coming to the Terms with the Field: Understanding and Doing Organisational Ethnography, *Journal of Management Studies*, no. 28, 1991, pp. 1–24.
M.J. Hatch, Irony and the Social Construction of Contradiction in the Humor of a Management Team, *Organization Studies*, 1997, pp. 275–288.

List of figures

List of tables

New Horizons in Management Sciences

Edited by Lukasz Sulkowski

Vol. 1 Lukasz Sulkowski: Neodarwinism in Organization and Management. 2012.

Vol. 2 Lukasz Sulkowski: Epistemology of Management. 2013.

Vol. 3 Barbara Kożuch / Zbysław Dobrowolski: Creating Public Trust. An Organisational Perspective. 2014.

Vol. 4 Konrad Raczkowski / Lukasz Sulkowski (eds.): Tax Management and Tax Evasion. 2014.

Vol. 5 Michał Chmielecki / Łukasz Sułkowski: Metaphors in Management – Blend of Theory and Practice. 2017.

Vol. 6 Łukasz Sułkowski (ed.): Management and Culture of the University. 2017.

Vol. 7 Barbara Kożuch / Łukasz Sułkowski (eds.): Reflections about Contemporary Management. 2017.

Vol. 8 Łukasz Sułkowski/Ewa Grandys (eds.): New Challenges in Change Management. 2018.

Vol. 9 Zuzana Bačíková(ed.): Marketing in the Digital Era. 2018.

Vol. 10 Łukasz Sułkowski / Jerzy Mączyński / Sylwia Przytuła (eds.): Leadership across Cultures. 2019.

Vol. 11 Łukasz Sułkowski: Cultural Reflection in Management. 2020.

www.peterlang.com

www.ingramcontent.com/pod-product-compliance
Ingram Content Group UK Ltd.
Pitfield, Milton Keynes, MK11 3LW, UK
UKHW021831100926
8556IPUK00004B/280

9 783631 640128